The Psychology of Employee Empowerment

Understanding, and effectively managing, the relationship between Empowerment and Leadership is one of the central issues of our time. Dr Huq's research and analysis not only makes an important scholarly contribution to the theory of the subject but, in her well-presented and readable book, she makes invaluable suggestions on the critical area of the practice of employee empowerment. All individuals with leadership roles urgently need to rethink their ideas, roles and behaviours within Dr Huq's insightful 'Framework for Implementing Employee Empowerment Model'.

Bruce Lloyd, London South Bank University, UK

This book makes a helpful contribution to employee involvement and empowerment in relation to organisational improvement. Much of the existing literature in this area comes from an operations management and TQM background. Hence the current work's grounding in psychology gives a much needed new perspective. This approach gives a more rounded view of employee empowerment from both theory and practice and avoids overly simple assumptions which often pervade the literature in this area. The work is effectively supported by Dr Huq's extensive experience of researching and consulting in this area. I strongly recommend this text to academics and practitioners seeking a fuller understanding of employee involvement and empowerment leading to increased organisational effectiveness.

Rodney McAdam, Ulster University Business School, UK

'Managerialism' is seen by many as the cause of social work's loss of professional confidence which can only be recovered through the reassertion of 'relationship' as the discipline's core. So it is intriguing to find in Huq a writer who looks to social work for key insights, not to fend off management but to strengthen it. With 'empowerment' as the bridge she shows how both disciplines can engage with one another to mutual benefit.

To achieve effective management through empowerment, Huq argues convincingly in her 'Framework for Implementing Employee Empowerment Model D' for a synergy of the managerial goals of effectiveness, efficiency and innovation with social work insights into power, personal relationship and psychological well-being. She challengingly highlights a paradox that if a sustainable, productive future is to be found, would-be powerful leaders need to learn the lessons of how to create enabling and empowering environments from a profession who works with those pushed to the social margins.

Professor John Pinkerton, School of Sociology, Social Policy and Social Work,
Queen's University Belfast, UK

To My Beloved Mother, Mahela Ahmad.
Thank you for your love and constant encouragement in
my pursuit of knowledge.

The Psychology of Employee Empowerment

Concepts, Critical Themes and a Framework for Implementation

ROZANA AHMAD HUQ

GOWER

Gower Applied Business Research
Our programme provides leaders, practitioners, scholars and researchers with thought provoking, cutting edge books that combine conceptual insights, interdisciplinary rigour and practical relevance in key areas of business and management.

Published by
Gower Publishing Limited
Wey Court East
Union Road
Farnham
Surrey, GU9 7PT
England

Gower Publishing Company
110 Cherry Street
Suite 3-1
Burlington, VT 05401-3818
USA

www.gowerpublishing.com

British Library Cataloguing in Publication Data
A catalogue record for this book is available from the British Library

Library of Congress Cataloging-in-Publication Data
Huq, Rozana Ahmad.
  The psychology of employee empowerment : concepts, critical themes and a framework for implementation / by Rozana Ahmad Huq.
     pages cm
  Includes bibliographical references and index.
   ISBN 978-1-4094-4890-7 (hardback) -- ISBN 978-1-4094-4891-4 (ebook) -- ISBN 978-1-4724-0800-6 (epub) 1. Employee empowerment. 2. Employee motivation. I. Title.
   HD50.5.H87 2015
   658.3'14--dc23

                                                                                    2015011232

ISBN 9781409448907 (hbk)
ISBN 9781409448914 (ebk – PDF)
ISBN 9781472408006 (ebk – ePUB)

MIX
Paper from
responsible sources
FSC
www.fsc.org   FSC® C013985

Printed in the United Kingdom by Henry Ling Limited,
at the Dorset Press, Dorchester, DT1 1HD

At first people refuse to believe that a strange new thing can be done, then they begin to hope it can be done, then they see it can be done – then it is done and all the world wonders why it was not done centuries ago.

Frances Hodgson Burnett, *The Secret Garden*

Contents

List of Figures

Abbreviations

CEO   Chief Executive Officer

CSF   Critical Success Factors

EFQM   European Foundation for Quality Management

NASW   National Association of Social Workers

PDP   Personal Development Plan

SHRM   Strategic Human Resource Management

TQM   Total Quality Management

Acknowledgements

Writing this book has been a delightful and most rewarding experience. I would like to express my thanks and gratitude to my family, my children and my husband, Amin Huq, for his encouragement and loving support during the writing of this book.

I am grateful to John Knowles (Library at Queen's University Belfast) for helping me to prepare the manuscript.

I wish to thank Professor John Pinkerton and Dr George Wilson (School of Sociology, Social Policy and Social Work, Queen's University Belfast) for taking a genuine interest in my research work, particularly, for their encouragement with regards to the multi-disciplinary literature reviews (management and social work) during my doctoral study, and for the continuation of their feedback while writing this book. I would also like to express my appreciation for being asked to provide teaching input into the Social Work, MSc Strategy and Leadership Programme, Modern Organisations Module.

Studying the literature in social work has been valuable in deepening my own understanding of empowerment and the importance of psychological empowerment, which helped me to create a framework for the implementation of employee empowerment (Huq's Model D). In this respect, I am thankful to Professor Pinkerton for his valuable comments, as he highlights how both disciplines (management and social work) can 'engage with one another to mutual benefit'. This sums up the essence of drawing knowledge from social work for *bridging the gap*.

I am equally thankful to Emeritus Professor Bruce Lloyd of South Bank University, London, and Professor Rodney McAdam, Business and Management Research Institute at Ulster University, for giving up their time to read the manuscript of my book and forwarding their valuable comments.

I wish to thank Natasha Huq for her input into the designing of the front cover of this book. My thanks go to the wonderful team at Gower Publishing who have been tremendous in putting this book together. There are many people to thank, Annette Bell, Sara Hutton, Donna Shanks, Caroline Spender, Gail Welsh, Shirley Wood, including the production and design team. I know there are several other people who worked behind the scenes, towards the final appearance of this book, who deserve an abundance of thanks.

I would like to thank Martin West (previous Commissioning Editor) of Gower Publishing for his encouragement to write this book, which was truly inspiring for me.

Finally, I am indebted to the CEO of Large Organisation and the Owner of Small Organisation and to all the participants who willingly shared their stories and experiences of 'empowerment'. Thank you for helping me to learn and understand 'empowerment' from different perspectives and allowing me to ask pertinent questions; without you this book would not have been written.

Prologue

Why Write a Book on Employee Empowerment?

There is high consensus in the management literature that employee empowerment is necessary for the success and survival of organisations. It is a management response to an increasingly complex and competitive external environment. Belasco (1989: 12) states: 'If we are to deal with the serious competitive problems facing our nation, we must change the way we do business. The only way to accomplish this needed change is to empower people to execute change ... The future of our country depends on our ability to become masters of empowerment.' In a similar vein, Ripley and Ripley (1993: 29) point out: 'Empowerment is critically important in enabling ... businesses and organisations to survive in this ever-expanding national and international marketplace.' Thus, an important management practice, such as employee empowerment, necessary to the 'survival' of organisations, is deserving of attention.

It is well established in management literature that the current state of knowledge about employee empowerment is not satisfactory and that organisations are introducing employee empowerment without fully understanding what it means or what they are committing themselves to. Hence, the danger is that organisations are also faced with another problem, namely, how to implement it (Huq, 2010).

Significant findings with regards to people's experiences of employee empowerment emanated from my doctorate research titled: *An Investigation of What Employee Empowerment Means in Theory and in Practice* (Huq, 2008). This evidence-based research is valuable for organisations and equally for leaders, who are grappling with 'how to' empower employees. Hence, I felt motivated to write this book, which is a great platform for me to share my knowledge and research findings.

The strength of my research is not just that it gives an in-depth understanding of the difficulties and problems surrounding the implementation of an employee empowerment programme; it is also enlightening about the wider issues with regards to this subject, including the much neglected aspect of psychological empowerment of individuals. In addition, as knowledge drawn from the management literature proved unsatisfactory, it was deemed necessary to draw knowledge from another discipline, namely, social work, where empowerment is an important construct. The key themes of empowerment from both disciplines, management and social work, are examined and reported in this book, named as Huq's Model A and Huq's Model B respectively. The merging of these important themes gave birth to the '*kaleidoscope of themes*', Huq's Model C, as explained in this book.

During my research interview, participants of my case study were extremely candid in talking about their expectations and feelings with regards to their experiences of employee empowerment. This gave me a chance to find out several important things: how do employees emotionally feel about employee empowerment? What methods do organisations employ to implement it and what do they actually achieve and potentially what could they achieve?

Two organisations in UK took part in my case study – one was a publicly owned subsidiary of a multinational communications company, employing over 2,000 people, during the time of my research (excluding agency staff); and the other was a privately owned manufacturing company with 54 employees. My research was qualitative in nature. I interviewed 235 people in total (ranging from CEOs, board members, people in management and non-management positions). It was important to get responses from people in non-management positions as well and not just from management, adding more credibility to the research evidence. Thus, according to Greasley et al. (2005: 366):

> *studies that have neglected employees' perspectives … do not provide a complete picture of the empowerment process. Thus, research that has attempted to measure levels of empowerment of the workforce through management responses alone may not be a true representation of the individual employees' perspectives.*

Multiple sources were used in collecting data for research. First, at each case organisation, information was gathered from three types of informants, that is, senior management, middle management and non-management personnel, to get different views and perspectives from each. Second, the interviews comprised two different types of interviewing, namely, one-to-one and focus group. Third, more than one form of data collection method was used, for example, in addition to interviewing people, evidence was drawn from company literature and other relevant company documents. A number of authors agree that triangulation is a successful technique for combining different data collection methods and enhancing credibility (Patton, 1987, 2002; Robson, 1993; Banister et al., 1994; Brewer, 2000; Flick, 2002; Ritchie, 2003; Fink, 2005).

The aim of my research was the examination of the differing perspectives, perceptions and experiences of people regarding 'employee empowerment' with the underlying assumptions and philosophical stance that, 'in different social worlds or groups, differing views can be found' (Flick, 2002: 165). Individuals and social groups perceive and make sense of the world differently; hence as human beings we are constantly constructing and reconstructing the social world. In this sense, Pring's (2000: 55) argument is valid, that there is a need for an interpretive way of looking at things 'in which we seek to understand the world from the perspective of the participants, or to understand a set of ideas from within an evolving tradition of which they are part'. In this sense, Zimmernann's (1990: 175) cautionary note was carefully considered: 'As long as we continue to use primarily quantitative methods we will have a limited understanding of the (empowerment) construct.'

In a similar vein, Snape and Spencer (2003: 23) argue: 'the social world is not governed by regularities that hold law-like properties. Hence, a social researcher has to explore and understand the social world through the participants' and their own perspectives'. And, as McLeod (2001: 1) points out, qualitative research is an inquiry that can offer 'a set of flexible and sensitive methods for opening up the meanings of areas of social life that were previously not well understood'. Through qualitative interviewing we can find out about how people feel and think about their experiences in the world, at least, and attempt to 'understand experiences and construct events in which you did not participate' (Rubin and Rubin, 1995: 1). Qualitative interviewing is about finding out from people those things we cannot directly observe. Hence, this method was appropriate to gather the rich, 'thick description' (Denzin, 1989: 83) of people's experiences and understandings of employee empowerment: 'thick descriptions are deep, dense, detailed accounts of problematic experiences'.

The popularity of the 'empowerment era' in the management literature is noted by a number of authors, particularly as organisations have taken steps in 'liberating the creative and innovative energies of employees to compete effectively in a global environment' (Gandz, 1990: 74). Pushing responsibility and decision-making down the organisation is viewed as one way to respond to turbulent environments and increased competition. Furthermore, a demand for quality and the need to provide customer satisfaction have added momentum to the need for employee empowerment at the workplace.

But, despite virtues extolled for employee empowerment and the perceived need to implement it at the workplace, there is concern in the management literature regarding the lack of published research findings, which has led to significant weaknesses and gaps in the existing body of knowledge. Several authors are concerned about the paucity of research with regards to employee empowerment, both at the theoretical and practical levels. Indeed, Morrell and Wilkinson (2002: 121) caution that, 'The term (empowerment) is complex and subject to different interpretations. The implications of this are that it will not be perceived in the same way by different organisations, nor will people within the same organisation think of empowerment in the same way.' Thus, our understanding of employee empowerment is restricted in terms of both theory and practice (Conger and Kanungo, 1988: 471–2).

Hence, although there are robust arguments for employee empowerment in the management literature, a number of authors raise concern with regards to the complexities and problems surrounding it. Undoubtedly, there is a lot of tension and potential for conflict surrounding employee empowerment. In Claydon and Doyle's (1996: 23) view: 'Empowerment is therefore no magic bullet providing a unitarist "cure" for organisational "pathologies"', while Hales (2000: 501) shows concern about 'the divergence between the widespread rhetoric of empowerment and the limited reality of empowerment programmes'. In a similar vein, Ogden et al. (2006: 522) report: 'Little attention has been given to the ways in which empowerment initiatives actually become enacted and incorporated into organisational practices. It is frequently noted that there is a considerable gap between rhetoric and practice.'

There are concerns with regards to these significant gaps in knowledge about employee empowerment; not only on the theoretical and practical levels, but also with regards to its implementation. These inadequacies have the potential to lead to conflict in organisations, arising from, for example, middle management defensiveness and alienation, and a mismatch between management expectations and perceptions, and those of non-management personnel (Huq, 2010). For management, the gaps in knowledge have serious implications, it is disabling organisations, as they do not achieve what they set out to achieve via employee empowerment (Huq, 2010).

Lack of appropriate definitions, models or frameworks have provided little evidence of how employee empowerment can be operationalised (Huq, 2008). A review of the management literature revealed considerable conceptual ambiguity. Thus, in an attempt at enlightenment, the secondary research was drawn from the social work literature (Huq, 2008), because empowerment is an important construct in this discipline. There is a strong consensus in social work that, in practice, empowerment is viewed as a core paradigm, 'the practice of empowerment is now a central paradigm' (Adams, 1996: xv).

There is hardly any information on issues that may arise when implementing employee empowerment or the conditions that are necessary for such an approach to be successful (Wilkinson, 1998). Thus, Hammuda and Dulaimi (1997: 289) point out: 'Misunderstanding of the concept and the steps needed to apply empowerment might lead to unsuccessful implementation, and to some adverse effects', as also demonstrated from the findings of my study. Another added problem is that as the term employee empowerment lacks clarity in its definition, it is confused with other management practices, such as employee involvement and employee participation. Lashley (2001: ix) observes: 'a critical analysis of the literature on empowerment does communicate an array of meanings'. Related to this, several authors are concerned about the interchangeable use of the term 'employee empowerment' with 'employee involvement' and 'employee participation'. Lashley (2001: 49) argues that it is unwise to use these terms 'interchangeably' as it creates confusion. This begs the question: *is employee empowerment a construct distinct from similar others, such as employee involvement or employee participation?* Attempts have been made to highlight the debate and reach a conclusion in this book.

There is high consensus in the management literature that employee empowerment is necessary for the survival and success of organisations. By not empowering employees, businesses have consistently failed to utilise the full potential of employees. With this view, Austen-Smith (1994) argues that since employees deal with customer issues on a daily basis, given the opportunity they would be able to come up with the best solutions to any problems.

Employees in an empowered organisation are viewed as people that hold the key to knowledge, experience and expertise. 'People are the source of ideas and innovation and their expertise, experience, knowledge and co-operation have to be harnessed to get these ideas implemented' (Oakland, 1989, cited in Wilkinson and Brown, 2003: 181).

Thus, there is a growing realisation that in the complexity of the post-modern world, it is becoming less and less feasible to concentrate leadership and decision-making at the top of the organisation. According to Hammer (in Gibson, 1997: 97) what is required is a model whereby employees 'at the front lines' are allocated considerable autonomy and responsibility for decision-making and problem-solving and management exists 'not to direct and control or to supervise, but rather to facilitate and enable', moving towards an employee empowerment culture. There is a shift in employees' attitudes as well. Their perception is that management is not always the expert, and hence employees are not keen to take orders and instructions from above, instead they ask questions and demand answers. This shift is described by Toffler (1991: 4) as the 'crack up of old style, authority and power in business and daily life' and this is accelerating everywhere, office, supermarkets, banks, hospitals, schools, at 'every level of human society'. For empowered organisations this shift is challenging and inevitable, particularly, with decentralisation, as decision-making is vested down the line to front-line employees. Furthermore, with the advance in information technology, it is no longer the case that knowledge is held in one department or by any one person. Hence, empowerment is all around us; people are empowered in more ways than they realise.

But, the lack of a critical analysis of power, together with the absence in mainstream management to address the link between power and empowerment, have been proposed as causes of the unsuccessful results of employee empowerment programmes (Hardy and Leiba-O'Sullivan, 1998). There are obvious tensions and potential for conflict between management and employees concerning the sharing of power. Daft (1999: 257) states that, 'Empowerment programmes can be difficult to implement ... because they destroy hierarchies and upset the familiar balance of power'. Throughout this book, I have continued the discussion of power and power-sharing in relevant places.

It is also interesting to note the importance of employee empowerment placed in the Strategic Human Resource Management (SHRM) literature, which strongly argues that if leaders empower their employees to have more control over their work, take decisions and responsibility at the operational level, this will free leaders to take decisions and responsibility at the strategic level, which in turn would lead to a more judicious utilisation of human resources at all levels.

The lack of knowledge surrounding the employee empowerment construct does not help organisations to get the desirable results or outcomes as argued in the SHRM literature, such as creative decision-making, problem-solving, taking responsibility – these are unlikely to materialise. Hence, leaders in organisations have a responsibility to think about how they are going to empower their employees and what leadership style is needed in an empowered organisation.

'Crisis in Leadership Underscores Global Challenges' – an article in the World Economic Forum (2015), states that: 'The World Economic Forum's Global Leadership Index says 86% of experts believe the world is in the midst of a leadership crisis'.

'This research reveals a massive shake-up … To reclaim leadership status, politicians need to be seen to be serving the greater good again, while international organizations must find new models of governance to demonstrate that they are capable of meeting expectations', said Martina Larkin, Senior Director, Head of Global Knowledge Networks, World Economic Forum (World Economic Forum, 2015).

Leadership is essential for empowered organisations and leaders need to play a crucial role, otherwise, the danger is organisations could be heading for 'crisis' due to lack of the right kind of leadership which is conducive to employee empowerment. If organisations are serious about employee empowerment, first, leaders need the knowledge to understand what employee empowerment means, second, they also need to be clear what they are seeking to achieve via employee empowerment, and third, what framework or model they are going to use to implement employee empowerment in the workplace? Furthermore, there is also a fourth issue, what kind of leadership style should they adopt in an empowered organisation to enable their employees to 'feel' empowered?

In enabling employees, leaders need to be aware of the importance of psychological empowerment of employees, which is paramount. This is based on the argument that empowerment comes from people's personal belief systems, that is, the notion that empowerment *'comes from within'* (Thomas and Velthouse, 1990; Huq, 2010). Believing in oneself, and feeling that *one can do the job* is crucial and underpins the behaviour of empowered employees. Hence, attention must be paid to the locus of control, the self-efficacy and self-esteem of individuals, because these help to shape how individuals view themselves in relation to their work environments and their perceptions of their own capabilities (Spreitzer, 1995).

Employee empowerment is a complex issue, irrespective of whether organisations adopt a formal or informal approach. Furthermore, organisations face several problems, which are exacerbated because of the lack of knowledge of what employee empowerment means and how to implement it. Leaders and CEOs are heading towards a crisis, they are accepting the need to empower employees without giving much thought to planning, evaluating or methods of implementation. A lack of 'framework' for implementation makes it difficult to carry out a comprehensive employee empowerment strategy.

This book makes a number of significant contributions to the subject of employee empowerment.

First, at the conceptual level, this book enhances the knowledge about empowerment through the literature review of two disciplines, social work and management literature (an interdisciplinary approach). The second review of literature (social work) was important to undertake, in order to further the understanding of empowerment.

Second, at the practice level, this book provides insight into the practice and experiences of employee empowerment in organisations from two important perspectives, from people in management (senior and middle) and people in non-management positions.

Third, a new framework for implementing employee empowerment is offered, the Model of Employee Empowerment, Huq's Model D, as a tool to enable implementation.

Fourth, this book sheds light on the kind of leadership style people prefer in an empowered organisation, that is, a 'people-oriented' leadership style. The key characteristics and traits of this kind of leadership style are also explained in this book.

The two organisations in my case study were attempting to embrace employee empowerment, but in different ways, one through a formal programme and the other through informal methods, thus making this study more interesting and challenging. Interviewing people from different positions in the organisational hierarchy, namely, senior management, middle management and non-management positions, was important, in order to gather a wide range of views with regards to employee empowerment. This was useful in order to interpret how different participants in different job positions understood and perceived the meaning of the same subject, thus, different perspectives can help to understand different understanding of the same topic (Rubin and Rubin, 1995).

To summarise, this book does not aspire to be a blueprint for employee empowerment. However, it makes a number of important contributions to knowledge with regards to this subject, which has frequently been criticised for its lack of research. This book has significantly contributed to knowledge with regards to the understanding of employee empowerment, not only at a conceptual level, but also at the practice level. If leaders in organisations are serious about employee empowerment, first, they need the knowledge to understand what employee empowerment means, second, they also need to be clear what they are seeking to achieve and, third, they need a 'framework' for implementation.

In the absence of a framework, how are they going to enable their employees to help them achieve whatever outcomes organisations are seeking, via employee empowerment? Recognising the global leadership 'crisis', in this book I have provided a framework for employee empowerment. It is hoped that through the help of this framework, the Model of Employee Empowerment, Huq's Model D, leaders will be able to provide an *enabling* environment for the success of employee empowerment in their organisation.

PART 1
What is Employee Empowerment About?

Chapter 1
Concept of Employee Empowerment in the Management Literature

Introduction

Within the context of intense competition, organisations are constantly seeking new sources of competitive advantage. What is required is a model whereby employees 'at the front lines' are allocated considerable autonomy and responsibility for decision-making and problem-solving and management exists 'not to direct and control or to supervise, but rather to facilitate and enable' (Hammer in Gibson, 1997: 97).

In line with such arguments, organisations responded to the competitive market by attempting to empower their employees; but, there are a number of problems. The first problem is the 'what' and the second problem, 'how?'. In other words, organisations do not grasp the real meaning of 'what' employee empowerment means and, second, 'how' to implement it?

Another problem is that employee empowerment is often confused with other management initiatives, such as 'employee involvement' and 'employee participation', and this also contributes to the complexity of implementation. Clearly, these kind of misconceptions can make it difficult for organisations to identify suitable methods and means to implement and sustain the practice of employee empowerment, with the result that 'its application in organisational settings is fraught with misunderstanding and tension' (Denham Lincoln et al., 2002: 271) leading to a 'frustration' amongst managers (Ford and Fottler, 1995: 22).

My research findings reveal that a number of 'themes' of employee empowerment exist, which are fragmented in the management literature.

These 'themes' are not found in any one place. This lack of information leads to further confusion when organisations try to implement employee empowerment.

This chapter begins by setting employee empowerment in a historical context; ironing out some of the ambiguity and confusion that surrounds the concept and bringing together the themes, under the umbrella of *Themes of Employee Empowerment Emanating from the Management Literature*, Huq's Model A (Figure 1.1) that is fundamental to the understanding of it.

Historical Context

A shortcoming of employee empowerment in the management literature is that although there is a plethora of articles and books available on this subject, very few attempt to set it within the historical context (Huq, 2010). Historically, there is neither one single definition of employee empowerment, nor one theoretical construction in the management literature.

> *There is no single nor simple definition of empowerment. Equally, its prescriptive dimensions cannot be directly traced to any dominant theoretical construction. (Cunningham and Hyman, 1999: 193)*

Several authors report that employee empowerment in the 1980s came to prominence as a management response to rapid economic and technological change, and an increasingly complex and competitive external environment (Block, 1987; Peters, 1987; Belasco, 1989; Gandz, 1990; Hammer and Champy, 1993; Hoepfl, 1994; Clutterbuck and Kernaghan, 1995; Lawler et al., 1995; Collins, 1996b; Kondo, 1997; Wilkinson, 1998; Potterfield, 1999; Sigler and Pearson, 2000; Huczynski and Buchanan, 2001; Morrell and Wilkinson; 2002; Psoinos and Smithson, 2002; Greasley et al., 2005).

Authors such as Morrell and Wilkinson (2002: 120) note that employee empowerment is associated with 'the "excellence" movement, where the customer is "king". In this sense, empowerment should enable organisations to be more immediately responsive to their customers, as decision-making is devolved'.

> *'Productivity through people', 'autonomy and entrepreneurship' summed up the new philosophy which when combined with 'the customer is king' provided the context for current empowerment ideas. (Wilkinson, 1998: 42)*

Certainly, the quality movement played an important part, underpinning the philosophy of employee empowerment. A number of authors agree that the term employee empowerment came about as organisations were trying to implement initiatives, such as Total Quality Management (TQM) (Lawler et al., 1995; Wilkinson, 1998; Sigler and Pearson, 2000; Morrell and Wilkinson, 2002; Psoinos and Smithson, 2002) and Business Process Re-Engineering (BPR) (Hammer and Champy, 1993; Psoinos and Smithson, 2002; Greasley et al., 2005).

> *The quality movement was also influential during this period. While its principles had been developed by Japanese companies in the late 1950s and 1960s, interest in the West peaked in the 1980s, and there appeared to be a strong message of empowerment (Wilkinson et al., 1992). Under TQM, continuous improvement is undertaken by those involved in a process and this introduces bottom-up issue identification and problem-solving. As a result TQM may empower employees by delegating functions that were previously the preserve of more senior organisational members. (Wilkinson, 1998: 43)*

Empowerment is seen 'in many respects as a rejection of the traditional classical model of management associated with Taylor and Ford where standardised products were made through economies of scale and the division of labour, and workers carried out fragmented and repetitive jobs' (Wilkinson, 1998: 44).

A major spur to the popularity of employee empowerment has been the quality movement and, in particular, TQM; both advocate an open style of management, with devolution of responsibility down the line. A key feature of TQM is empowering employees (Crosby, 1979; Deming, 1986; Juran, 1988; Oakland, 1989; Farnham et al., 2005). TQM stipulates that continuous improvement should be undertaken by those involved in a process, thereby introducing elements of bottom-up identification of issues and problems (Wilkinson, 1998; Farnham et al., 2005).

It is also important to note the negative force that has driven the employee empowerment initiative historically, such as rationalisation and downsizing during the 1980s and 1990s. This has created the conception that employee empowerment is for the benefit of organisations only to combat cost-effectiveness and does not relay any benefits to its employees.

> *In the 1980s and 1990s rationalisation and downsizing were very much the order of the day. In this context empowerment became a business necessity, as the destaffed and delayered organisation could no*

> *longer function as before. In this set of circumstances, empowerment*
> *was inevitable, as tasks had to be allocated to the survivors in the new*
> *organisation. (Wilkinson, 1998: 43–4)*

From the human resource management point of view, employee empowerment in the 1990s was underpinned by the notion that competitive advantage can only be achieved by unleashing the power of the workforce (Pfeffer, 1994).

Hence, in general, organisations accept the notion of employee empowerment as a good thing, but in practice struggle with its implementation.

Ambiguity and Confusion

Significant problems regarding employee empowerment range from the vagueness of what it means, to the practicalities of implementing it. 'Guidelines on making it happen are typically vague and over-generalized' (Wilson, 2004: 167). Furthermore, this confusion is exacerbated by the 'interchangeable' use of the word employee empowerment with 'employee involvement' and 'employee participation'. This gives rise to ambiguity and confusion surrounding it. Hence, 'a critical analysis of the literature on empowerment does communicate an array of meanings' (Lashley, 2001: ix).

It is hardly surprising then, that as Ghoshal and Bartlett (1997: 312) point out, in practice, employee empowerment encompasses anything from employee suggestion schemes to the restructuring of the organisation around self-managed teams. It is also argued that different meanings of employee empowerment held by organisations can be problematic, as noted by Clutterbuck and Kernaghan (1995: 7):

> *it is almost impossible to gain any kind of rational consensus as to*
> *exactly what it (empowerment) is. In visiting companies around the*
> *world, I have encountered organisations that perceive empowerment*
> *to be a total dismantling of the managerial structure in favour of a*
> *semi-egalitarian ideal; companies that consider empowerment to be*
> *little more than delegation; and others that see it simply as an element*
> *of some other change programme, such as total quality management.*

It is interesting to note that: 'Many companies (if not the majority), and the managers and human resource people, within them, do not truly understand what empowerment is or exactly what it entails' (Pastor, 1996: 7). Hence, in practice, there are problems in implementing employee empowerment, as organisations struggle with the meaning of it. This is illustrated by Lashley (2001: 6):

> In the hospitality industry, for example, employee empowerment is a term that had been used to describe quality circles (Accor group), suggestion schemes (McDonald's Restaurants), customer care programmes (Scott's Hotels), employee involvement in devising departmental standards (Hilton Hotels), autonomous work groups (Harvester Restaurants) and delayering the organisation (Bass Taverns).

Obviously, if management do not have clarity in their understanding of what employee empowerment means, it can be difficult for them to communicate to employees what they are trying to implement. In the absence of a clear message, the danger is that employees can then formulate their own definitions that, in turn, will influence their expectations (Cunningham et al., 1996; Denham et al., 1997; Morrell and Wilkinson, 2002), which may be different from those of management.

Hence, there is concern not only about the ambiguity regarding the meaning of employee empowerment, but also how employees perceive it, 'when we talk about empowerment do we all mean the same thing?' (Burdett, 1991: 23). Another danger is that some managers believe empowering means letting people 'loose' on a project as if they are now empowered to do whatever they want (Pastor, 1996: 5). Hales (2000: 503) draws a cautionary note for those who extol employee empowerment's virtue and highlights the lack of clarity with regards to who is to be empowered and to what extent:

> Certainly, the burgeoning prescriptive or celebratory literature on empowerment is replete with equivocation, tautology and contradiction in equal measure about what 'empowerment' is, for whom, to what extent, where and why empowerment should occur and what else accompanies it.

Obviously, one of the problems is that organisations are trying to implement employee empowerment without having a great deal of knowledge about this subject.

Unravelling the Mystery

Several authors agree that the concept of employee empowerment in the management literature is diverse and loose (Wilkinson, 1998; Thomas and Velthouse, 1990). For example, in Gandz's (1990: 75) view: 'Empowerment means that management vests decision-making or approval authority in employees where, traditionally, such authority was a managerial prerogative.' Authors such as, Huczynski and Buchanan (2001: 262) view autonomy and decision-making to be fundamental elements in employee empowerment, as illustrated: 'Empowerment is the term given to organisational arrangements that allow employees more autonomy, discretion and unsupervised decision-making responsibility.' Similarly, Martin (2005: 241) describes empowering employees where 'Employees are given the freedom (within defined boundaries) to take action without the need to seek approval.'

Interestingly, some authors view employee empowerment simply as a concept or philosophy such as, Ripley and Ripley (1992: 21), who define empowerment as 'a concept, philosophy, set of organisational behavioural practices, and an organisational programme'. According to other authors, distribution of power is fundamental in employee empowerment (Conger and Kanungo, 1988; Bolin, 1989; Thomas and Velthouse, 1990).

Expanding on Conger and Kanungo's (1988) study, Thomas and Velthouse (1990: 677) identify employee empowerment from the psychological point of view and describe it as: 'an emerging, non-traditional paradigm of management' and further go on to stress: 'We have argued that the motivational content of this paradigm involves the fostering of intrinsic task motivation among workers.' Thus, employee empowerment is also viewed as a psychological concept leading to intrinsic motivation (Conger and Kanungo, 1988; Thomas and Velthouse, 1990; Siegall and Gardner, 2000) and self-efficacy (Conger and Kanungo, 1988; Thomas and Velthouse, 1990; Spreitzer, 1995, 1996; Hartline and Ferrell, 1996; Heslin, 1999; Siegall and Gardner, 2000).

These different meanings of employee empowerment held by organisations can be problematic, as noted by Clutterbuck and Kernaghan (1995: 7):

> it is almost impossible to gain any kind of rational consensus as to exactly what it is. In visiting companies around the world, I have encountered organisations that perceive empowerment to be a total dismantling of the managerial structure in favour of a semi-egalitarian ideal; companies that consider empowerment to be little more than

delegation; and others that see it simply as an element of some other change programme, such as total quality management.

Clearly, such confusion and ambiguity have implications for organisations seeking to implement employee empowerment. The term employee empowerment does have a number of themes attached to it and therefore it produces a number of meanings.

As already mentioned, employee empowerment is blamed for communicating *an array* of meanings. At the outset, employee empowerment does seem mysterious with so many different interpretations accompanying it. In reality, there is no mystery regarding employee empowerment; simply, a multi-dimensional approach is necessary with regards to understanding the notion of employee empowerment. It is not possible to capture the essence of empowerment in a single concept (Thomas and Velthouse, 1990).

Honold (1997: 210) rightfully states: 'it seems that employee empowerment is multi-dimensional. No single set of contingencies can describe it.' In a similar tone, authors such as Greasley et al. (2005) are also in agreement and they too assert the need for a multi-dimensional approach, particularly in order to sustain the employee empowerment strategy in organisations. This is what is largely missing with regards to employee empowerment in the management literature; the fact that it has more than one dimension or themes and that all of these themes need to be considered.

In this book, I have attempted to pull the themes of employee empowerment from the management literature discussed next.

Themes of Employee Empowerment Emanating from Management Literature: Huq's Model A

It is agreed that a number of themes surround employee empowerment. A review of the management literature highlights power-sharing; participative decision-making; devolution of responsibility and people-oriented leadership style – Huq's Model A (see Figure 1.1). These are some of the key themes of employee empowerment emanating from the management literature.

- Theme: Power-sharing

- Theme: Participative decision-making

- Theme: Devolution of responsibility

- Theme: People-oriented leadership style

Figure 1.1   Huq's Model A: themes of employee empowerment emanating from management literature

It is evident that employee empowerment is not viewed as a one-dimensional management practice, there are several themes associated with it. The importance and significance of these aforementioned themes are explained next.

Power-Sharing

The *Concise Oxford Dictionary*'s (p. 339) definition of 'empower' is to 'give power', thus to 'empower' is to:

> *Authorise, license, (person to do);*
> *Give power to, make able, (person to do).*

In the literal sense, empowerment is about giving power. This needs to be highlighted, and several authors do this. For example, Lashley (2001) emphasises that the power dimension is fundamental to understanding the concept of empowerment. Dupuy (2004: 217) recognises that to empower is to acquire '*more power*', which is the literal translation of the word 'empowerment'. Other authors, such as Wilson (2004: 167), stress that in order to empower employees, power needs to be shared: 'it concerns an individual's power and control relative to others, as well as the sharing of power and control, and the transmitting of power from one individual to another with less'. In a similar vein, Neumann (1992/3: 25) defines empowerment as 'passing on previously withheld power and authority to employees further down the hierarchy'.

There is agreement in the literature that the distribution of power is more important than the hoarding of power (Kanter, 1984; Goski and Belfry, 1991; Daft, 1999; Greenberg and Baron, 2000). It makes sense to give employees power, especially 'to make certain decisions and resolve certain issues themselves' (Lashley, 2001: 7). But, the question is does this really happen in organisations? The problem is that management hide their heads in the sand when it comes to power-sharing, despite the fact that it is widely agreed that power-sharing is an essential part of employee empowerment (Kanter, 1984; Block, 1987; Conger and Kanungo, 1988; Bowen and Lawler, 1992; Martin and Vogt, 1992; Neumann, 1992/3; Ashness and Lashley, 1995; Hardy and Leiba-O'Sullivan, 1998; Wilkinson, 1998; Daft, 1999; Quinn and Davies, 1999; Greenberg and Baron, 2000; Lashley, 2001; Denham Lincoln et al., 2002; Dupuy, 2004; Wilson, 2004).

But, there are tensions and often conflict surrounding the sharing and distribution of power. Undoubtedly, in empowered organisations, power structures will be challenged. Lashley (2001: 160) notes: 'empowerment essentially implies that organisational power structures are being altered so as to allow individuals (operatives or managers) more power.' The removal of hierarchies and the implementation of flat structures in empowered organisations give rise to some questions, such as, what happens to power held by people and how is it shared, if at all? These are challenging questions for empowered organisations where employees expect managers to be flexible in their sharing of power. But, the literature does not provide clear information on how management should share power and management feel they are caught in a dilemma because they are not sure how they can do this, without diminishing their own power (Tjosvold et al., 1998).

The ambiguity concerning the meaning of employee empowerment is seen by some authors, such as Edmonstone and Havergal (1993), to be perhaps an unfortunate source of ambivalence among managers. They may see employee empowerment as a structural form of control as far as workers are concerned. Fincham and Rhodes (2005: 430) conclude that traditional organisational hierarchies are 'structures of deeply entrenched power, and this has also proved to be a major constraint on work humanization'. Often, people with power at the top, such as leaders or chief executives, are uncomfortable with changes, and feel so threatened by the fear of losing their control, that projects can encounter great resistance, with the result that they are sometimes even dropped. The problem is that management are not sure how to share power in organisations without diminishing their own power (Tjosvold et al., 1998) and they fail to understand that the transformation of power helps to build dynamism and energy in organisations (Murrell, 1985; Morgan, 1986). For example, Murrell (1985: 36) explains that: 'to empower is to create power'.

Although power and employee empowerment are inextricably linked, several authors have expressed concern about management's reluctance to share power (Conger and Kanungo, 1988; Hardy and Leiba-O'Sullivan, 1998; Wilkinson, 1998; Quinn and Davies, 1999; Lashley, 2001; Denham Lincoln et al., 2002), as disempowered employees can suffer from low self-efficacy and low self-esteem. In such cases, instead of feeling empowered, the danger is that employees can feel de-motivated and lose their belief in the organisation's strategy of empowering employees. Daft (1999: 10) argues: 'Today's leaders need to share power rather than hoard it and find ways to increase an organisation's brain power.' This is a crucial issue – it is management's task to ensure that the organisation derives maximum benefit for its investment in human resources, utilising all their skills and expertise and this also leads to employees feeling valued, and an increase in their self-efficacy, self-esteem and self-confidence.

Participative Decision-Making

A number of authors agree on the importance of participative decision-making with regards to employee empowerment (Conger and Kanungo, 1988; Gandz, 1990; Goski and Belfry, 1991; Bowen and Lawler III, 1992; Ripley and Ripley, 1992; Clement, 1994; Johnson, 1994; Ashness and Lashley, 1995; Besterfield et al., 1995; Ford and Fottler, 1995; Cunningham et al., 1996; Kondo, 1997; Wilkinson, 1998; Greenberg and Baron, 2000; Hales, 2000; Huczynski and Buchanan, 2001; Lashley, 2001; Martin, 2005; Beirne, 2006; Hasan, 2010). This stems from the economic argument that employees should be allowed to take decisions and given the requisite authority, as this will contribute to the effectiveness of the organisation (Gandz, 1990; Wilkinson, 1998).

It is argued that one of the reasons for empowering employees is that employees are able to take decisions quickly, without looking for manager's approval, in a participative decision-making capacity. Hence, 'Authority to make decisions and take action must increasingly be vested in those who are closest to the problem if maximum speed is to be achieved ... Empowered people respond faster' (Gandz, 1990: 75).

But, there is concern with regards to participative decision-making that although employees are told they are empowered, as Ashness and Lashley's (1995) study reveals, significant decisions still tended to be taken by the team manager at unit level. In a similar vein, Cunningham et al.'s (1996) research also reveals that those organisations which allowed participative decision-making did so only to a limited extent. Arguments also exist that often employees are unwilling, for fear of the consequences of taking wrong decisions, in case they are penalised or lose their jobs (Ripley and Ripley, 1992). In such cases, empowering employees will be counter-productive, as employees will be reluctant to take decisions.

In reality, it seems that participative decision-making does not always give employees the confidence to take decisions, due to the negative psychological implication of the fear of being reprimanded. However, in order to respond to customers' needs in a timely and effective manner, it is essential for empowered employees at all levels to be free to take decisions without constant worry and apprehension.

Devolution of Responsibility

It is agreed in the management literature that the devolution of responsibility is also necessary in order to empower employees (Hellriegel et al., 1989; Gandz, 1990; Jones and Davies, 1991; Clement, 1994; Johnson, 1994; Peters, 1994; Ashness and Lashley, 1995; Clutterbuck and Kernaghan, 1995; Ford and Fottler, 1995; Marchington, 1995; Claydon and Doyle, 1996; Cunningham et al., 1996; Kondo, 1997; Wilkinson, 1998; Walton, 1999; Greenberg and Baron, 2000; Hales, 2000; Lashley, 2001; McAuley et al., 2007; Sahoo and Das, 2011).

As previously stated, if managers empower non-managerial employees to take responsibility for decision-making and problem-solving at the operational level, this would empower managers to exercise their responsibilities at the strategic level. On a psychological level, it is also argued, for example, that the positive effects of self-efficacy and self-esteem can enable employees to cope with the extra responsibilities that employee empowerment brings. In a similar vein, Nesan and Holt (2002: 201) state:

Authorising employees to be responsible for their own work makes them simultaneously an inspector and processor. Consequently, this approach greatly reduces and/or eliminates unnecessary non-value added procedures and enables individuals to be involved in the improvement of their business.

In many cases, people like taking on responsibility, because they feel work becomes more meaningful. Ashness and Lashley (1995) note in their study that several employees gained a great deal through the devolution of responsibilities, making them feel more involved and more trusted. However, there are some critical issues concerning devolution of responsibility, particularly, with lack of clarity with regards to salary, parameters and boundaries of people's jobs. In addition to these problems, devolution of responsibility is also perceived as a means of giving employees more responsibility for less, or sometimes no reward. There is a danger that employees might interpret devolution of responsibility as simply abdication of management responsibility.

An important point to note is that the devolution of responsibility without authority is meaningless, as employees need to have the requisite authority to carry out the decisions they have made. The absence of the requisite authority to carry out decisions would lead to subsequent low motivation and morale; this is often overlooked and ignored by leaders in organisations. There is evidence that people like to take responsibility, it not only makes them feel valued, it *empowers* them. 'Providing opportunities to be responsible *empowers* people' (Hellriegel et al., 1989: 576).

However, implementing employee empowerment is not easy; leaders fail to understand the significant role that they need to play in the empowerment process in organisations; this theme is discussed next.

People-Oriented Leadership Style

It is generally agreed that there are problems in understanding what leadership is on a general level because leadership can mean different things to different people, and, in the context of employee empowerment, it is even more complex (Bennis, 1984; Pearlstein, 1991; Graen and Uhl-Bien, 1995).

One of the biggest challenges for empowered organisations concerns the role of leaders. How should leaders lead in an empowered organisation? What roles should leaders play? What kind of qualities do they need to have to support employee empowerment and how should they develop their skills? The answers to these questions are not easily found because historically there has been a lack of education regarding the development of leadership skills (Bennis, 1984; Pearlstein, 1991). There is an argument that 'we teach people how to be good technicians and good staff people, but we don't train people for leadership' (Bennis, 1984: 17).

In this sense, it needs to be pointed out that developing a people-oriented leadership style that supports employee empowerment is a significant part of the employee empowerment process. However, a review of the literature on leadership in the context of employee empowerment has been unsatisfactory. There is inadequate discussion and research in the management literature, yet leadership is critical; it can be the difference between success and failure in the practice of employee empowerment in organisations.

> *If I have learned anything from my research, it is this: The factor that empowers the work force and ultimately determines which organisations succeed or fail is the leadership of those organisations. (Bennis, 1984: 16)*

It is useful to note Ripley and Ripley's (1992) argument regarding the differences between a leader who is empowering and one who is not; they describe an empowering leader as having characteristics, such as, being interactive; encouraging participation; sharing power and information willingly and leaning towards a democratic people-oriented leadership style. By way of contrast, the traditional authoritarian leader is predisposed to operate in command control mode and is unwilling to share power and information. Hence, a more democratic type of people-oriented leadership style, where leaders discuss and collaborate with employees, is desirable in empowered organisations.

In Block's (1987) view, the traditional contract between employees and employers is patriarchal in nature and that means high control by leaders and submission to authority by employees. With this kind of mindset the assumption is that if employees are given authority and responsibility, it will be counter-productive for the organisation. Therefore, the belief is that authority from the top must be constantly reinforced. Block (1987: 29) describes this as the 'pessimistic view of human nature'. Leaders who have patriarchal attitudes and a passion for control will find it difficult to lead effectively in an empowered organisation. Hence, balancing between a democratic and an authoritative approach is a 'major dilemma' facing leaders (Wilson, 2004: 239).

Clearly, leaders need to change and adopt new skills in an empowered organisation in order to develop a people-oriented leadership style, discussed in Part VI of this book.

Employee Empowerment, How Does it Differ From Other Management Practices?

There is major concern with employee empowerment with regards to the confusion with other management practices, such as employee involvement or employee participation. Although this book is not about these aforementioned management practices, nevertheless, I feel it is important to briefly discuss the ways in which employee empowerment is different from these practices.

Several authors report the lack of clarity between employee empowerment and employee involvement or employee participation, which has also given rise to concern (Conger and Kanungo, 1988; Alpander, 1991; Goski and Belfry, 1991; Cotton, 1993; Ripley and Ripley, 1993; Hammuda and Dulaimi, 1997; Lashley, 2001; Lee and Koh, 2001; Denham Lincoln et al., 2002; Psoinos and Smithson, 2002). For example, Cotton (1993) and Lashley (2001) draw attention to the 'interchangeable use' of the terms 'employee involvement' and 'employee empowerment' by management writers. A major problem is that 'there is rarely a recognition of, let alone an attempt to explain or define, the boundaries between them' (Lashley, 2001: 5–6), and this has the potential to create significant misunderstanding, hence the argument that it is unwise to use the above terms 'interchangeably' as it creates confusion (Lashley, 2001: 49).

Historically, employee empowerment has evolved from management initiatives, such as employee involvement and employee participation. However, sometimes these terms are used interchangeably with employee empowerment, which creates confusion. This has the potential which can lead to the failure of employee empowerment initiatives (Lashley, 2001; Psoinos and Smithson, 2002). Obviously, there is cause to be concerned with regards to the lack of clarity between these terms.

Employee empowerment is different from other management practices, such as employee involvement and participation, and needs to be viewed differently. A number of authors argue that clearly it is power-sharing which differentiates employee empowerment from employee involvement and participation (Ford and Fottler, 1995; Wilkinson, 1998; Lashley, 2001; Martin, 2005). Other authors, such as Psoinos and Smithson (2002: 134), propose that the main difference between employee involvement, participation and employee involvement is to do with the 'transfer' of decision-making authority, as explained below:

> *Whereas in both involvement and participation, management retains control, in empowerment employees have – at least to some degree – authority to make and implement their own decisions.*

Employee involvement (EI) is defined by Fincham and Rhodes (2005: 437) as: 'a recent movement of work improvement ... which emphasises a wide range of methods including communications and changes in work culture, as well as work redesign'. In their investigation they found that, although not dramatic, changes in work design allow low levels of input from employees, as there were 'some signs of a move away from strictly Taylorist methods towards more broadly based work flows' (Fincham and Rhodes, 2005: 436); but there is no power-sharing involved. Employee involvement is as it states, simply an involvement of employees in organisational strategy or decisions. It is important to note that it is only an '*involvement*'; it does not mean that management allows strategic decisions to be taken by employees, as in employee empowerment.

Even participation is viewed by several authors as at best a 'consultative' process without any real sharing of power (Arnold and Feldman, 1986; Hellriegel et al., 1989). For example, 'Participative leadership characterises a leader who, when faced with a decision, consults with subordinates, solicits their suggestions, and takes ideas seriously in arriving at a decision' (Arnold and Feldman, 1986: 131). However, it is the leader who actually takes the decision in the end. Another problem is that many organisations mistakenly define participatory management as employee empowerment, but participatory management does not necessarily include employees all the time in decisions that may affect their jobs (Alpander, 1991; Goski and Belfry, 1991; Ford and Fottler, 1995). Thus, Alpander (1991: 14) argues: 'simply equating empowerment with participative management does not adequately address the process as experienced by subordinates'.

Notable, the tendency in employee involvement and participation is that employees are told by management to be involved or to participate in particular projects, or to put forward ideas and suggestions for specific purposes. Under these initiatives employees are asked for input but they do not make the final decisions. This kind of involvement or participation 'by invitation' only, is not viewed as employee empowerment. Empowered employees should have the freedom and be able to bring forward ideas and suggestions on their own initiative, and not only when being asked or told to do so.

Clearly, it is power-sharing which differentiates employee empowerment from employee involvement and participation (Ford and Fottler, 1995; Wilkinson, 1998; Lashley, 2001; Greasley et al., 2005; Martin, 2005). For example, Lashley (2001: 161) argues that as far as quality circles, team briefings or suggestion schemes are concerned, these are implemented to increase commitment in employees, but there is no 'significant attempt to redistribute organisational power'. Greasley et al. (2005: 365) emphasise: 'the main barriers [to employee empowerment] can be associated with whether the leader is reluctant to share power or has a set way of doing work and is inflexible to change.'

To put it simply, the argument is that it is not possible to empower employees without a meaningful sharing of power by management with their subordinates. This is clearly illustrated by Wilkinson (1998: 45):

> *At its simplest, empowerment would commonsensically be associated with the redistribution of power, but in practice empowerment is usually seen as a form of employee involvement, designed by management and intended to generate commitment and enhance employee contributions to the organisation. While some forms of employee involvement may provide employees with new channels through which their influence is enhanced, employee involvement does not involve any de jure sharing of authority or power.*

Sharing power is the purposeful act of giving employees the authority to make decisions. Viewed in this way, Ford and Fottler (1995: 22) vehemently argue that 'the concept of empowerment is something broader than the traditional concepts of delegation, decentralisation and participatory management as the responsibility for the decision-making process is stretched beyond a mere contribution to a specific decision area'. Similarly, Goski and Belfry (1991: 213) argue: 'Empowerment is not just a new term for what many organisations have defined as participatory or incentive management. Empowerment is broader than these, in that it fosters the inclusion of all employees in the decisions that affect their job functions and performance.'

Adhering to these arguments, employee involvement cannot be seen as employee empowerment since the former does not give power to employees or an opportunity for input into the decision-making process in the organisation as and when appropriate. The potential to give employees more control over their working lives is an important point that differentiates employee empowerment from employee involvement or participation.

There is consensus in the management literature that the most significant area of difference between employee empowerment and other management initiatives is power-sharing. By distributing and sharing power with employees, management passes on authority and opportunities for employees to take decisions. This means that, in an empowered organisation, operational decisions are not made hierarchically because employees are allowed to have a say in both strategic and operational decision-making, which makes it totally different from employee involvement or participation. Hence on the basis of power-sharing alone, employee empowerment emerges as a distinct construct, separate from employee involvement or employee participation. Based on these reasoning, it may be concluded that employee empowerment is a unique concept and that this uniqueness should not be substituted with any of the aforementioned terms.

Conclusion

As indicated, a review of the management literature reveals that there are several themes of employee empowerment. If organisations want to implement employee empowerment, then they need to address these themes in practice, namely, power-sharing, participative decision-making, devolution of responsibility and a people-oriented leadership style (Huq's Model A).

One argument supporting the merits of employee empowerment is that through the distribution and sharing of power, the domination of subordinate groups by more powerful ones can be reduced. This is where the major difference lies between employee empowerment and other management initiatives, such as employee involvement or employee participation.

A significant contribution of this chapter is that it highlights how employee empowerment differs from other management initiatives such as employee involvement and employee participation. Primarily, the latter initiatives do not necessitate the sharing of power by management with their subordinates. Further, this chapter suggests that the former, that is, employee empowerment, comprises particular themes, namely, power-sharing, participative decision-making, devolution of responsibility and a people-oriented leadership style (Huq's Model A), which are not necessarily associated with employee involvement or employee participation.

It is evident from the management literature that there is misunderstanding and misconception with regards to the knowledge about employee empowerment; this is further exacerbated by the lack of information with regards to implementation. It is abundantly clear that there are some key themes with regards to the practice of employee empowerment and the problem is that these are fragmented. Different authors talk about these themes in different ways, hence employee empowerment sounds confusing and ambiguous.

The themes of employee empowerment (Huq's Model A) enable us to recognise that employee empowerment is multi-dimensional and holds a number of themes. If organisations are serious about practising employee empowerment, then they need to address these key themes before the employee empowerment process can begin, namely, power-sharing; participative decision-making; devolution of responsibility and, furthermore, organisations need to be alert that employee empowerment needs a particular kind of leadership style, namely a people-oriented one.

An empowered organisation also means that the structure needs to change from a command and control mode to a power-sharing, decentralised form. These aforementioned themes of employee empowerment potentially can enable organisations to move to a flatter structure; decentralise power and authority, thus, moving towards de-bureaucratisation.

Chapter 2
The Debate: Why Empower and Why Not?

Introduction

Chapter 2 sets the scene with a crucial discussion of the arguments underpinning Strategic Human Resource Management (SHRM) theory and neo-modernist organisation theory; both strongly argue the need for employee empowerment in organisations.

Theories are important, as Greenberg and Baron (2000: 43) explain: 'we define a theory as being a set of statements about the interrelationships between concepts that allow us to predict and to explain various processes and events'. In line with these arguments I would also like to offer the debate from three perspectives, which I describe as the '*Triangular Perspective of Employee Empowerment*', namely, the economic, psychological and critical perspectives, discussed in this chapter.

Strategic Human Resource Management (SHRM) Theory and Neo-Modernist Organisation Theory

The competitive nature of the global market place and business environment has made effective utilisation of human resources a strategic issue for organisations. There is a growing realisation that traditional hierarchical 'command and control' organisations are struggling to meet the increasing demands for flexibility and quality. It is widely accepted also, that in the complexity of the post-modern world, it is becoming less and less feasible to concentrate leadership at the top of organisations. Rather, it needs to be diffused, and responsibility for decision-making and problem-solving devolved down to lower level employees. Even service organisations are feeling vulnerable – with a greater level of uncertainty and an increase in demanding customers.

It is a challenge for them to retain loyal customers. Empowering front-line employees is an absolute necessity.

SHRM theory stems from the premise that an organisation's only sustainable competitive advantage is its people (Peters and Waterman, 1982; Peters, 1987; du Gay and Salaman, 1998; Huselid, 1998; Mabey et al., 1998; Corsun and Enz, 1999; Schuler and Jackson, 1999; Walton, 1999; Siegall and Gardner, 2000; Leach et al., 2003; Beirne, 2006; Hitt et al., 2006; Silzer and Dowell, 2010). There is strong agreement in the management literature that the human resources of an organisation are a source of competitive advantage. Hence, if organisations are going down the route of empowering employees then they need to have congruence between their policies and SHRM goals. The argument in the domain of SHRM is organisations that pursue an employee empowerment strategy actually enable their employees to build up 'distinctive skills' and 'competencies', such as decision-making, problem-solving, taking responsibility. These 'distinctive skills' (Walton, 1999) of employees in turn help the organisation to compete and cope with the changes in the marketplace. Thus, SHRM is important, it helps to diagnose the needs of human resources according to talent. Hence, talent management is crucial for organisations in order to develop a competitive SHRM strategy to be different and unique in serving its customers and to achieve organisational goals (Silzer and Dowell, 2010). This requires a radical change in human resources recruiting, matching talents to the needs of the organisation.

> Organisations are beginning to understand the strategic value of talent and the impact that strong talent can have on financial outcomes. This represents a major shift in how business executives view the value of Human Resources. Companies realised that successful buying or building critical talent would create competitive advantage in the global market place. (Silzer and Dowell, 2010: xxi)

SHRM has an important role to play. It can improve the function of human resource department, enabling it to link with the strategic objectives of the organisation in order to improve performance and be effective. Referring to the major organisation-wide changes and initiatives that are taking place, Walton (1999: 3) observes that, 'people are the only truly sustainable resource providing long-term competitive and customer advantage. Any organisation can quickly access the elements of new technology … what is scarcer are the distinctive skills or competencies which individuals bring to, and acquire, during their stay with a given enterprise'. In line with this, Barney (1991) emphasises that the purpose of SHRM is to create a sustainable competitive advantage, and this can be achieved through the *talents* of people.

From the human resource perspective, valuing people and developing their potential is also resonant with neo-modernist thinking. In the neo-modernist paradigm, 'people' play an important role in organisations. Thus, neo-modernism challenges the 'place of the "human" in organisations' and is 'concerned with putting people at the heart of the organisation' (McAuley et al., 2007: 101), as illustrated below:

> *Neo-modernism is 'neo' in the sense that it is an organisation theory that is concerned with putting people at the heart of the organisation; it is 'modernist' in the sense that it assumes that effective 'organisations' are fundamental to human progress.*

The traditional model of the manager being in control and employees being controlled can no longer be sustained in organisations; this is the essence behind the argument of SHRM theory. Thus, it is essential to develop human resource skills. Accordingly, Huselid (1998: 194) argues: 'a firm's current and potential human resources are important considerations in the development and execution of its strategic business plan.'

Undoubtedly, *an organisation's human resources are the backbone of the development and execution of its strategic business plan.* It has been noted that an increasing number of organisations are considering employee empowerment as part of their human resource strategy for competitive advantage (Lashley and McGoldrick, 1994). Furthermore, employees do not want to be regarded as subjects to be controlled and mere 'attendants' to machinery, and in this sense employee empowerment is viewed as 'a rejection of a strict division of labour, with workers seen as "attendants" to machinery, carrying out fragmented and repetitive jobs' (Marchington and Wilkinson, 2000: 342).

Within the discourse of the enterprising organisation, it is argued in SHRM that, 'Governing the business in an enterprising manner is therefore said to involve "empowering", "responsibilizing" and "enabling" all members of that organisation to "add value" – both to the company for which they work and to themselves' (du Gay and Salaman, 1998: 61). It is important to emphasise here that this includes enabling employees to add value to themselves.

Hence, organisational effectiveness derives from judicious utilisation of human resources and all organisational members need to be engaged and active for a company to be successful (Siegall and Gardner, 2000). Shipper and Manz (1992: 48) note: 'In attempting to use their human resources more fully, many organisations have moved beyond the mentality that managers make decisions and employees are simply expected to do what they're told.'

Clearly, there are strong arguments within the domain of SHRM that employees need to be empowered, so that all members in the organisation can 'add value' in order to achieve organisational goals. Hence, in the words of Siegall and Gardner (2000: 703): 'The concept of empowerment is closely aligned with this thrust to gain organisational effectiveness through the wise utilisation of human resources.' This has resonance with neo-modernist theory, which argues that in order to develop effective organisations; there is a need to integrate the person into the organisation. Interestingly, neo-modernism favours democratic values in organisations, and 'emphasises the idea of empowerment of *all* members of the organisation' (Siegall and Gardner, 2000: 101). Based on this, the potential for everyone in an organisation, when empowered, leads to more possibility of the organisation to achieve its business goals.

Triangular Perspectives of Employee Empowerment

INTRODUCTION

From the review of the management literature, it is apparent that the understanding of employee empowerment is parochial in nature. Just having knowledge of employee empowerment from one perspective is not helpful.

There is a lack of a holistic approach to understand employee empowerment from different perspectives. Hence, a triangular perspective is offered which can assist in demonstrating that employee empowerment is a concept that needs to be understood from more than one perspective. This is in line with my argument that employee empowerment is multi-dimensional and has more than one theme; similarly it has more than one perspective. I have termed these the *'Triangular Perspectives of Employee Empowerment'*, which include the economic, psychological and critical perspectives, and it is necessary to consider all of them, leading to a better understanding of employee empowerment.

ECONOMIC PERSPECTIVE

On what economic grounds should an organisation consider employee empowerment? Beirne (2006: 1) argues that 'empowerment is a matter of straightforward economics, of acknowledging the potential value in untapped human resources'.

It is easy to forget that there is an economic perspective to the concept of employee empowerment. From the economic perspective, it is recognised that an organisation's sustainable competitive advantage is its people (Peters, 1987; Barrett et al., 1993; du Gay and Salaman, 1998; Huselid, 1998; Mabey et al., 1998; Wilkinson, 1998; Schuler and Jackson, 1999; Walton, 1999; Siegall and Gardner, 2000; Bernstein, 2003; Beirne, 2006; Hitt et al., 2006). In order to compete in the global market and to respond to customer needs speedily, there needs to be less control at the top and more and more decision-making devolved right down the organisation, especially to front-line workers. Hence, there is a need to move away from 'dysfunctional systems of control' which lead to decreases in organisational efficiency (Wilkinson, 1998: 45).

Support for employee empowerment stems from the premise that as employees are close to their work situation, empowering them will mean that they have the freedom, flexibility and the authority to take decisions at the right time. This can help employees to make speedy responses to customers, engage in creative problem-solving to reduce costs, and make the organisation more effective. Thus, employee empowerment is viewed as an organisational strategy for the 'optimum utilisation of all human resources'.

Thus, from the economic perspective, the practice of employee empowerment is advocated on the grounds that it can reduce costs and make organisations more effective (Walton, 1985; Peters, 1987; Gandz, 1990; Thomas and Velthouse, 1990; Herschel and Andrews, 1993; Peters, 1994; Spreitzer, 1995; Kappelman and Richards, 1996; Pearson and Chatterjee, 1996; Hammuda and Dulaimi, 1997; Kondo, 1997; Forrest, 2000; Beirne, 2006).

In this sense, Wilkinson (1998: 44–5) sums up the economic argument as follows:

> there is an economic case for empowerment which is essentially pragmatic. It is assumed first that workers have the opportunity to contribute to organisational success and, as they are closer to the work situation, they may be able to suggest improvements which management would be unable to by virtue of their position in the hierarchy.

It is essential that employees are enabled to make day-to-day decisions with regards to problems. It does make sense, as employees are closer to their work situation they know best what the problems are and hence they will be able to come up with the best solutions. But, sometimes employees' suggestions are not welcome or worse not listened to. Furthermore, decision-making and responsibility should not be the prerogative of management only in an increasingly complex world, because managers are not always the experts. As knowledge and expertise can be found in different locations in the workplace, devolving responsibility and decision-making to front-line personnel is vital. Gandz (1990: 75) strengthens the economic argument and emphasises that by having authority to make decisions at the right time, employees in organisations can help reduce costs: 'The overhead cost of excessive bureaucratic controls, people checking up on people, layers of supervision and so on can be avoided by those organisations that work in an empowered mode. Innovative ways of working can drive down costs, and human and capital resources can be uitilized more effectively.'

A vast amount of knowledge exists in organisations that remains unused and untapped, and alluding to this, Clutterbuck and Kernaghan (1995: 12) point out: 'Most companies still squander it (knowledge) in a way they would never dream of if they were wasting tangible raw materials.' Worse still, a high level of educated human capital is being wasted, as people are not allowed to contribute their intelligence:

> We have relatively highly educated human assets, many of whom are working and contributing at a fraction of their potential; the creative, innovative energy in this asset base is enormous. If it is to be liberated, we must start to think much more seriously than we have traditionally done of investing in human resource development rather than expensing people. Only through making such investments will we be able to improve our business processes continuously, utilising both our human and other assets to maximum benefit for the business organisations, employees within those organisations and our society as a whole. (Gandz, 1990: 79)

In a competitive market, organisations need talented, empowered people, as customers expect problems to be solved and decisions to be made in 'real time', and so if employees are not empowered to take decisions, this may have negative implications for organisations, resulting in loss of customers and revenues. Moreover, Carter's (2009) study reports that giving people more responsibility generates greater productivity, morale and commitment. Silzer and Dowell (2010) emphasise the need to recognise the importance of 'talent'. Relating to this, these authors point out that organisations need to ask if they have people who have the right talent to make the right decisions and to achieve organisational strategies.

Empowering people also means the optimum use of employees' talents, as they are given the freedom to be innovative and creative, thus adding value to organisations. There is high consensus in the literature that these talents remain largely unused and untapped in many organisations. In the SHRM literature, it is noted that 'managers should pursue policies that increase employee commitment, motivation and flexibility, in place of control and standardisation' (Rosenthal et al., 1998: 170). Further, as indicated above, if employees are empowered to take decisions and responsibility at the operational level, this will free managers to take decisions and responsibilities at the strategic level, which in turn would lead to a more judicious utilisation of all human resources.

PSYCHOLOGICAL PERSPECTIVE

Employees' perceptions and experiences of employee empowerment at work (Conger and Kanungo, 1988; Spreitzer, 1995; Holt et al., 2000; Greasley et al., 2005) are important from a psychological perspective. There is a lack of robust debate and discussion about the importance of employees' psychological perspective and the significant role this plays with regards to employee empowerment. Several authors warn that organisations are largely unaware of the impact of this.

The argument from the psychological perspective is that people need to be empowered at a personal level before they can feel empowered. Such an approach emphasises the need to give attention not only to the structural aspect of employee empowerment but also to the psychological aspects, such as locus of control, self-efficacy and self-esteem of people, leading to psychological empowerment (discussed in Part III of this book).

It is important for management to acknowledge that some people are motivated by higher level intrinsic needs (Conger and Kanungo, 1988). Several studies imply the motivational benefits of employee empowerment (Conger and Kanungo, 1988; Thomas and Velthouse, 1990; Spreitzer, 1995, 1996; Nesan and Holt, 2002; Bernstein, 2003; Seibert et al., 2004), which anchors the psychological perspective. This follows the argument that when employees are empowered and have the authority to make decisions, it makes them more motivated to help organisations achieve their goals and objectives. By way of contrast 'disempowered employees tend to become over-reliant, dependent, demoralised and not very willing to use their initiative' (Heslin, 1999: 54).

In line with this, Lee and Koh (2001) argue that empowered employees may be motivated, but motivated employees may not necessarily feel empowered. There are numerous ways to motivate employees, employee empowerment may be one of the methods (Lee and Koh, 2001).

There is a growing realisation that as pressures for survival grow in organisations it impacts on managers' work load as well. On a psychological level, Heslin (1999: 53) notes that: 'Coping with these pressures requires that managers empower their staff to make decisions and take actions.' Furthermore, this psychological perspective ties in with the economic perspective, as discussed earlier, that is, empowering employees to take responsibility also frees up managers to do other things: 'Managers need to get things done, not do them' (Heslin, 1999: 52). Besides, it is not in an organisation's interest if its managers are spending excessive time and effort on operational issues rather than strategic ones.

Hence, employee empowerment is advocated because of its perceived positive psychological benefits for the individual, such as an increase in internal locus of control; an increase in self-efficacy and self-esteem, which benefits the organisation as well. Furthermore, it is implied in the management literature that employees with high self-efficacy and self-esteem are able to take decisions and solve problems better (than those who have low self-efficacy and low self-esteem), thereby enabling individuals to use their full potential.

An important aspect of empowerment, which is given greater prominence in the social work literature, is the proposition that empowerment comes from within, and that people need to believe and feel that they are empowered. Hence, employee initiatives in organisations are unlikely to produce the desired results unless employees believe themselves to be, and feel, empowered. Spreitzer (1995) observes that individuals with a strong internal locus of control are more likely to feel capable of performing their tasks, and as mentioned earlier, it can also lead individuals to be innovative and creative, which are the 'distinctive skills' organisations particularly look for in employees (Walton, 1999), as described in SHRM (Strategic Human Resource Management) theory.

It is evident from the psychological perspective that there are benefits in empowering employees, as it leads to strong locus of control; positively raises self-efficacy, self-esteem and self-confidence, leading to the potential for an individual to gain psychological empowerment, which is essential for empowered employees.

Thus, employee empowerment is viewed as part of best management practice for the optimum utilisation of people's talents in organisations.

CRITICAL PERSPECTIVE

One of the arguments from the critical perspective is the inconsistency with regards to what actually constitutes employee empowerment, leaving it open to variety of interpretations (Honold, 1997; Hales, 2000; Denham Lincoln et al., 2002; Ogden et al., 2006); or what the impact of it may be (Ogden et al., 2006).

> *Empowerment initiatives have become popular in recent years in programmes of organisational change, but their impact as a practical managerial policy remains shrouded in ambiguities. (Ogden et al., 2006: 521)*

Although several authors extol the positive benefits and outcomes of employee empowerment, it is not all 'motherhood and apple pie' (Ojeifo and Winstanley, 1999: 277). Appelbaum et al. (1999: 233) state:

> *On one hand, there are those who extol its virtues and preach about its potential as a response to increasingly intense competitive forces in the market place, the rapidly changing nature of work, downsizing and restructuring, and shifting employee expectations, while on the other, there are those who see it as an old formula in a new package, denounce its problem-solving potential and point out possible risks and disadvantages such as loss of control by management.*

A number of authors caution that employee empowerment can, in practice, be nothing more than work intensification and giving employees more responsibility (Legge, 1995; Marchington, 1995; Claydon and Doyle, 1996; Hardy and Leiba-O'Sullivan, 1998; Wilkinson, 1998; Christensen Hughes, 1999; Ojeifo and Winstanley, 1999; Hales, 2000), 'which has nothing to do with meeting the needs of workers at all' (Ojeifo and Winstanley, 1999: 277). Christensen Hughes (1999: 127) highlights that: 'In practice, however, organisations have responded to current pressures by downsizing their operations and implementing strategies of responsible autonomy. While often being labelled "empowerment", such strategies have proven ineffective at either masking or responding to the tension that has always existed, and will likely always continue to exist, between owners of capital and those who provide their labour.'

In a similar vein, Beirne (2006: 81) reports that, 'Many companies that claim to empower employees in practice do nothing of the sort. There is evidence of window dressing and appearance management, with lots of schemes in various contexts favouring rhetoric over substance'. Furthermore, there are other issues, such as how much empowerment employees should be given and how much control management should retain.

An ongoing argument from the critical perspective is with regards to the lack of understanding of how power is going to be shared. Without a clear conceptualisation of power it is hard to understand what role the sharing of power plays in the practice of employee empowerment. Hence, Gilbert (1995: 865) rightly raises the question: 'how do we work to empower others when we have no clear notion of what power is?' People have difficulty in defining power, as it seems most people only have an 'intuitive notion' of what it means (Dahl, 1957: 201).

Writers from the critical perspective describe their view of how power works in organisations, stating that dominant groups can legitimise their demands over other disadvantaged groups, and, in the process, decrease these groups' awareness of their disadvantaged positions and the existence of any political issues (Hardy, 1985). Peters (1994: 87) blames the very nature of organisations to a large extent for individual powerlessness:

> By their very nature, organisations run roughshod over individuals. They produce powerlessness and humiliation for most participants with more skill than they produce widgets.

Another criticism is the lack of power-sharing with lower level employees. According to Dupuy (2004: 217) empowerment is to acquire *'more power'* (Dupuy's emphasis), 'which is the literal translation of the word (empowerment)'. However, referring to employee empowerment in practice, Marchington (1995: 56) notes:

> its practice has been some way short of its literal meaning, which is to give an employee the power, authority and influence to do things at work. In reality, the term is typically much more dilute, likely to refer to the opportunity for employees to make suggestions for change or have the responsibility for decision making in severely constrained boundaries.

Moreover, according to Marchington (1995: 61), even if employee empowerment leads to a 'lowering of informal and interpersonal barriers between management and employees, this does little itself to reduce formal hierarchies or the power of management prerogatives'. Cunningham et al. (1996) conclude from their study that participants hardly experienced any increase in their power, instead they felt an increase in managerial control. Another study by Cunningham and Hyman (1999: 195) reveals that despite the implementation of an 'ostensibly extensive empowerment programme' in reality there were 'few elements of the employee-centred empowerment prescription in evidence' in their case study. These authors also conclude that instead of giving employees more control over their work situations, the organisation had reinforced more control over their employees:

> *After reviewing the findings of the case study, the paper arrives at conclusions which suggest that in contrast to providing employees with added control, discretion, responsibility, moral rewards or even more co-operative relationships with managers, the empowerment process can be directly aligned to managerial pressures to operate low cost, directive systems of employee control, in which empowerment serves as an emblematic device to reinforce rather than reallocate managerial authority. (Cunningham and Hyman, 1999: 195)*

Several authors caution of the danger of employee empowerment being another form of worker control (Willmott, 1994; Cunningham et al., 1996; Wilkinson, 1998; D'Annunzio-Green and Macandrew, 1999; Morrell and Wilkinson, 2002). In this sense, Morrell and Wilkinson (2002: 121) describe the dangers as follows: 'empowerment can become a weasel word, framed in smoke, aggrandized by mirrors. The "smoke" of empowerment may hide the fact that there is no real increase in or reconstitution of workers' power; instead empowerment proves to be a more insidious mechanism for control'.

There are concerns because ways to share power and the meaning of employee empowerment are not articulated properly in organisations; this can lead to uncertainty amongst managers as to how they can empower their employees without diminishing their own power. It is necessary that decisions regarding day-to-day operations need to be pushed lower and lower down the organisational hierarchy. This process of delegating power from higher to lower level employees constitutes decentralisation. But, on a practical level, for management there are obvious difficulties and problems with power-sharing, such as, how much power should be shared with employees with regard to decision-making. This is illustrated by Hales (2000: 503) who states that although there is considerable agreement in the management literature that employee empowerment refers to the enhancement of the capacity of some people to take decisions, there is ambiguity and disagreement regarding what this 'capacity' refers to, in what way it is 'enhanced' and to which 'decisions' and 'agents' it applies. Furthermore, it is unclear 'whether this capacity refers to *responsibility* for decisions (or outcomes) or the *power* to discharge that responsibility'.

From the critical approach, Hardy and Leiba-O'Sullivan (1998: 472) criticise the lack of power-sharing and argue that 'much of the research conducted in the *mainstream* management tradition tends to skirt the issue of power and, in so doing, adopts assumptions and protocols that restrict the redistribution of power in empowerment initiatives'. Hence, in their view, as power is seen as domination by *critical* theorists, employee empowerment needs to provide the means to 'combat the sources of domination' (1998: 475). It is instructive for organisations to pay attention to this, as Appelbaum et al. (1999: 238) report that it is the critical perspective of power which highlights the importance of power-sharing, whereas mainstream management research 'often compounds this problem because of its lack of attention to power'.

Employee empowerment may take different forms in organisations and therefore reflects different managerial strategies, and related to this is the argument that some initiatives can be 'participatory whilst others are more immediately concerned with involvement and commitment' (Lashley, 1996: 335). Studies also reveal that often employees are concerned about the consequences of taking the wrong decisions – will they be penalised or lose their jobs? (Ripley and Ripley, 1992). If such is the case, then clearly empowering employees will be counter-productive, as employees will be reluctant to take decisions.

In addition to these problems, the devolution of responsibility is also perceived as a means of giving employees more responsibility for less, or sometimes no reward. Many writers taking a critical perspective view the devolution of responsibility as producing more stress and intensification of work (Marchington, 1995; Claydon and Doyle, 1996; Wilkinson, 1998; Hales, 2000; Lashley, 2001).

> *Adding extra responsibilities to a person's job can increase the burden of work, produce more stress and represent an intensification of work ... For some workers, empowerment in the form of added responsibilities can be an unwelcome development. (Lashley, 2001: 7)*

There is also a danger, as mentioned previously, that employees might interpret devolution of responsibility as simply abdication of management responsibility.

Further, an important point often ignored in organisations is that the devolution of responsibility without authority is meaningless, as employees need to have the requisite authority to carry out the decisions they have made. The absence of the requisite authority to carry out decisions would lead to subsequent low motivation and morale.

However, in reality, Moon and Stanworth (1999: 333) argue that in many cases employee empowerment is not extended to lower-level workers: 'empowerment, where it exists, is most likely to be something that top management creates for other managers, but is often not extended to lower-order workers'. Thus, Greasley et al. (2005: 358–9) note, 'employees may consider empowerment to be just empty rhetoric and yet another management attempt to exploit them'.

The critical perspective highlights the danger of employee empowerment being used as a means to exploit and manipulate employees. If organisations are serious about empowering their employees, then it is instructive for organisations to pay attention to the concerns raised by the arguments from this perspective. In the long run, it will help organisations as they will recognise the pitfalls before it is too late (Huq, 2010).

Conclusion

The economic, psychological and critical – all these three perspectives are important to take into consideration before embarking on any employee empowerment initiative.

On one hand, the economic and psychological perspectives make employee empowerment an *attractive* necessity for businesses and, on the other, the critical perspective draws attention to the downside of employee empowerment. Hence, it is essential to look at these perspectives in order to come to a balanced understanding of employee empowerment. Being alert to the debate from all these perspectives can enable organisations to formulate their strategy and take decisions based on a thorough knowledge of what employee empowerment is and the pros and cons related to it, leading to a planned, successful implementation.

At the conceptual level, there is considerable ambiguity and confusion surrounding the debate regarding whether or not employee empowerment is a distinct construct, different from employee involvement or employee participation. It is important to clear this confusion. There is strong agreement in the management literature that employee empowerment is indeed different from management practices, such as employee involvement and employee participation.

At the practice level, there is also concern with regards to the implementation of employee empowerment in organisations: 'its application in organisational settings is fraught with misunderstanding and tension' (Denham Lincoln et al., 2002: 271). This is mainly due to the lack of understanding of employee empowerment as a concept and the multi-dimensional themes which surround it. A review of the management literature reveals that there are several themes of employee empowerment. Hence, employee empowerment should not be viewed as one-dimensional or having just one theme. 'It seems that employee empowerment is one-dimensional. No single set of contingencies can describe it' (Honold, 1997: 210). As indicated in earlier discussions, different authors conceptualise employee empowerment according to different themes. Hence, if organisations want to implement employee empowerment, they need to be alert and take into account that employee empowerment has several themes, namely, power-sharing; participative decision-making; devolution of responsibility and people-oriented leadership style (Huq's Model A).

The divergence between the widespread rhetoric of employee empowerment and the limited reality of employee empowerment programmes can lead to significant conflict and tension in organisations (Hales, 2000; Huq, 2010). Therefore, organisations need to have a clear understanding of what employee empowerment is; be familiar not just with the structural processes but also be aware of the psychological implications of it. Questions need to be asked and answers sought as to why they want to empower people, and for what purpose.

Strategic human resource management supports employee empowerment based on the argument that when people are empowered they can take decisions, act responsibly and are not deterred by challenges to deliver organisational goals. The logic is that technological superiority alone cannot provide competitive advantage; organisations need empowered employees to provide competitive advantage and uniqueness. It is important to understand that SHRM is not just about hiring people, it is a planned approach to achieve a competitive edge through people, who are empowered to take decisions and responsibility. The uniqueness of the skills, talents of people (and this includes people in non-management and management positions, who may be leaders and managers) who not only feel empowered, but psychologically empowered. These empowered people have confidence, high self-efficacy, self-esteem and resilience to assist organisations to achieve organisational goals and 'be the best'.

But, despite strong arguments for employee empowerment in the management literature, several authors raise concern with regards to the complexities and problems surrounding it. The relative paucity of empirical research in the management context has led to limited understanding of empowerment and provided little evidence of empowerment as a distinct construct and how it can be operationalised (Huq and Hill, 1999). The knowledge from the management literature review proved unsatisfactory, hence it was deemed necessary to draw knowledge from another discipline, namely social work (Huq and Hill, 2005), where empowerment is an important construct. The review of the social work literature is discussed next.

PART II
What Does Social Work Have to Do With It?

Chapter 3
Concept of Empowerment in Social Work

Introduction

A review of the management literature alone did little to reduce the conceptual ambiguity surrounding employee empowerment. Hence, the purpose of delving into social work literature is broadly to understand what is meant by empowerment in social work; what are the methods used from the practising point of view and more importantly what knowledge can be drawn.

There is value in reviewing other disciplines, as important lessons can be learnt. It is also advocated by a number of authors as they argue that a multi-disciplinary approach is necessary to put employee empowerment in a richer, contextual setting (Zimmermann, 1990; Collins, 1996a; Denham Lincoln et al., 2002). Thus, this second review of literature was undertaken in order to explore and further the understanding of empowerment by drawing knowledge from social work (Huq, 2008). This is because, as stated previously, empowerment is a central construct in social work.

The psychological implications of empowerment, such as locus of control, self-efficacy and self-esteem, are particularly emphasised in social work but less importance is placed on them in the management literature. 'Empowerment conveys both a psychological sense of personal control or influence and a concern with actual social influence, political power, and legal rights' (Rappaport, 1987: 121). Furthermore, in social work literature, the importance of feeling empowered from within is viewed to be important. This essential aspect of psychological empowerment, *'feeling empowered within'*, is rarely highlighted in the management literature.

A Paradigm Shift

A paradigm shift in the practice of social work is gradually moving towards empowerment. Empowerment in social work is now a central paradigm that has replaced the old paradigm of 'client treatment' (Adams, 1996: xv) which dominated social work in the past, and the empowerment of service users is becoming '*the* central, energising feature of social work' (Adams, 1996: 2–3). Empowerment is central to social work theory and practice, 'without empowerment, it could be argued that something fundamental is missing from the social work being practised' (Adams, 1996: 3). Undoubtedly, as Adams (1996: xvi) states: 'the development of an empowering practice in social work is a professional necessity'.

However, an important point needs to be highlighted, that is, just by telling people they are empowered does not necessarily produce results; there must be strategies to enable employees *to be* and *feel* empowered. Empowerment needs to be supported by leaders. Resources and training are also essential – these are viewed as enablers of the empowerment process in practice. Furthermore, the social work literature argues that besides power-sharing, there are other essential aspects that are necessary in the practice of empowerment, namely, access to information, collaboration and enablement – these are missing in the management literature as part of the employee empowerment model.

It should be noted that empowerment in the management literature is largely about the empowerment of employees; hence it is referred to as 'employee empowerment'. However, in this chapter the term used is 'empowerment', as in social work although 'empowerment' is about empowering employees (that is social workers), there is a strong emphasis that service users (individuals, groups or communities) must also be empowered. Hence, using the term 'employee empowerment' would not be appropriate here, as there are citizens and service users involved as well. In this context, the term 'service user' is a generic term that can be used in preference to 'client', 'patient' and 'lay person' (Williams, 1995: 38).

There is agreement in the social work literature that powerlessness is a common condition experienced by different groups in society, for example, women, the aged and people from ethnic minority backgrounds. Frans (1993: 312) explains how social movements in the 1960s and 1970s contributed to the 'spotlight' on powerlessness. Thus empowerment is viewed as a necessary response to powerlessness, and regarded both as a process and goal. It is important to note that a paradigm shift in the practice of social work is steadily moving towards empowerment (Stanton, 1990; Parsons, 1991; Frans, 1993; Sheppard, 1995; Adams, 1996; Guterman and Bargal, 1996; Kirst-Ashman, 2003; Fook, 2012). Thus, the post-modernism approach in social work is about 'understanding of power inequalities and a commitment to the empowerment of powerless people' (Fook, 2012: 53).

Stanton (1990: 122) observes:

> *we've seen a distinct expansion, with terms like ... 'empowerment' becoming widely used. For instance, in 1989, the British Association of Social Workers made 'the empowerment of both service users and workers' the theme of its annual conference.*

An observation from the review of the management literature is that employee empowerment is always a top-down management agenda in organisations. In contrast to this, in the social work literature, there is a shift in attitude; Kirst-Ashman (2003: 203) advocates that empowering people needs a 'bottom-up' approach.

> *A 'grassroots, bottom-up approach' means that people at the bottom of the formal power structure, such as ordinary citizens, band together to establish a power base.*

By taking a 'bottom-up' approach at the grassroots level, service users collectively and individually challenge authorities and attempt to bring about changes in their lives. This has resonance with the definition of empowerment offered by *The Blackwell Encyclopaedia of Social Work* (Davies, 2000: 116): 'For service users, *empowerment* means challenging their disempowerment, having more control over their lives, being able to influence others and bring about change'. This kind of attention to employees having control over their working lives, that is, at the 'grassroots' level, was largely missing in both case organisations of my study, particularly with regards to agency workers in the Large Organisation, discussed later.

However, as noted in the management literature, there may be resistance to change by different levels of management in social work too. An understanding of the barriers to empowerment is important in order to create a skilled workforce. Braye and Preston-Shoot (1995: 116) state: 'Such understandings will also form the basis for staff development and training policies which are geared to creating a *skilled workforce*, able to overcome some of the barriers ... and take on the challenge of empowerment', which is to do with enablement.

Clearly, there is a noticeable shift in attitudes as well, which has led to the growing realisation that empowerment is regarded highly not only as an important construct but also an important 'value' in social work (Kirst-Ashman, 2003: 21), as it helps service users to gain more control over their environment to improve their life situations. In this sense, Sheppard (1995: 7) notices a change whereby service providers share power with service users and describes empowerment as 'giving users and carers greater power and control ... than was previously the case'. In this sense, there has been a recognised paradigm shift in social work, where power inequalities are consciously being addressed. Relating to this, Fook (2012: 53) states: 'An understanding of power inequalities and a commitment to the empowerment of powerless people has been a cornerstone of more modernist critical social work approaches.'

In management, there is a lot of writing and rhetoric about employee empowerment (Clutterbuck and Kernaghan, 1995; Wilkinson, 1998; Pearson and Chatterjee, 1996; Hales, 2000; Huq, 2010), but there is very little practical guidance. It is important to note that the notion of empowerment is right at the heart of social work (Parsons, 1991); something that is clearly not the case in the management literature. Parsons (1991) states that empowerment is the purpose of social work and points out that, historically, social workers have worked towards enabling the transaction between individuals and their environments for the purposes of problem-solving, using empowerment as a mechanism for intervention. This is an important skill leaders in management need to develop.

Concept of Empowerment

A key question addressed in this chapter is, 'what does empowerment mean in the social work literature?'. By raising this question, aspects of empowerment in this discipline are examined.

Interestingly, the concept of empowerment in social work also has diverse meanings (Kieffer, 1984; Rappaport, 1987; Lord and Hutchinson, 1993; Dalrymple and Burke, 1995; Sheppard, 1995; Adams, 1990, 1996). But, unlike in management where the diverse meanings create confusion, in social work 'the diversity of interpretation' is viewed positively because it makes sense. The reason for the diversity is because empowerment not only applies to a wide variety of service users from diverse backgrounds of race, colour and creed, but it also applies to the different professionals who provide the services. Hence, Sheppard (1995: 30) argues that, 'It (empowerment) can have as many meanings as social and political creeds available'. Nevertheless, some writers have sought to achieve greater consensus. For example, according to Adams (2003: 8), in social work empowerment is defined as: 'The means by which individuals, groups and/or communities become able to take control of their circumstances and achieve their own goals, thereby being able to work towards helping themselves and others to maximise the quality of their lives.' According to some (Adams, 1996, 2003; Guterman and Bargal, 1996; Fook, 2012), attention to client powerlessness and systems and methods to empower people has re-emerged as a central theme in social work practice.

Historically, the idea of empowerment in social work comes from the traditional activities of mutual aid and self-help (Kieffer, 1984; Frans, 1993; Adams, 1990, 1996). Frans (1993) describes empowerment as a notion that has grown out of social action and ideology and self-help perspectives. Based on the concept of self-help, empowerment can enable people to work towards helping themselves and others to maximise the quality of their lives and to achieve their own goals (Adams, 1990). Viewed in this way empowerment is therefore a process (Adams, 1990; Beresford and Croft, 1993; Frans, 1993; Adams, 1996; Parrott, 2007; Fook, 2012; Saleebey, 2013) that enables people to take greater control and responsibility of their lives. This is an important point which needs to be emphasised in the management literature; employees need to take and be given greater control and responsibility for their work. This can lead to motivation and pride in their jobs.

There is high consensus in social work literature that empowerment can enable people to achieve control in their lives and to achieve their goals (Adams, 1990; Frans, 1993). In practice, this is how empowerment in social work is viewed by individuals, groups and/or communities, namely as a way of taking control of their lives, thereby achieving empowerment from within (Parsons, 1991). Although empowerment is described as a means whereby social workers, groups of people and/or communities are enabled to take control of their lives, the growth of the individual is also considered important (Rappaport, 1987; Adams, 1990).

> The concept (of empowerment) suggests both individual determination
> over one's own life and democratic participation in the life of one's
> community. (Rappaport, 1987: 121)

Hence, empowerment needs to be understood on both individual and collective levels (Rappaport, 1987; Adams, 1990, 1996; Parrott, 2002); again something that is missing in the management literature. Beresford and Croft (1993: 50) define 'empower' to mean 'making it possible for people to exercise power and have more control over their lives', through the process of self-help, which is enablement. Hence, having some control over people's lives and situations is regarded to be crucial in social work (Kieffer, 1984; Rappaport, 1987; Adams, 1990; Prestby et al., 1990; Zimmerman, 1990; Fahlberg et al., 1991; Beresford and Croft, 1993; Lord and Hutchinson, 1993; Williams, 1995; Sheppard, 1995; Adams, 1996, 2003; Kirst-Ashman, 2003; DuBois and Miley, 2005; Fook, 2012; Saleebey, 2013).

The diverse meanings of empowerment in social work are captured by Rappaport's (1987: 130) definition which demonstrates that empowerment is not just an individual construct, or for one group of people; rather it is diverse and at the same time global, as illustrated:

> *Empowerment is not only an individual psychological construct, it is also organisational, political, sociological, economic and spiritual. Our interests in racial and economic justice, in legal rights as well as in human needs, in health care and educational justice, in competence as well as in a sense of community, are all captured by the idea of empowerment.*

Thus, at this level empowerment is a societal issue across the world.

Power, Oppression and Powerlessness

It is very rare to find a discussion on power, oppression and powerlessness which provides an understanding of how these are linked, leading to a better understanding of empowerment and the importance of why oppressed people need to be empowered.

Clearly, it is argued in social work that people need to gain control, particularly over factors, whether they are social, political or psychological, that are critical to overcoming oppression, powerlessness and disempowerment; otherwise the danger is that 'disenfranchisement' and 'hopelessness' may set in (Kieffer, 1984: 16):

> *the sense of powerlessness is viewed as a construction of continuous interaction between the person and his/her environment. It combines an attitude of self-blame, a sense of generalized distrust, a feeling of alienation from resources for social influence, an experience of disenfranchisement and economic vulnerability, and a sense of hopelessness in socio-political struggle.*

The problem with the concept of 'power' is that it is viewed as 'being invested to particular people, often by virtue of their position in the social structure' (Fook, 2012: 119). Furthermore, it is seen as '"possessed" rather than "exercised", and this is more fixed and less accessible to change' (Fook, 2012: 119). Viewed in this way, this can make some people feel disempowered and unable to bring about any positive changes in their lives. The results of the negative feelings of powerlessness can be damaging as the individual feels that his or her actions will be unsuccessful and futile in influencing the outcomes of events (Kieffer, 1984). Under these conditions an unsettling air of oppression can set in.

A critical analysis of oppression leads to the question 'what is oppression'? A definition of oppression offered by Kirst-Ashman (2003: 50), '*Oppression …* is the longer-term result of putting extreme limitations on or discriminating against some designated group'. Further, it is also worthwhile noting how oppression can be a result of people (or oppressors) holding negative views about other people, as Kirst-Ashman (2003: 54–5) explains:

> *Discrimination and oppression often result from stereotypes – fixed mental images of members belonging to a group based on assumed attributes that reflect overly simplified opinions about that group. People who hold stereotypes neither consider nor appreciate individual differences.*

There are negative forces of oppression, as explained by Dalrymple and Burke (1995: 57): 'it is best understood if it is seen as a system of *colliding explosive forces*, which, if they collide randomly, are more likely to be oppressive'. However, if the forces are channelled and controlled in a positive manner, they can open new opportunities for the way ahead, otherwise, the actual process of empowerment can be disempowering and oppressive, leaving people powerless to change things or their situation. Such an understanding of oppression may explain a number of scenarios concerning potential discrimination in organisations. An example of this concerns agency workers (Hill and Huq, 2001, 2004), many of whom, as the findings of this research suggest, may be serious victims of disempowerment. Agency staff not only felt marginalised, but tended to be perceived as 'marginal' (Hill and Huq, 2004: 1040) by permanent employees and management. As agency workers were not allowed to have a 'say' in the employee empowerment programme at Large Organisation (explained elsewhere) they were in danger of being oppressed. It is worth noting this kind of 'oppression' causes powerlessness – where organisations' policies are such that people's 'voices' are suppressed.

In social work, having a 'voice' is argued to be critical for both social workers and service users (Kieffer, 1984; Adams, 1990; Friedmann, 1992; Fook, 2012). However, it is important to note Bricker-Jenkins et al.'s (2013: 266) argument that social workers do not give voice to clients: 'the notion that social workers "give voice to the voiceless" is a disempowering bromide. All people have a voice; our work is to make sure that all voices are heard'. Hence, it is about social workers facilitating their client's 'voice' to be heard.

It is agreed that empowerment can facilitate the entry of people and communities into different areas of policy-making where previously they did not have any means or process to put their 'voice' forward – in shaping politics, education, communities or services. Kieffer's study (1984: 32) concludes that empowerment at the individual level includes the development of skills removing the feelings of 'helplessness'. Thus: 'The fundamental empowering transformation, then, is in the transition from sense of self as helpless victim to acceptance of self as assertive and efficacious citizen.' From the individual and community perspective this is vital, as it means all members of community can have a say in shaping the environment in which they live or work, thus creating a broader base for problem-solving in a collective manner. Parallel examples can be drawn from management; it is argued by Bowen and Lawler III (1992: 34) that giving front-line employees a chance to have a say in 'how we do things here can lead to improved service delivery and ideas for new services'.

Addressing the inequality in power is a fundamental issue in social work, as Parsloe (1996: 56) states: 'Power is a central notion in empowerment'. Even in social work it is recognised that, in practice, empowerment is not easy. Fook (2012: 55) warns: 'it [empowerment] is not so easy to apply in practice'. A number of authors in the social work literature agree that inequalities in power come from oppression, and therefore there is a need to address power imbalances (Freire, 1972: Friedmann, 1992; Breton, 1994; Dalrymple and Burke, 1995; Sheppard, 1995; Parsloe, 1996; Kirst-Ashman, 2003; Fook, 2012).

Clearly, empowerment is about change on several levels, for example, people having to learn new behaviours and new skills, and new ways of interacting with other people, the environment, social conditions and systems that may be oppressive. As Freire (1972) argues, it is about the development of critical consciousness, and the ability to think against the status quo that enables people to act together, to change oppressive social conditions. The process of liberation, freedom and empowerment is through education and consciousness-raising of individuals and groups. The corollary of this is the absence of empowerment means alienation, helplessness and feelings of powerlessness (Rappaport, 1984). Hence, individuals need to be enabled to overcome feelings of helplessness and despair through measures that increase confidence, internal locus of control, self-efficacy and self-esteem (Bandura, 1977; Kieffer, 1984; Rappaport, 1987; Conger and Kanungo, 1988). From Kieffer's (1984: 32) study, it is enlightening to note from the psychological perspective, how participants in his study did not view themselves as '*having* more power', but rather as '*feeling* more powerful'.

In the management literature, the concepts of power and oppression are rarely examined. The emphasis with regards to people having to learn new behaviours and new skills are not given much attention by management; the social work literature is an important vehicle to further our knowledge with regards to these aforementioned issues. Feelings of powerlessness occur when people believe they are unable to cope with the physical and social demands of the environment (Conger and Kanungo, 1988; Spreitzer, 1995; Greenberg and Baron, 2000; Fook, 2012). This perceived feeling of being unable to cope could be damaging in a variety of situations including the workplace, as it creates stress (Spreitzer, 1995; Greenberg and Baron, 2000; Wilson, 2004; Laschinger et al., 2009), leading to further feelings of powerlessness. Even in social work discipline, Fook (2012: 124) states that the 'idea of powerlessness is almost universal in accounts of practice in which workers feel they are caught in a dilemma or impasse'. Referring to a series of critical reflection workshops with a group of social workers, she reports that: 'Workers felt caught underneath the power of a manager or supervisor, the power of bureaucratic rule, or even of agency or community culture.' In this case, the conclusion is that social workers did not see themselves as powerful.

In line with this, in the management literature, it is acknowledged that the danger is that disempowered employees can begin to feel disenfranchised, hence Peters (1994: 87) emphasises that the 'central ethical issue in the workplace should be protection and support for people who are unempowered, especially the frontline worker'. Thus, employee empowerment can be enhanced if organisations remove all impediments that lead to a sense of powerlessness, such as unnecessary rules and regulations and limited participation. But, it is surprising how many of the aforementioned impediments still remain in organisations. Pearlstein (1991), in the management literature, notes that many organisations are so bureaucratic that even routine actions need some form of permission or approval from the top.

Without the sharing of power, empowerment in social work is viewed as having no meaning. It is worthwhile noting the theory of empowerment described in the *Dictionary of Social Work*:

> *Theory concerned with how people may gain collective control over their lives, so as to achieve their interests as a group, and a method by which social workers seek to enhance the power of people who lack it. (Thomas and Pierson, 1995: 134)*

The sharing of power should concern people who genuinely lack power and are effectively deprived of power (that is oppressed people). Breton (1994) emphasises that this does not include people who either have power but choose not to exercise it, or people who simply feel that they lack power. It is worthwhile noting Breton's (1994: 24) argument that 'oppressed' people are not people who lack personal, moral, spiritual strengths or resources, but they are people whose chances and choices in life are considerably affected by inequalities in the distribution of resources including social, economic and political power:

> *the issue of empowerment is one that concerns people who lack power – not people who have power but choose not to exercise it, not people who 'feel' or have 'a sense' that they lack power, but people who are effectively deprived of power. Put starkly, empowerment, as discussed herein, concerns oppressed people. Oppressed people are not people who are without personal, moral, or spiritual strengths or resources, but rather people whose life chances and choices are significantly curtailed by inequalities in the distribution of social, economic and political power and resources.*

Similarly, in community health, empowerment is seen as taking control of one's health. Fahlberg et al. (1991) emphasise that a definition of empowerment must include the development of both the individual's and the community's capacity to improve their own health. These authors view empowerment as the result of the removal of social and structural barriers that may hinder the attainment of good health, similar to enablement. Such an approach clearly challenges the traditional medical model of health, whereby the professional is no longer viewed as the *expert* in possession of specialist knowledge. Thus, having control over decisions that affect people's lives is seen to be central in empowerment.

In the context of empowerment it is abundantly clear that powerless people need to gain control over the factors that keep them in a state of oppression. Hence, it is important to include those who are marginalised and that empowerment should not be used to 'serve only to strengthen the power of dominant groups by increasing their hold' (Fook, 2012: 58). This is described as the 'downside of empowerment' (Fook, 2012: 58). Denham Lincoln et al. (2002: 285) acknowledge that: 'the underlying interpretation of the word (empowerment) is one of mobilizing the oppressed by helping them to believe in themselves, increasing their self-efficacy', which also leads to a sense of control. This is parallel to a report by Breton (1994: 24): 'Following a solid consensus, empowerment is defined as gaining control over one's life, that is, gaining control over the factors which are critical in accounting for one's state of oppression or disempowerment.' Clearly, it is important that people need to gain control and these include social, political and psychological aspects – all critical to overcoming oppression, powerlessness and disempowerment.

It is evident that power itself is a complex construct and has different connotations for different groups, nevertheless, it needs to be recognised that sharing of power is an important aspect of employee empowerment and therefore must be firmly rooted in all discussions in order to implement it. Lashley (2001: 160) emphasises that: 'The power dimensions is fundamental to understanding the concept of empowerment and variations in its form and application.' The underpinning argument here is that as decision-making is pushed down the line, employees will need power to make decisions and deliver outcomes.

The lack of a critical analysis of power together with the reluctance of researchers from *mainstream* management to address the link between power and empowerment, have been proposed as causes of the disappointing results for the success of employee empowerment programmes (Hardy and Leiba-O'Sullivan, 1998). Without a clear conceptualisation of power it is hard to understand what role power plays in the practice of employee empowerment, and how it is to be shared. Gilbert (1995: 865) rightfully raises the question: 'how do we work to empower others when we have no clear notion of what power is?' Power is difficult to define, as it seems most people only have an 'intuitive notion' of what it means (Dahl, 1957: 201). But, the concept of power in employee empowerment 'demands a very specific consideration' (Gilbert, 1995: 865). Failure to do so may have serious implications, as illustrated:

> *The consequence of leaving power under-conceptualised is a tendency to consider that empowerment can be achieved solely through enabling strategies such as providing information. (Gilbert, 1995: 866)*

The concept of power is linked with empowerment, this is fundamental in social work. 'It is the conception of power that gives life to empowerment' (Parsloe, 1996: 56). In order to understand empowerment, we need to clarify first a conception of the condition from which it evolves, that counterpoint is referred to as the 'sense of powerlessness' (Kieffer, 1984: 15). However, without the mobilisation of power, the issue of powerlessness cannot be addressed, as Staub-Bernasconi (1991: 47) argues: 'Empowerment means the mobilization of any power source for pursuing legitimate needs and goals'.

Powerlessness can be a common condition experienced by many groups discriminated against by society, for example women, the aged, ethnic minorities and the disabled. From the results of their study on the process of empowerment, Lord and Hutchinson (1993: 9) report how participants experienced extensive powerlessness in their lives, and they described in great detail specifically 'the anguish' of feeling powerless. Further, Lord and Hutchinson (1993: 9) also note that 'No single factor or experience created a sense of powerlessness; rather, it was a build-up of factors and experiences that developed into a disempowering situation'. Hence, the emergence of empowerment is viewed to rectify powerlessness and regarded both as a process and a goal in overcoming it (Frans, 1993: 312).

A number of authors agree that inequalities in power come from oppression, and therefore there is a need to address power imbalances (Freire, 1972: Friedmann, 1992; Breton, 1994; Dalrymple and Burke; 1995; Sheppard, 1995; Parsloe, 1996; Kirst-Ashman, 2003). This is highly essential, as disempowered and oppressed people lack control over their lives, in part because they lack control over the decisions and the resources that affect the quality and direction of their lives (Breton, 1994). In management, this is crucial for leaders to take into account, particularly if front-line employees are to be empowered. Employee empowerment will necessarily entail leaders and managers relinquishing at least some of their control over resources and decision-making to other employees.

In a similar vein, Braye and Preston-Shoot (1995: 154–5) warn of the dangers of 'internalized oppression' and argue that power imbalance is a crucial factor that needs to be addressed for empowering practices to be successful. Hence, the concept of empowerment is also viewed as a process whereby oppressed people can gain control of their lives: 'empowerment is taken to mean a process by which oppressed persons gain some control over their lives by taking part with others in development of activities and structures that allow people increased involvement in matters which affect them directly' (Bystydzienski, 1992: 3).

Although power and employee empowerment are inextricably linked, much of the literature in management has omitted in-depth discussion of power, as indicated previously. In contrast, without the sharing of power, empowerment in social work is viewed as having no meaning.

Challenges for Social Workers, Managers and Leaders

The implementation and management of empowerment in social work is not without its problems. Despite the widespread advocacy and adoption of the practice of empowerment in social work, Adams (1996: xv) highlights that: 'it is dangerous to assume that practice is enhanced, and people's interests advanced, simply by tacking a few paragraphs on empowerment on to circulars, procedures and guidelines as they stand'. Parallel examples of this can be drawn in the management sector, where the problem is that the word 'empowerment' is *tacked* onto organisations' policy, or any quality award application forms without giving much thought to the practice and implementation of it.

It is generally recognised that individuals and groups have unequal power in society, and with this in mind, Parsons (1991) argues that the common goal of social work activities must be the empowerment of service users. Hence, Braye and Preston-Shoot (1995: 115) emphasise the need for an 'organisational change' where power-sharing with service users is advocated:

> For empowerment in social care to have meaning, the organisational culture must move away from that of power (control of the expert) and role (emphasis on given tasks and procedures) to that of community (learning with users).

An important point emphasised in social work is that in order to enable service users to bring about change and feel empowered, it is essential that social workers must feel empowered themselves (Adams, 1996; Guterman and Bargal, 1996). In this sense, the argument is that social workers who feel empowered are more likely to possess the motivation and capacity to enable and help empower other individuals and groups. This is an important lesson to learn for leaders in management. In line with this argument, it can be accepted that managers and leaders who feel empowered are more likely to motivate, enable and empower other individuals and groups.

Empowerment must bring about change so that people can take control over their own lives in communities or groups, or as individuals, with a view to improving their lives – and this is the essence of '*self-help*'. It (self-help) relates to empowerment as a process, where groups of people get together and share an experience or a problem with a view to individual and/or mutual benefit. Hence, empowerment can be on an individual and collective level. Parrott (2007) explains that empowerment in social work requires the development not only of personal, but also interpersonal and political power to allow individuals or people in communities to enhance their life situation. Viewed in this way, it requires the full participation of all people in the formulation, implementation and evaluation of decisions determining the well-being of people and their community and social environment.

In the social work discipline, it is considered the job of social workers to facilitate the transaction between individuals and their environments for the purposes of problem-solving, thus enabling service users to be empowered in order to gain more control over their environment and improve their life situations. Empowerment is viewed as a process that enables people to take greater control of their lives; this is an important conceptualisation that is largely missing in the management literature. In practice, this is how empowerment in social work is viewed by individuals, groups and/ or communities, namely as a way of taking control of their lives, thereby achieving empowerment from within (Parsons, 1991). Thus, Davies and Mills (1999: 179) argue that real employee empowerment requires 'a certain minimal *degree of control* over one's activities in the workplace'. Hence, having some control over people's lives and situations is regarded to be crucial in social work.

In the context of empowerment it is abundantly clear that powerless people need to gain control over the factors that keep them in a state of oppression. The reason why disempowered and oppressed people find themselves powerless is because they lack control over the decisions and the resources that affect their lives. In this sense, empowerment must be viewed as an anti-oppressive practice; that is, to humanise as far as possible the oppressive circumstances which users of services may face. Therefore, practitioners need to make sure that through the sharing of power, users can make decisions, particularly those that affect their life situations (Denney, 1998; Means et al., 2003).

However, in some cases, power may not be shared at all. Denney (1998: 221) points out that, although at the lower end of the ladder users' views are sought before taking decisions, this does not indicate whether any meaningful power is shared with the users or not, or whether they have any control over what decisions are going to be taken. Hence, simply participation and consultation of users does not mean empowerment of service users, as illustrated by Parrott (2002: 148):

> A commitment to empowerment requires local authority to open up their own organisations to change and involve service users at every level of the organisation. Local authorities need to provide information, help users, attend meetings and be clear what areas of decision-making are open for consultation.

This is instructive for leaders and managers not only in social work but in management too. This scenario may be common in both the aforementioned disciplines. Referring to the implementation of empowerment in social work, Fook (2012: 55) reports, 'it is not so easy to apply in practice'. The issue of power and control are a contentious subject of great debate, as seen in the management literature as well. Breton (1994: 24) stresses that there is a moral aspect to power and control, as illustrated:

> there are constraints on power and on control – and by extension on empowerment, not the least of them being the moral constraint that the empowerment of one disempowered individual or group or class of people should not come at the expense of other disempowered individuals, groups or classes of people. This moral imperative is also an existential and operational imperative, for as long as society allows for the oppression of one of its constituent groups, no other constituent group is completely free from the threat of oppression.

Sometimes the organisational structure itself in social work can be a hindrance in the distribution of power; just as it is in management. Shera and Page (1995) note that the bureaucratic, top-down nature of some social work organisations can lead to vulnerability, loss of control and helplessness in employees, leading to powerlessness, which in turn negatively affects service users. It is important to note that management in social work may also suffer from oppression and disempowerment; hence they too need to be empowered (Stanton, 1990; Shera and Page, 1995; Guterman and Bargal, 1996; Parsloe, 1996). Parsloe's (1996) concern is that social workers will find it difficult to empower service users if they do not feel empowered themselves. It is often overlooked that empowerment is not just for service users, it extends wider than that and must include everyone, namely employees, leaders, managers, social workers, service users and relevant partners (Adams, 1990). Clearly, empowerment does not concern subordinates only, leaders and managers need to feel empowered too.

Although practitioners in social work are encouraged to empower their service users, the truth is that sometimes they can feel disempowered themselves within their organisations (Shera and Page, 1995; Guterman and Bargal, 1996). Thus, a valid question is how can social workers empower their service users if they suffer from disempowerment themselves? This obviously puts them in a precarious situation in the delivery of services:

> *If workers themselves serve in positions laden with power-related problems, then it is plausible that their own abilities to assist clients with parallel concerns may be jeopardized. For example, workers who have difficulty manoeuvring within their agencies, who have difficulty tapping needed resources and supports, or who appear powerless to their clients, may show impaired efficacy in their own direct service delivery attempts. (Guterman and Bargal, 1996: 2)*

Sharing power has implications not only for service users, but for social workers and service providers as well (Shera and Page, 1995; Guterman and Bargal, 1996). Thus, everyone, including leaders, managers and social workers, are essential to the delivery of the empowerment process, and, the critical point is they may also suffer from oppression, and hence need to be empowered. This leads to an important question raised by Stanton (1990: 122), that is, whether the 'Empowerment of staff' is a 'prerequisite for the empowerment of users?' As mentioned previously, an area often overlooked is that empowerment is not just for users of services, it extends wider than that, and, must include all parties to social work including employees, organisations, leaders, managers, social workers, service users and relevant networks and partners. Similarly, this is also an issue in management. Sometimes it is not just about empowerment of subordinates or lower-level employees, leaders, managers, suppliers, contractors may also need to be empowered; it needs to be all inclusive. As Fook (2012: 55) points out: 'People do not fit easily into "powerful" or "powerless" groupings, sometimes having membership of both at the same time.'

Lack of resources can also be a disempowering factor and this is recognised as a serious challenge for social work practitioners (Kieffer, 1984; Guterman and Bargal, 1996; Parrott, 2002). Thus, a valid question is how can social workers empower their service users if they are suffering from disempowerment themselves? This puts them in a precarious situation in the delivery of services, and this is a significant concern in management as well. Under such circumstances, social workers may be at risk of acting as 'bare-footed shoemakers' (Guterman and Bargal, 1996: 2) who are in fact trying to solve service users' power problems, without addressing similar problems that they might suffer themselves, which these authors describe as 'their own parallel predicaments'. The concern is that these power-related difficulties can lead to low self-efficacy and perceived lack of control for social workers, resulting in poor delivery of services (Guterman and Bargal, 1996). Furthermore, lack of resources can also be a disempowering factor and this is recognised as a seriously challenging issue for practitioners (Kieffer, 1984; Guterman and Bargal, 1996; Parrott, 2002).

Even though self-help is related to groups, it can also be an individual process initiated by individuals for themselves (Adams, 1990). Viewed in this way, self-help may thus be seen as one form of psychological empowerment that enables people to feel empowered from within. Kieffer's (1984: 32) study shows personal control and self-efficacy to be the positive results of psychological empowerment:

> The participants in this study did not view themselves as 'having more power', but rather as 'feeling more powerful'. They had not necessarily gained significant social influence or political control, but they did see themselves becoming more efficacious participants in the political process and local decision making. While they did not assess themselves as having acquired any more absolute power to dictate the shape of their environments, they did believe they were growing better able to engage effectively in the dynamics of social and political change.

Apart from personal control, there is also a growing realisation of the collective benefit of self-help as people gain control over their own lives, thus, improving their participation in the community. It is worthwhile noting that in practice, as empowerment is viewed as a means whereby social workers, individuals, groups and/or communities are enabled to take control of their lives, it is not just about groups of people, but the growth of the individual is also important (Rappaport, 1987; Adams, 1990).

Empowerment is thus viewed as an interaction between individuals, communities and their environments (Prestby et al., 1990; Zimmermann, 1990). Environmental influences and neighbourhood conditions are seen as catalysts for changes in empowerment and therefore an opportunity to participate in decision-making enhances empowerment for residents in the community. Hence, empowerment in social work advocates that it must bring about changes in people's lives, especially for people who are disempowered. Sheppard (1995: 31) emphasises that: 'The task of empowerment is to change the individual from their (current) empirical self – who is actually disempowered – to their empowered potential self.' In order to bring about change people also need to develop the necessary skills needed to participate effectively in community decision-making.

Although psychological empowerment on an individual level is meant to bring about positive changes in people within themselves leading to increases in self-efficacy and self-confidence, it is also important to bear in mind that people need to have the necessary skills. Kieffer's study (1984: 32) study concludes that empowerment at the individual level includes the development of skills necessary to participate effectively in community decision-making: 'The fundamental empowering transformation, then, is in the transition from the sense of self as helpless victim to acceptance of self as assertive and efficacious citizen.'

Thus, in social work, empowerment is seen as a strategy for dealing with powerlessness, for helping individuals to gain control of key aspects of their lives and to improve their situations, which includes clients and social workers too. Guterman and Bargal (1996: 13) conclude from their studies that social workers with less power are more likely to report 'low feelings of service effectiveness, lower feelings of accomplishments with their service users, greater emotional exhaustion, and a greater intent to leave their jobs'. Hence, social workers who believe themselves to be 'powerless' are unlikely to be able to reduce such feelings in others. On the contrary, those who feel empowered are more likely to have the capacity to encourage and support others to be empowered. Therefore, in practice, social workers need to have higher feelings of accomplishment, self-esteem and self-empowerment. This stems from the argument that as part of social workers' jobs is to support their clients in taking greater control over their own lives, and assisting them to address personal difficulties, then the management of their own individual self-efficacy, self-esteem and self-empowerment is vital. However, despite the important role self-empowerment plays in the empowerment process, this vital area can sometimes be neglected. 'In view of the centrality of empowering the self to the concept of empowerment, it is surprising that self-empowerment is one of the most neglected aspects of empowerment theory and practice' (Adams, 2003: 48).

It is worthwhile noting the NASW (National Association of Social Workers) Code of Ethics for social workers (Kirst-Ashman, 2003: 31), particularly in the absence of any guidance or code of ethics for leaders and managers in management. The 'six core values' are as follows:

1.   *Service*: providing help, resources, and benefits so that people can achieve their maximum potential.

2.   *Social justice*: upholding the condition that in a perfect world all citizens would have identical 'rights, protection, opportunities, obligations, and social benefits' regardless of their backgrounds and membership in diverse groups (Barker, 1999: 451; cited in Kirst-Ashman, 2003: 31).

3.   *Dignity and worth of the person*: holding in high esteem and appreciating individual value.

4.   *Importance of human relationships*: valuing 'the mutual emotional exchange; dynamic interaction; and affective, cognitive, and behavioural connections that exist between the social worker and the client to create the working and helping atmosphere' (Barker, 1999: 407; cited in Kirst-Ashman, 2003: 31).

5.   *Integrity*: maintaining trustworthiness and sound adherence to moral ideals.

6.   *Competence*: having the necessary skills and abilities to work effectively with clients.

It is easy to disregard the implications of the practice of empowerment on a macro and micro level, something that might be instructive for management to be aware of. A number of authors argue that the practice of empowerment does have great significance on both these levels (Parsons, 1991; Dalrymple and Burke, 1995). According to Parsons (1991: 13), because individuals have unequal power in society, the common goal of social work activities must be empowerment of client systems, and hence empowerment-oriented practice needs to be directed towards both micro and macro systems. In the micro systems, users and clients need to be educated about their own situations and the situations of other groups or individuals like them, for validation of experience and mutual support that is so important in the empowerment process. On the macro level, large system intervention strategies include models of campaigning, legislative lobbying and social planning, which must include consultation and facilitation of skill building of disempowered people. These collective based interventions result in both the process and product of empowerment.

Another important point in the social work literature regarding a strategy for empowerment-oriented practice is the use of consciousness-raising (Breton, 1994; Freire, 1996; Adams, 2003; Kirst-Ashman, 2003). Related to this, Adams (2003: 10) takes the view that consciousness-raising 'is implicit in the process of empowerment'. On a practice level, Breton (1994: 31) calls for the need for practitioners to understand the importance of the consciousness-raising process; not only as a 'politicization' but also a 'liberation' process, as illustrated:

> another necessary condition for empowerment-oriented practice is that practitioners conceptualise and understand the consciousness-raising process not only as a personal process of cognitive restructuring, but as a politicization process and a liberation process which create a demand for socio-political restructuring.

Viewed in this way, empowerment has the potential to have positive effects, both for social workers and their clients.

Conclusion

Clearly, significant knowledge can be drawn from social work with regards to understanding empowerment. In social work practice, it is apparent that empowerment is seen as a means and a process by which individuals, groups and/or communities become able to take control of their lives in order to have power and control over the factors that are critical to overcome oppression and disempowerment. The practice of social work therefore as Kirst-Ashman (2003: 53) pointed out is to 'empower users in general and members of oppressed groups in particular'. In line with this, consciousness-raising is also viewed as a strategy for empowerment-oriented practice.

Several authors in social work highlight that the significant impact of empowerment in many cases has resulted in 'oppressed' citizens having a better quality of life, thus enabling them to contribute and participate democratically in decision-making processes. In such cases, empowerment is seen as facilitating the entry of people into different areas of policy-making where previously they did not have any 'say' in shaping politics, education, communities or services.

In management, such knowledge can help to enhance the process of employee empowerment. From social work, learning can be on several levels, such as the importance of empowering lower-level employees so that they too can have a 'say' or voice their 'opinion' in the decisions that may affect their job or improve the organisation's effectiveness. Lower-level employees can often bring solutions to customer satisfaction. Empowerment can give them an opportunity to increase their locus of control, self-efficacy and self-esteem and give them the confidence to 'speak up'. This psychological boost can help them to be better 'efficacious' employees who are motivated to do better for the organisation.

Chapter 4

Knowledge Drawn from Social Work Literature

Introduction

Drawing knowledge from social work literature has been a valuable exercise to enhance understanding of employee empowerment from a multi-disciplinary approach, because as mentioned before, empowerment in social work is an important construct.

There are several themes with regards to 'empowerment' in social work, but it was important to pay attention to the themes that were particularly missing in management literature, namely, access to information, collaboration and enablement. Participants who were interviewed in my research study commented that these themes were not mentioned during the 'employee empowerment' programme in their organisation. However, these themes are vital with regards to the psychological empowerment of individuals in organisations.

After scoping the important themes of empowerment from social work literature, it was also deemed necessary to revisit themes from management literature in order to have a comprehensive list of themes to generate a holistic understanding of employee empowerment from a multi-disciplinary approach.

Themes of Empowerment Emanating from Social Work Literature

We need to pay attention to three key themes emanating from the social work literature that are largely missing in the management literature, namely, access to information, collaboration and enablement.

ACCESS TO INFORMATION

In order to be empowering, organisations need to make information available to individuals in a relevant way. Kouzes and Posner (1987: 157) state that 'without information, you can be certain that people will not extend themselves to take responsibility or vent their creative energies'.

> *Although access to information seems obvious, as people must have information to be empowered to make choices and decisions, surprisingly information can often be the most difficult thing to access. In many cases, this is due to a lack of planning with regards to who the information is for [target audience], what it should contain and how it should be disseminated. (Pierson and Thomas, 2002)*

It is essential to remember that social work deals with a diverse group of individuals from different backgrounds, and in this sense it is vital that information is tailored to suit the needs of various groups. For example, information leaflets for younger people may be different from those designed for an adult group with learning difficulties. Keeping this important issue in mind, Pierson and Thomas (2002: 236) state:

> *Organisations need an information strategy to inform potential users of all services. The strategy should include an analysis of the most likely points of contact with particular client groups and an appreciation of the forms of communication most suitable to their needs. For example, a leaflet for children might have to be written in a different way from one designed for young people or adults.*

Access to information is viewed as empowering in social work, particularly by service users (Beresford and Croft, 1993; Wilson, 1995; Payne, 2000; Pierson and Thomas, 2002). An example of this is provided by Wilson (1995: 83): 'Group members valued the opportunity to gain knowledge about the condition or issue on which the group was based; to get information about services they could use and ask for; and to learn ways of coping.' Hence, access to information is 'fundamental and a necessary requisite for any service that aspires to have user participation' (Pierson and Thomas, 2002: 237).

It is worth noting the psychological benefits can also be gained from having access to information, such as self-confidence: 'One of the results of gaining more information … was that people felt more confident' (Wilson, 1995: 84). An important point to note is that it is not just service users, but professionals working in the discipline of social work who need access to information, otherwise they too can suffer from disempowerment.

Hence, in order to be empowering, organisations need to make more information available to people. But, a major problem for organisations can be that they are not aware of the various ways of letting employees have access to information. Leaders need to collaborate with their teams and employees to find out the best way information can be accessed and to make sure everyone has access to appropriate information.

COLLABORATION

It is important to understand what collaboration means and how it can play a part in the process of empowerment. It has already been noted that the *Blackwell Encyclopaedia of Social Work* (Davies, 2000: 67) offers the following definition of collaboration: '*Collaboration* refers to working together to achieve common goals'. In a similar vein, the *Concise Oxford Dictionary* (Sykes, 1976: 196) also explains 'collaborate' as meaning to 'work jointly'. These definitions help one understand what an important role collaboration plays in the empowerment of people in social work (Adams, 1996; Mattaini et al., 1998; Kirst-Ashman, 2003; Weinstein et al., 2003; DuBois and Miley, 2005; Saleebey, 2013).

Collaboration is an important part of empowerment, as 'much of social work involves collaborating with organisations and communities to improve social and health services' (Kirst-Ashman, 2003: 5). In a similar manner, DuBois and Miley (2005: 27) state: 'Empowerment-oriented social workers work collaboratively with their clients. They focus on clients' strengths and adaptive skills as well as clients' competencies and potential.'

Social workers deal with an enormous range of human problems and issues concerning service users from a variety of different backgrounds and communities. Collaboration can be a complex process in such cases. Hence, it is acknowledged that collaboration is not without problems. The *Blackwell Encyclopaedia of Social Work*'s (Davies, 2000: 67) expansion of the definition of collaboration goes on to explain: 'Collaboration and conflict are "both sides of the same coin" in that conflict may be part of the process of achieving collaboration, the process of working together may lead ultimately to a relationship that ends in either conflict or collaboration.' One conflict can arise when social workers assume that they know best what the needs of service users are, rather than collaborating or 'working jointly' with service users to find out what they think their needs are. Payne (2000: 87) cautions: 'assumptions about what is required do not meet the needs of diverse populations'. Hence, Whittington (2003: 58) points out that, 'Effective *interprofessional* collaboration appears to require practitioners to learn, negotiate and apply understanding of what is *common* to the professions involved; their *distinctive contributions*; what is *complementary* between them; what may be *in conflict*; and *how to work together*' (emphasis in original).

In order to enable and maximise service users' capabilities, it is imperative that social workers do not assume the role of experts. Breton (1994: 29) highlights:

> *If professionals accept that they don't know best, and if they accept to let go of the role of expert, they will be able to engage in a genuine dialogue with the oppressed and will be ready to learn from them. This necessitates a non-authoritarian approach – not easy for practitioners who find themselves in more or less authoritarian settings.*

Hence, it is emphasised that social workers need to: 'replace paternalistic and elitist forms of intervention (those that assume the worker knows best) with approaches that maximise people's rights, strengths, and capabilities' (Mattaini et al., 1998: 221).

In a similar manner, DuBois and Miley (2005: 27) warn: 'The embedded patriarchal organisational culture of social service delivery thwarts collaborative work with clients.' In this sense, it should be remembered that power is not a commodity, it is something that needs to be used, rather than simply possessed. Relating to this, Fook (2012: 60) states that: 'it [power] is created out of social relations and is not finite. It is therefore conceivable that both less and more powerful people can work together to create situations in which all experience empowerment. In effect, more power can potentially be created through collaboration'. In other words, as Saleebey (2013: 288) explains: 'Collaboration means that each of the parties to the contract has control.' Both parties are independent but they come together for a particular project.

Collaboration in social work can enable individuals to be empowered. Many clients are competent and knowledgeable. Social workers need to acknowledge these clients as *experts* in defining their needs. In this respect, the attitude of the social worker must be one that appreciates the clients' expertise. In order to empower clients, hence, social workers need to identify clients' skills and strengths and enable them to use their abilities to help them achieve personal goals. This is an essential outcome of empowerment in social work.

Another important point is that not only do social workers need to collaborate with their service users, they also need to collaborate with different service agencies who are responsible for providing services for the users. In this case too, social workers need to collaborate with service providers, to get the best outcome possible for individuals and groups whom they are trying to empower. Hence, it is imperative that they 'work jointly' with service providers as well, in order to enable their service users to achieve their needs and feel empowered. Collaboration and working in partnerships are essential roles for social workers, irrespective of which client group they serve (Leiba and Weinstein, 2003).

From the aspect of collaboration, if organisations want to practise employee empowerment, then leaders need to work in collaboration with all employees (management and non-management personnel), that is, work jointly with them to achieve common goals. In such cases, a command and control culture is disempowering and disabling; and works against the practice of employee empowerment.

ENABLEMENT

There is high consensus in the social work literature that empowerment can enable people to achieve control in their lives and to achieve their goals (Adams, 1990; Frans, 1993). At the practice level, although empowerment is viewed as a means whereby social workers, groups of people and/or communities are enabled to take control of their lives, the growth of the individual is also considered important (Rappaport, 1987; Adams, 1990).

> The concept (of empowerment) suggests both individual determination over one's own life and democratic participation in the life of one's community. (Rappaport, 1987: 121)

In social work, enablement is viewed as a process that empowers people to take greater control over their lives (Adams, 1990; Beresford and Croft, 1993; Frans, 1993), hence, it is an important concept in social work with regards to empowerment (Kieffer, 1984; Adams, 1990, 1996; Frans, 1993; Means et al., 1993; Parsloe, 1996; Mattaini et al., 1998; Kirst-Ashman, 2003; Zastrow, 2003). The problem in the management literature is that the majority of management researchers referred to empowerment in the sense of delegation rather than in the sense of enabling (Conger and Kanungo, 1988). It is useful to note the definition to 'enable' in the *Concise Oxford Dictionary*:

> *Authorize, empower, (person to do); supply (person etc.) with means to*
> *(do); make possible. (Sykes, 1976: 340)*

Zastrow (2003: 13) emphasises that one of the roles social workers must assume is that of an 'enabler', which has resonance with the above definition. The role of the enabler is thus, to help, or facilitate, or make it possible for the person concerned to achieve his/her goals:

> *In this role a worker helps individuals or groups articulate their needs,*
> *clarify and identify their problems, explore resolution strategies,*
> *select and develop their capacities to deal with their own problems*
> *more effectively.*

There are two elements of enablement, one is giving people more control over their lives and the other is to help them to exercise this control effectively. In this sense, facilitation becomes an important skill for social workers, as enabling is not only about equipping people with skills to have control over their lives, but sometimes social workers also have to act as facilitators to help achieve this (Kieffer, 1984: 28).

> *While we cannot stimulate or cognitively duplicate the fundamental*
> *dynamic of empowering learning, we can actively facilitate individuals, or*
> *citizen organisations, in their own critical and constructive examination*
> *of their efforts toward changing social and political situations.*

In social work literature, people having some control over their lives is regarded to be highly essential (Kieffer, 1984; Rappaport, 1987; Adams, 1990; Prestby et al., 1990; Zimmerman, 1990; Fahlberg et al., 1991; Beresford and Croft, 1993; Lord and Hutchison, 1993; Sheppard, 1995; Williams, 1995; Adams, 1996, 2003; Kirst-Ashman, 2003; DuBois and Miley, 2005). Interestingly this has resonance with the results of some studies in the management literature. For example, the conclusions of Conger and Kanungo's (1988) studies revealed that employee empowerment gives employees more control over their work; and Parker and Price (1994: 911) conclude from their studies that 'high levels of worker control over decision-making are associated with high levels of psychological well-being and job satisfaction'. Noted also in the management literature are the negative consequences that can result from a lack of control, such as withdrawal, decrease in performance, stress and depression (Bandura, 1995).

In management literature, there are some authors who propose that organisational strategies which strengthen employees' internal locus of control, are considered to be empowering and enabling (Conger and Kanungo, 1988; Thomas and Velthouse, 1990; Alpander, 1991; Greasley et al., 2005; Logan and Ganster, 2007; Sahoo and Das, 2011). Interestingly, from the management literature it is also noted that having control at work can lead individuals to be innovative and creative (Peters and Waterman, 1982; Velthouse, 1990; Whetten and Cameron, 1991; Sahoo and Das, 2011).

However, in order to enable people to achieve more control over their lives, training, educating and supporting them is crucial, as enablement is not just about giving people opportunities to take control or to perform tasks, but also equipping them adequately to do so (Beresford and Croft, 1993). Training and education are important processes of enablement, something that is easily overlooked; this applies to both social workers and service users. Braye and Preston-Shoot (1995: 116) emphasise the need to create a skilled workforce, where staff development and training should be seen as vital; a skilled workforce will be able to 'take on the challenge of empowerment'.

Clearly, in order to empower others, enablement is a challenge for leaders to re-skill and develop, whether they are in industry, hospitality, manufacturing, health, hospital and patient care or social work sectors. There are two important function of leaders – on the one hand to create the conditions that are necessary to enable employees/individuals/service users (as the case may be) to take control (in their lives or at work) and develop their individual competencies, and on the other hand, to remove all impediments that may hinder this. It is important to note that there is potential for tension, as the roles of leaders change to facilitators or enablers. Some leaders may not be able to carry out these roles and there may be resistance to change.

Revisiting Themes from Management and Social Work Literatures

This multi-disciplinary research has been extremely valuable, as it enabled me to bring together key themes of employee empowerment from both disciplines, namely, management and social work, as illustrated below, Huq's Model A (Figure 4.1) and Huq's Model B (Figure 4.2).

■ Theme: Power-sharing

■ Theme: Participative decision-making

■ Theme: Devolution of responsibility

■ Theme: People-oriented leadership style

Figure 4.1   Huq's Model A: themes of employee empowerment emanating from management literature

■ Theme: Access to Information

■ Theme: Collaboration

■ Theme: Enablement

Figure 4.2   Huq's Model B: themes of empowerment emanating from social work literature

From the in-depth reviews of the management and social work literatures respectively, some conclusions about meaning of employee empowerment can now be drawn. In the management literature, employee empowerment means that an organisation needs to address power-sharing, participative decision-making, devolution of responsibility and people-oriented leadership style (Huq's Model A). In social work literature, empowerment embraces not only the themes in Huq's Model A, but in addition emphasises that access to information, collaboration and enablement are also essential aspects of empowerment (Huq's Model B). Hence, considering the themes from both management and social work literatures, it may make sense that those organisations that wish to embrace an employee empowerment culture should address all these seven themes as in Huq's Models A and B.

Thus, the potential of the *combined synergy* of themes from both the literatures, management and social work, is powerful, which will have a positive impact on the understanding and acceptance of employee empowerment in management, and it is hoped that the social work discipline may benefit too.

Conclusion

It is clear from the review of social work literature that such an exercise is necessary to bridge some of the gaps with regards to the understanding of empowerment at the conceptual and practice levels. A number of important themes have emanated from the social work literature, which may help to understand employee empowerment in a wider context.

An in-depth review of the social work literature with regards to empowerment reveal some common themes that were found in management literature, namely, power-sharing, participative decision-making, devolution of responsibility and people-oriented leadership style (Huq's Model A). However, themes that were also viewed as empowering in social work, namely, access to information, collaboration and enablement (Huq's Model B), were largely missing in the management literature, in the employee empowerment context. In this respect, knowledge from social work has been extremely enlightening.

With respect to this finding, it is important that an organisation needs to address all these seven themes (Huq's Models A and B) if they want to empower their employees.

As defined by *The Concise Oxford Dictionary* (Sykes, 1976: 339) to 'empower' also means to 'give power', thus to 'empower' is to:

> *Authorise, license, (person to do);*
> *Give power to, make able, (person to do).*

It is recognised in both management and social work literatures that there are significant implications with regards to lack of power. For example, when people feel powerless they have low self-esteem and low self-efficacy.

This creates doubt in employees about their capability to achieve anything positive or productive at work. Heslin (1999) describes how disempowered employees are more likely to become over-reliant, dependent, demoralised and demotivated. Therefore, feelings of powerlessness and disempowerment can cause damage not only to individuals, but in the end the organisation suffers as well. One of the ways management can meet the higher motivational needs of employees is to shift power down from the top of the organisational hierarchy and share it with subordinates (Daft, 1999; Greenberg and Baron, 2000). Hence, empowerment is seen as a process where power is shared with a view to tackle oppression and to address the unequal balance of power experienced by vulnerable and powerless people in the community.

However, it should be remembered that empowerment in social work is not just about power-sharing it is also about problem-solving and decision-making and it entails people taking responsibility for their own choices and actions. In social work, giving people access to information is vital. It is also clear that in social work, empowerment is a collaborative process in which leaders, social workers and clients work together as partners. Hence, empowerment is also about enablement.

In social work practice, it is apparent that empowerment is seen as a means and a process by which individuals, groups and/or communities are enabled to take control of their lives in order to have power and control over the factors that are critical to overcome oppression and disempowerment. The practice of social work therefore is 'to empower users in general and members of oppressed groups in particular' (Kirst-Ashman, 2003: 53).

A significant impact of empowerment in many cases has resulted in people who are 'oppressed' to have a better quality of life, thus enabling them to contribute and participate democratically in decision-making processes. In such cases, empowerment is seen as facilitating the entry of people into different areas of policy-making where previously they did not have a means to put forward their 'voice' in shaping politics, education, communities or services.

It is also useful to take into account Kieffer's (1984) argument that empowerment is not just a commodity to be acquired, but it must be viewed as a process of transforming people's lives that is developed through action and learning. Thus, it means to enable and develop an individual's ability to help themselves (Humphries, 1996).

Apart from the importance of power-sharing, the social work literature also argues there are three other themes that are necessary in the practice of empowerment, namely, access to information, collaboration and enablement. Access to information is essential, from two points of view. First, without access to information, professionals and social workers are unable to help service users, leading them to feel helpless. Second, service users feel helpless and disempowered without having access to information. An important point related to this is the psychological benefits that can be gained by service users, from having access to information, such as self-confidence. But it is also instructive to note from the social work literature that it is not just service users, but also professionals working in this discipline who need access to information, otherwise they too can suffer from disempowerment. While both Large and Small Organisations attempted to provide access to information to some employees, they did not seek to empower all their employees.

Collaboration is also viewed as an important theme in the practice of empowerment in social work. An essential point to note is that not only do social workers need to collaborate with their service users, they also need to collaborate with different service agencies who are responsible for providing services for the users. Empowerment initiatives are unlikely to produce the desired results unless there is appropriate collaboration between social workers and service users. Furthermore, the social work literature also emphasises that it is essential for service users to feel and believe themselves to be empowered, and that they are enabled to do so. In this respect, it is instructive for leaders to understand that they must enable employees to feel empowered, because enablement is a process that empowers people to take greater control over their lives.

An important point made by Kieffer (1984: 27) is that it is not just about learning new skills, it is also about '(individuals) reconstructing and reorienting deeply engrained personal systems of social relations'. Thus, empowerment is about change on several levels, for example, people having to learn new behaviours and new skills, and new ways of interacting with other people, the environment, social conditions and systems that may be oppressive. As Freire (1972) argues, it is about the development of critical consciousness, and the ability to think against the status quo that enables people to act together, to change oppressive social conditions. The process of liberation, freedom and empowerment is through education and consciousness-raising of individuals and groups. The corollary of this is the absence of empowerment, which means alienation, helplessness and feelings of powerlessness. Hence, individuals need to be enabled to overcome feelings of helplessness and despair through measures that increase confidence, internal locus of control, self-efficacy and self-esteem.

From Kieffer's (1984: 32) study, it is enlightening to note with regards to the psychological perspective, how participants in his study did not view themselves as *'having* more power', but rather as *'feeling* more powerful' (Kieffer's emphasis). This has resonance with my research findings, discussed in this book.

Chapter 4 concludes by synthesising the learning from the reviews of the two literatures (management and social work). It presents the key themes of employee empowerment, namely, power-sharing, participative decision-making, devolution of responsibility and a people-oriented leadership style, emanating from the management literature (Huq's Model A) and access to information, collaboration and enablement, which are the key themes emanating from social work literature (Huq's Model B).

As previously mentioned, in this respect, knowledge from social work has been extremely enlightening. This may help to reduce the gap with regards to understanding the concept of employee empowerment and, furthermore, it is important if an organisation wants to empower their employees, they need to address all these themes, namely, power-sharing, participative decision-making, devolution of responsibility, people-oriented leadership style (Huq's Model A) and access to information, collaboration and enablement (Huq's Model B).

It is wise to accept that empowerment does not happen overnight and it is not a 'quick fix', hence Kieffer (1984: 27) cautions: 'Empowerment is inescapably labour-intensive.' In the management world, the realities of culture change, training, learning skills and so on related to empowerment and the realisation of the time and resources needed, have not been given adequate attention.

This chapter draws knowledge from the social work literature to enhance a wider understanding of empowerment. Moving from a parochial and narrow information base of empowerment in the management literature, knowledge drawn from the social work literature has been emancipatory. It has also been a valuable exercise to understand the concept of empowerment in a wider context which is beneficial for leaders in organisations.

PART III
What Does Psychology Have to Do With It?

Chapter 5

Psychological Implications

Introduction

Employee empowerment is advocated because of its perceived psychological benefits, such as an increase in internal locus of control, self-efficacy and self-esteem of employees. There is abundant literature to support this view (Maslow, 1943; Bandura, 1977; Kieffer, 1984; Gist, 1987; Conger and Kanungo, 1988; Conger, 1989; Thomas and Velthouse, 1990; Weber, 1991; Ivancevich and Matteson, 1993; Dubrin, 1994; Parker and Price, 1994; Spreitzer, 1995; Zimmerman, 1995; Kappelman and Richards, 1996; Corsun and Enz, 1999; Menon, 1999; Siegall and Gardner, 2000; Kark et al., 2003; Greasley et al., 2005; Logan and Ganster, 2007; Tuuli and Rowlinson, 2009; Sahoo and Das, 2011; Hashemi et al., 2012; Burke et al., 2014; Mangundjaya, 2014).

It should also be highlighted that if organisations pay 'lip service' to employee empowerment and fail to address all the themes as in Huq's Models A and B, it may have negative psychological implications on an individual's internal locus of control, self-efficacy and self-esteem, and employees may feel 'disempowered', which is counter-productive. This is important to mention here, as the findings from my research evidently show that some employees did feel 'disempowered'. For example, in one of my case study organisations, employees were told that they could make decisions, but when they used their empowerment initiative and took decisions they were not allowed and discouraged to do so. Employees in this situation commented that they did not feel 'empowered', in fact they felt more 'disempowered' since the introduction of 'employee empowerment' in the organisation, which led to confusion. Some employees did not believe that their organisation was serious in the first place and remarked that the introduction of employee empowerment was just a 'paper exercise'.

Hence, attention needs to be paid to the psychological implications (positive and negative) of employee empowerment. These are viewed as significant and can lead to employees perceiving themselves as being empowered or not. In this sense, Siegall and Gardner (2000: 705) argue:

> *While one can change attitudes by first shaping behaviours, we believe that the true benefits of empowerment (however defined) will not be seen unless people first perceive themselves as being empowered.*

By supporting and creating the appropriate environment, leaders in organisations can help to enhance internal locus of control; self-efficacy; self-esteem and self-confidence in employees; and vice versa.

Internal Locus of Control

Locus of control concerns the extent to which people believe they have control over what happens to them in life and it may be internal or external (Kieffer, 1984; Arnold and Feldman, 1986; Conger and Kanungo, 1988; Thomas and Velthouse, 1990; Alpander, 1991; Whetten and Cameron, 1991; Ivancevich and Matteson, 1993; Spreitzer, 1995; Kappelman and Richards, 1996; Menon, 1999; Wilson, 2004; Greasley et al., 2005; Logan and Ganster, 2007).

Internal locus of control refers to people's perception that events which happen to them in life are primarily, though not exclusively, within their direct control and influence; whereas an external locus of control refers to people's perceptions that events which happen to them are determined by matters outside their control, such as the behaviour of other people, chance, external circumstances, fate and so on.

Conclusions of Conger and Kanungo's (1988) studies reveal that employee empowerment has positive implications on employees' locus of control. Locus of control is therefore the belief that each person holds regarding the relationships between their actions and outcomes and, as mentioned before, it may be internal or external. Whetten and Cameron (1991: 72) explain internal locus of control as referring to: 'the attitude people develop regarding the extent to which they are in control of their own destiny'. In this context, Wilson (2004: 167) notes: 'Potentially empowerment can mean workers take more control over their jobs and working environment. They should be able to enhance the contributions they make as individuals and members of a team and also seize opportunities for personal growth and fulfilment.'

The need for employees to feel that they have some control, not only over their work, but also their own lives, is regarded to be essential, as du Gay and Salaman (1998: 61) emphasise: 'Enterprising companies "make meaning for people" by encouraging them to believe that they have control over their own lives; that no matter what position they may hold within an organisation their contribution is vital, not only to the success of the company but to the enterprise of their own lives.' When people feel they have some control over their work and are empowered to take decisions, they are also more likely to accept the consequences of them. In other words, employees are more committed to actions based on decisions that they have taken themselves than they are to actions that are based on decisions taken by others (Greenberg and Baron, 2000).

Employees with a strong internal locus of control are more likely to feel capable of performing their tasks, and it can also lead individuals to be innovative and creative (Peters and Waterman, 1982; Velthouse, 1990; Whetten and Cameron, 1991; Spreitzer; 1995; Knol and Linge, 2009; Sahoo and Das, 2011), hence this is a skill particularly sought after by organisations. A number of authors propose that managerial strategies that strengthen employees' self-determination or locus of control can be considered as empowering and enabling (Conger and Kanungo, 1988; Thomas and Velthouse, 1990; Alpander, 1991; Greasley et al., 2005; Logan and Ganster, 2007).

Thus, the need for personal control can be a powerful motivator for people at work. But, in order to help employees enhance and develop their internal locus of control, managers need to believe, and have trust in the potential of their people throughout the process of empowering their employees. Managers must also give up control over a variety of decision-making that takes place in organisations, and let their employees act independently, especially at lower levels (Simons, 1995). This has resonance with the social work literature: '*the most oppressed people in society*' need to be empowered.

Conclusions drawn from Conger and Kanungo's (1988) studies reveal that employee empowerment gives employees more personal control. This is essential, particularly, for front-line employees. Employee empowerment is necessary because they (front-line employees) need the flexibility and the self-confidence to make on-the-spot decisions to satisfy customers, or respond quickly to customers' needs, thus making the organisation more efficient, leading to the optimum utilisation of human resources.

A range of unwanted consequences can result from low, or less than desired, levels of control, such as withdrawal, decrease in performance, stress and even depression (Bandura, 1995). In contrast, a number of benefits of feeling in control highlighted by several authors include a reduction in an individual's feelings of helplessness, fears of insecurity and manifestations of stress.

Self-Efficacy

Self-efficacy is a 'critical ingredient' in employee empowerment, because it is to do with people's confidence in their ability to perform effectively in their empowered roles (Heslin, 1999: 52). In this context, Conger and Kanungo (1988: 474) define empowerment as 'a process of enhancing feelings of self-efficacy among organisational members through the identification of conditions that foster powerlessness and through their removal by both formal organisational practices and informal techniques of providing efficacy information'.

Drawing on Conger and Kanungo's (1988) study, it is clear that managerial strategies have a direct influence on individuals' self-efficacy beliefs. Hence, the argument that organisational strategies that strengthen self-efficacy beliefs will make individuals feel more powerful, and in contrast, any strategies that weaken self-efficacy beliefs will result in an increase in the individual's feelings of powerlessness, thus leading to feelings of oppression (Freire, 1972; Friedmann, 1992).

According to Bandura (1977: 34), self-efficacy is a person's belief in their capability to be competent in performing tasks, reaching a goal or overcoming obstacles in life:

> Personal efficacy is valued not because of reverence for individualism but because a strong sense of personal efficacy is vital for successful adaptation and change regardless of whether it is achieved individually or by group members working together.

Borrowing from Bandura (1977), Greenberg and Baron (2000: 107) offer a definition of self-efficacy as 'an individual's beliefs concerning his or her ability to perform specific tasks successfully'.

Several authors (Bandura, 1977, 1986; Gist, 1987; Conger and Kanungo, 1988; Baron and Greenberg, 1990; Thomas and Velthouse, 1990; Weber, 1991; Spreitzer, 1995, 1996; Corsun and Enz, 1999; Heslin, 1999; Baron and Byrne, 2000; Greenberg and Baron, 2000; Siegall and Gardner, 2000; Dessler, 2001; Nesan and Holt, 2002; Bernstein, 2003; Seibert et al., 2004; Hashemi et al., 2012) conclude that self-efficacy has a strong influence on any individual's task performance and has motivational benefits. As self-efficacy enhances people's competence, it has a positive effect on their psychological well-being and motivation; it boosts the individual's belief in their capacity to perform tasks.

In this sense, employee empowerment is advocated as a useful tool to motivate employees to take decisions on their own without constant referral to their managers, which in turn enhances their self-efficacy beliefs (Greenberg and Baron, 2000). There is strong agreement in the literature that by creating conditions to increase motivation, organisations can enable employees to accomplish their tasks in a confident manner, and build a strong sense of self-efficacy (Conger and Kanungo, 1988; Peters, 1994; Daft, 1999; Greeenberg and Baron, 2000; Hashemi et al., 2012).

Some of these psychological benefits of empowerment are also noted in other disciplines and not just in management, for example, Denham Lincoln et al. (2002: 285) observe the wide usage of the term 'empowerment' across a large number of non-management disciplines, such as feminism, minority groups, education, community care and politics, to enable oppressed people to increase their self-efficacy:

> From this review of the use of the term empowerment across several disciplines, it would seem that the underlying interpretation of the word is one of mobilizing the oppressed by helping them believe in themselves, increasing their self-efficacy.

Thus, in an empowered organisation, self-efficacy can potentially have a strong impact on an individual's task performance (Baron and Greenberg, 1990; Hartline and Ferrell, 1996; Holt et al., 2000; Dessler, 2001; Psoinos and Smithson, 2002; Greasley et al., 2005). It is worthwhile noting the components of self-efficacy; Greenberg and Baron (2000: 107) explain that self-efficacy consists of three basic components:

1. Magnitude: The level at which an individual believes she or he can perform.

2. Strength: The person's confidence that she or he can perform at that level.

3. Generality: The extent to which self-efficacy in one situation or for one task extends to other situations and other tasks.

Conger and Kanungo (1988: 478) describe factors that can lower an individual's self-efficacy, for example, when jobs do not provide challenge and meaning; when there is role ambiguity; role conflict and work overload. Clearly, for individuals to feel empowered, leaders need to give consideration to the positive aspects of self-efficacy and understand that the lack of this can lead to negative results, such as under-performance and mistakes made by employees, which is not desirable in organisations. The danger is that when employees have low self-efficacy, they tend to blame other people in the organisation when things go wrong.

In line with this argument, Johnson (1994: 18) states: 'Empowerment refers to a process whereby an individual's belief in his or her self-efficacy is enhanced.' Studies have also shown that self-efficacy influences not only the amount of work but also the quality of effort a person will apply to complete tasks (Barling and Beatlie, 1983; Ellis and Taylor, 1983). Similarly, self-esteem also plays an important role within a person's internal perception of 'the sense of feeling worthwhile' (Dubrin, 1994: 80); this leads to the argument that individuals with high self-esteem tend to view themselves positively, and vice versa, individuals with low self-esteem view themselves negatively. These contrasting views obviously have an impact on a person's task outcomes.

Tasks become intrinsically motivating when employees derive positively valued experiences directly from a completed task (Conger and Kanungo, 1988; Thomas and Velthouse, 1990; Spreitzer, 1995). So, it is understandable that managerial strategies which strengthen employees' self-efficacy beliefs will make them feel powerful while strategies that weaken employees' self-efficacy beliefs will result in feelings of powerlessness. The argument here is that by creating conditions that will increase motivation, organisations can enable people in accomplishing their tasks and build a strong sense of self-efficacy.

Self-Esteem

Self-esteem is to do with how people feel about themselves and how they evaluate themselves (Bandura, 1977; Kieffer, 1984; Hellriegel et al., 1989; Baron and Greenberg, 1990; Dubrin, 1994; Yoon et al., 1996; Baron and Byrne, 2000; Huczynski and Buchanan, 2001). It is the part of the self that is concerned with self-evaluation or the judgement people make about themselves. Hence, self-esteem is 'the sense of feeling worthwhile' that plays an important role in a person's life (Dubrin, 1994: 80), since it determines whether they hold positive or negative attitudes about themselves (Baron and Greenberg, 1990; Dubrin, 1994; Baron and Byrne, 2000). Several studies conclude that employee empowerment can enable employees to raise their self-esteem (Conger and Kanungo, 1988; Thomas and Velthouse, 1990; Herschel and Andrews, 1993; Spreitzer, 1995; Joo and Shim, 2010; Sahoo and Das, 2011; Burke et al., 2014).

Individuals who have high self-esteem tend to evaluate themselves positively and more favourably, because they believe they have the traits and qualities needed to do the job, and view themselves as valued resources. In contrast, individuals who have low self-esteem evaluate themselves negatively and less favourably because of their belief that they lack the desired traits and qualities required for task performance. Obviously, individuals with high self-esteem are essential in an empowered organisation because it allows them to take risks, accept responsibility and be resilient (Thomas and Velthouse, 1990; Herschel and Andrews, 1993; Joo and Shim, 2010). Thus, managers should regard self-esteem highly at work, especially if employees are expected to be creative, imaginative and take risks on an organisation's behalf. Recognising this, Yoon et al. (1996) point out that it is important that efforts and contributions of employees are appreciated and rewarded, as this satisfies their need for approval, affiliation and self-esteem.

From the psychological point of view, different factors that can help or hinder the employee empowerment process are necessary for organisations to take into account. For example, self-esteem and locus of control are seen as antecedents of empowerment. Spreitzer (1995) explains that the reason is that they help to shape how individuals view themselves in relation to their work environments.

All individuals have a need for a high evaluation of themselves, or self-esteem, and this is illustrated by Maslow (1954: 90):

All people in our society ... have a need or desire for a stable, firmly based, usually high evaluation of themselves, for self-respect, or self-esteem, and for the esteem of others. These needs may therefore be classified into two subsidiary sets. These are, first, the desire for strength, for achievement, for adequacy, for mastery and competence, for confidence, in the face of the world, and for independence and freedom (Allport, 1937). Second, we have what we may call the desire for reputation or prestige (defining it as respect or esteem from other people), status, dominance, recognition, attention, importance, or appreciation.

In this respect, it is interesting to note Maslow's (1943) conceptualisation of human needs in organisations, from basic needs such as physiological and safety needs to personal development and growth needs, namely, self-esteem and self-actualisation needs (Maslow's Hierarchy of Needs). Interestingly, neo-modernism is based on the argument that people work in organisation for a variety of reasons, and not just for economic reward, but also 'individual satisfaction, membership of a social group, "belonging" to an organisation, having a say in the running of the organisation – and for organisations to be *effective*, account needs to be given to these different aspects of human motivation' (McAuley et al., 2007: 102). Clearly, these aspects of human motivation have resonance with Maslow's (1943) theory and interestingly the discipline of social work. Hence, it is important for management to pay attention to the argument that some people are motivated by higher level intrinsic needs (Conger and Kanungo, 1988). Furthermore, Bernstein (2003: 75) implies that when intrinsic rewards such as 'feedback, mastery or self-knowledge' are valued more than extrinsic rewards such as 'money, status, promotion', people are thought to be more 'empowered'.

Thus, managers should regard self-esteem highly at work, especially if employees are expected to be creative, imaginative and take risks on an organisation's behalf.

Stimulating Innovation and Creativity

In relation to employee empowerment, as discussed, several authors note the effects of positive psychological implications of locus of control, self-efficacy and self-esteem leading to encouraging innovative and creative behaviours in people (Peters and Waterman, 1982; Kanter, 1984; Peters, 1987, 1994; Gandz, 1990; Thomas and Velthouse, 1990; Velthouse, 1990; Whetten and Cameron,

1991; Shipper and Manz, 1992; Herschel and Andrews, 1993; Simons, 1995; Spreitzer, 1995; Pearson and Chatterjee, 1996; Hammuda and Dulaimi, 1997; Kondo, 1997; Marchington and Wilkinson, 2000; Carter, 2009; Knol and Linge, 2009; Yang and Choi, 2009; Joo and Shim, 2010; Zhang and Bartol, 2010; Sahoo and Das, 2011).

As Gandz (1990: 78) states: 'Intensified competition requires more and more innovation', thus, the psychological implications cannot be ignored. In the competitive marketplace, recruiting employees who have the potential to be creative and innovative is highly desirable, as they can create value for organisations. Allowing people to be innovative and creative can help to drive down costs and make the organisation more effective, which has resonance with SHRM theory and views from the economic perspective debate, as illustrated:

> The overhead costs of excessive bureaucratic controls, people checking up on people, layers of supervision and so on can be avoided by those organisations that work in an empowered mode. Innovative ways of working can drive down costs, and human and capital resources can be utilised more effectively. (Gandz, 1990: 75)

According to Walton (1985: 77), 'workers respond best – and most creatively – not when they are tightly controlled by management, placed in narrowly defined jobs, and treated like unwelcome necessity, but, instead, when they are given broader responsibilities, encouraged to contribute, and helped to take satisfaction in their work'. It is true to say that people who have always been supervised are also anxious and fearful of being watched all the time, as Marchington and Wilkinson (2000: 40) point out: 'individuals empowered to make decisions may be unwilling to use their discretion if they feel continually under the watchful eye of "Big Brother"'. Under such conditions, innovation and creativity, which are seen as important skills in SHRM, may be stifled.

Competitive organisations are always seeking ways and methods to be innovative. Several authors report that employee empowerment is positively related to innovation and capability and it is also viewed as being motivational, 'innovative work practices can increase motivation by providing more interesting work, increasing flexibility and improving individual and organisational performance' (Marchington and Wilkinson, 2000: 342). On a psychological level, innovative organisations are seen to have positive benefits, 'fostering more self-esteem and self-worth' in individuals (Ripley and Ripley, 1993: 30).

Hence, the arguments behind innovation and creativity are that when organisations encourage these behaviours in individuals or even teams, it can enable employees to be imaginative, creative and feel empowered. Velthouse (1990: 13) explains how creativity is defined as the 'spark of the soul, *joie de vivre*'. In theory, employee empowerment is supposed to help unleash the potential and creative side of people, as Kondo (1997: 256) highlights: 'Creativity is the driving force behind the discovery of better ways of doing things.' In a similar vein, Ripley and Ripley (1993: 29) point out that innovative organisations can 'achieve long-term competitiveness with an ever increasing market share'.

However, Simons (1995: 80) cautions that although innovation and creativity can create opportunities for organisations and employees, it is also important to exercise some control to avoid exposing organisations to adverse situations, as illustrated:

> *A fundamental problem facing managers in the 1990s is how to exercise adequate control in organisations that demand flexibility, innovation, and creativity. Competitive businesses with demanding and informed customers must rely on employee initiative to seek out opportunities and respond to customers' needs. But pursuing some opportunities can expose businesses to excessive risk or invite behaviours that can damage a company's integrity.*

This is an important point and it is necessary for organisations to be tolerant of risk-taking and of employees making mistakes. Interestingly, implied in employee empowerment is not only the development of innovative and creative behaviours of employees, but risk-taking as well. Velthouse (1990: 14) highlights that there is a complementary relationship between creativity and employee empowerment and they are similar in many aspects, such as 'individual expressions of independence, risk-taking, confidence and commitment'.

However, encouraging risk-taking is not always easy for organisations, due to the potential for mistakes (sometimes costly) made by employees. Hence, in an environment of risk-taking, organisations must make sure that employees are encouraged to learn from their mistakes. Where there is risk involved, clear parameters need to be communicated to employees, and having trust and confidence in employees is vital.

Conclusion

There are strong arguments in the literature regarding the psychological implications of employee empowerment for locus of control, self-efficacy and self-esteem of employees. These are viewed as significant and important, as employee empowerment can help individuals achieve personal growth, by enhancing their internal locus of control, self-efficacy and self-esteem. Drawing on Conger and Kanungo's (1988) study, it is clear that managerial strategies have a direct influence on individuals' self-efficacy beliefs. Hence, the argument is that organisational strategies that strengthen self-efficacy beliefs will make individuals feel more powerful, and in contrast, any strategies that weaken self-efficacy beliefs will result in an increase in the individual's feelings of powerlessness, thus leading to feelings of oppression (Freire, 1972; Friedmann, 1992).

An individual's belief in himself or herself, in being able to do a job, is vital in empowered organisations. It enables employees to feel that they can perform their job competently. Psychological implications of locus of control, self-efficacy and self-esteem are critical to take into consideration during any employee empowerment initiative. Hence, 'Potentially empowerment can mean workers take more control over their jobs and working environments' (Wilson, 2004: 167). Thus, as a concept employee empowerment is also viewed as linking individual strengths and competencies.

Clearly, a number of authors support the view that when organisations encourage the behaviours of innovation and creativity in employees, it can enable employees to display their innovative and creative talents, leading to empowerment, and vice versa; if employees are empowered it can lead to innovative and creative behaviours amongst them. It is in the interest of the organisation to be aware and understand that people need to have the confidence and belief in themselves to carry out their tasks positively, leading to a sense of control and well-being at work, whether they are in management or non-management positions. Hence, the psychological implications of employee empowerment are viewed as significant and important; as employee empowerment can lead to personal development by enhancing an individual's internal locus of control, self-efficacy, self-esteem, and self-actualisation leading to self-confidence.

Chapter 6

Psychological Empowerment

Introduction

It is clear from the discussions in Chapter 5 that there are psychological implications with regards to empowering employees and it plays an important part with regards to the outcomes of employee empowerment. There is also an argument that unless people feel empowered 'from within' they cannot grasp the meaning of what empowerment is and how could they should work or behave in an empowered way. Hence, understanding the concept of psychological empowerment is vital.

Psychological empowerment refers to a set of positive psychological states that are necessary for individuals to feel a sense of control in relation to their work through, for example, locus of control, self-efficacy and self-esteem.

This chapter highlights the three components of psychological empowerment, namely, intrapersonal, interactional and behavioural components, which enables an individual to gain the inner confidence needed to feel empowered. Tasks can become intrinsically motivating when employees derive positively valued experiences directly from a completed task. This results in self-confidence and an inner self-belief of 'can do' leading to psychological empowerment.

Psychological Empowerment

An understanding of psychological empowerment is essential, without which the concept of empowerment and its implementation remains problematic and unsatisfactory.

The theory of psychological empowerment suggests 'interventions that provide genuine opportunities for individuals to participate may help them develop a sense of psychological empowerment' (Zimmerman et al., 1992: 724). In this sense, it is worthwhile noting Zimmerman et al.'s (1992: 708) study, which highlights three components of psychological empowerment, namely, intrapersonal, interactional and behavioural components, as illustrated:

> The intrapersonal component refers to how people think about their capacity to influence social and political systems important to them ... The interactional component refers to the transactions between persons and environments that enable one to successfully master social or political systems ... The behavioural component refers to the specific actions one takes to exercise influence on the social and political environment through participation in community organisations and activities.

It is worth noting for leaders, CEOs and human resources departments that sources of employees' feelings of empowerment – how and when people feel empowered – is important in all employee empowerment strategies in organisations. Chiles and Zorn (1995: 2) highlight that:

> to feel empowered in an organisation, an employee must (a) feel capable of competently performing the tasks of her or his job, and (b) believe that she or he has the authority or freedom to make the necessary decisions for performing the tasks of the job.

In a similar vein, Siegall and Gardner (2000: 705) report:

> if a person has the organisation's 'permission' to act autonomously but does not believe that she or he has the capability of acting effectively, then the autonomy will not result in improved outcomes for either the organisation or the person.

This further strengthens the earlier arguments with regards to locus of control, self-esteem and self-efficacy and how these play an important role within an individual's self-belief. The implications of these can be positive or negative which can enable employees to believe in themselves and in their capabilities to carry out a task with confidence, or vice versa.

But, despite some organisations actively practising employee empowerment, 'the exact meaning of "psychological empowerment", does not seem to be well considered' (Lee and Koh, 2001: 684). Psychological empowerment is advocated because of its perceived psychological benefits and there is abundant literature to support this view. Drawing on a number of studies, it is evident that psychological empowerment is important and can have a positive influence with regards to employee empowerment (Kanter, 1984; Kieffer, 1984; Kouzes and Posner, 1987; Conger and Kanungo, 1988; Kizilos, 1990; Thomas and Velthouse, 1990; Zimmerman et al., 1992; Lord and Hutchinson, 1993; Chiles and Zorn, 1995; Spreitzer, 1995, 1996; Spreitzer et al., 1997; Corsun and Enz, 1999; Heslin, 1999; Menon, 1999; Siegall and Gardner, 2000; Lee and Koh, 2001; Seibert et al., 2004; Chiang and Jang, 2008; Laschinger et al,, 2009; Tuuli and Rowlinson, 2009; Joo and Shim, 2010; Stewart et al., 2010; Hashemi et al., 2012; Burke et al., 2014; Farzaneh et al., 2014; Islam et al., 2014; Mangundjaya, 2014).

An interesting finding from a number of studies is that psychological empowerment has been associated with a broad range of positive outcomes that are beneficial to organisations and individuals, such as managing stress and burnout (Laschinger et al., 2009; Boudrias et al., 2012); stimulating creative and innovative behaviours in individuals (Peters and Waterman, 1982; Kanter, 1984; Peters, 1987, 1994; Gandz, 1990; Thomas and Velthouse, 1990; Velthouse, 1990; Whetten and Cameron, 1991; Shipper and Manz, 1992; Herschel and Andrews, 1993; Simons, 1995; Spreitzer, 1995; Pearson and Chatterjee, 1996; Hammuda and Dulaimi, 1997; Marchington and Wilkinson, 2000; Knol and Linge, 2009; Zhang and Bartol, 2010; Sahoo and Das, 2011); and motivation, job satisfaction and job commitment (Conger and Kanungo, 1988; Kanter 1984; Spreitzer, 1995, 1996; Kizilos, 1990; Kouzes and Posner, 1987; Thomas and Velthouse, 1990; Seibert et al., 2004; Chiang and Jang, 2008; Laschinger et al., 2009; Tuuli and Rowlinson, 2009; Stewart et al., 2010; Burke et al., 2014; Farzaneh et al., 2014; Hashemi et al., 2012; Mangundjaya, 2014; Islam et al., 2014).

A study by Mangundjaya (2014) revealed that psychological empowerment plays a positive role with regards to employees' commitment to organisational change. There is strong agreement in the management and social work literatures that stress is a factor that incurs huge costs and losses for organisations. Referring to this particular issue Boudrias et al. (2012: 8) point out that psychological empowerment was found to be a 'protective factor for burnout among workers exposed to work-related stressors (e.g. daily hassles, overload, job changes)'. This finding is also noteworthy for other professionals, such as social workers who also suffer from burnout and emotional exhaustion.

For front-line employees, psychological empowerment is necessary because, as discussed previously, they need the confidence to make on-the-spot decisions to keep customers happy and/or respond quickly to customer needs. Similarly, Conger and Kanungo (1988) and Besterfield et al. (1995) argue that if employees are empowered and have the authority to make decisions, it makes them more motivated to help organisations achieve their goals and objectives. By way of contrast, as Heslin (1999) warns, disempowered employees can easily become over-reliant and dependent, leading to employees feeling demoralised and not willing to use their initiative.

It is easy for the disempowered to feel disenfranchised, hence Peters (1994: 87) emphasises that the 'central ethical issue in the workplace should be protection and support for people who are not empowered, especially the frontline worker'. Employee empowerment can be enhanced if organisations remove all impediments that lead to a sense of powerlessness, such as unnecessary rules and regulations and limited participation. But, it is surprising how many of the aforementioned impediments still remain in the workplace. As Pearlstein (1991) notes, many organisations are so bureaucratic that even routine actions need some form of approval.

There is strong evidence by a number of authors that psychological empowerment increases workplace effectiveness and innovation. On an individual level, when people believe in their own ability, it gives them confidence, leading to psychological empowerment.

Critical Concerns

Referring to the themes of employee empowerment emanating from the management literature (Huq's Model A), there are several concerns about the psychological implications when expectations are not met with regards to the themes, such as power-sharing, participative decision-making and devolution of responsibility and people-oriented leadership style. The argument is that unmet expectations have the potential to lead to conflict and dissatisfaction at work. For example, participative decision-making has been noted to be given in a limited form as far as the employees are concerned, as Honold (1997: 209) argues:

> The critiques of employee empowerment emanate from what appears to be half-hearted attempts by employers that allow for a very limited degree of decision-making and control by employees.

Similarly, although power-sharing is supposed to be an important part of employee empowerment, the reluctance of management to share power is another concern (Hardy and Leiba-O'Sullivan, 1998). Related to this, Marchington (1995: 56) notes that although employee empowerment means giving 'an employee the power, authority and influence to do things at work', in reality, this rarely occurs. Kaler (1999: 110) criticises that empowerment is a 'one-sided deal', in reality there is no loss of power by management, whereas employees may acquire more responsibility without the commensurate authority:

> *All in all, empowerment would seem to be a somewhat one-sided deal. Management gains from being partly relieved of its responsibilities while losing none of its power. Employees gain responsibilities while acquiring nothing by way of power within the organisation. (Kaler, 1999: 110)*

Several studies have revealed that participants hardly experienced any increase in their power, on the contrary they reported that they felt an increase in managerial control (Cunningham et al., 1996; Cunningham and Hyman, 1999; Morrell and Wilkinson, 2002). These authors conclude that instead of giving employees more control over their work situations, the organisation had reinforced more control over their employees. This has resonance with my own research findings with the case organisations.

The notion of employee empowerment is that it 'involves the workforce being provided with a greater degree of flexibility and more freedom to make decisions relating to work' (Greasley et al., 2005: 354). In reality, such a notion of employee empowerment can sometimes be just empty rhetoric (Ogden et al., 2006; Huq, 2010).

According to Ogden et al. (2006: 522):

> *Little attention has been given to the ways in which empowerment initiatives actually become enacted and incorporated into organisational practices. It is frequently noted that there is a considerable gap between rhetoric and practice.*

A noticeable change in employees' outlooks and expectations for a more meaningful way of life at work should not be under-estimated. To illustrate, Davies and Quinn (1999: 1) observe the changing and demanding expectations of employees regarding the role of business and their attitudes towards working life:

the public's overall ethical expectations of the role of business in wider
global society has coincided with the individual's changing expectations
for a more meaningful, more empowered, and less controlled, working life

In order to respond to customers' needs in a timely and effective manner, it is essential for employees at all levels to be free to take decisions without the 'constant intervention of supervisors and the incessant surveillance of controllers' (Gandz, 1990: 74). From their studies, Greasley et al. (2005: 363) conclude: 'if decision-making opportunities are facilitated, the employees argue that productivity is improved as they can make the most efficient decisions. However, when they feel unable to influence a particular decision, a sense of frustration can occur as they feel that they know a better way but because of their position they are unable to decide the best course of action.'

Related to this, Beirne (2006: 81) argues that in reality several companies that claim to empower their employees in practice actually do 'nothing of the sort'. Instead, he cautions: 'There is evidence of window dressing and appearance management, with lots of schemes in various contexts favouring rhetoric over substance' (2006: 81). Hence, as previously noted, Morrell and Wilkinson (2002: 121) describe the danger that: 'empowerment can become a weasel word, framed in smoke, aggrandized by mirrors'.

Several studies reveal that employees hardly experienced any increase in their power; on the contrary they reported an increase in managerial control (Cunningham et al., 1996; Cunningham and Hyman, 1999; Morrell and Wilkinson, 2002). These authors conclude that instead of giving employees more control over their work situations, the organisation had reinforced more control over their employees.

Not Just Structural Empowerment, Psychological Empowerment is Also Necessary

There is an argument that empowered management strategies are only a set of conditions that are to do with the structure of employee empowerment, but that they may not necessary empower employees (Conger and Kanungo, 1988; Siegall and Gardner, 2000).

Clearly, for employee empowerment to be successful, leaders and CEOs need to pay attention not only to the structural aspects of employee empowerment, such as the themes of employee empowerment (Huq's Models A and B), but also to the 'psychological empowerment' of individuals, that is factors that strengthen the locus of control, self-efficacy and self-esteem of people. In this sense, Albrecht's (1988) argument is valid (cited in Chiles and Zorn, 1995: 3):

> empowerment may be influenced by other people and macro-level influences, but ultimately resides within the individuals. Since individuals symbolically interact with their environment, empowerment is simultaneously influenced by self-initiated actions, interpersonal interactions, and 'organisational interactions' or generalized perceptions of patterns of behaviours and symbols associated with the organisation.

Building on Conger and Kanungo's (1988) studies, Thomas and Velthouse (1990) argue that empowerment comes from people's personal belief systems, that is, the notion that empowerment 'comes from within'.

When people believe in their own ability, make assessments and judgements regarding their own tasks, they become self-empowering (Simons, 1995; Siegall and Gardner, 2000). Believing in oneself that one feels *one can do the job* is crucial and underpins employee empowerment, as illustrated by Siegall and Gardner (2000: 705).

> While one can change attitudes by first shaping behaviours, we believe that the true benefits of empowerment (however defined) will not be seen unless people first perceive themselves as being empowered. For example, if a person has the organisation's 'permission' to act autonomously but does not believe that she or he has the capability of acting effectively, then the autonomy will not result in improved outcomes for either the organisation or the person.

A study by Wagner et al. (2010) examined the relationship between structural empowerment and psychological empowerment and they found a link between the two. They concluded that creation of an environment in the organisation that provides structural empowerment contributes to psychological empowerment, which in turn leads to 'job satisfaction and retention' (p. 448). This is an important finding, as it strengthens my argument that *not just structural empowerment, psychological empowerment is also necessary.*

As indicated previously, from the economic perspective, empowerment is necessary for front-line employees, because they need to make quick decisions to satisfy customers, or respond quickly to customer needs. Conger and Kanungo

(1988) and Besterfield et al. (1995) argue that if employees are empowered and have the authority to make decisions, it makes them more motivated to help organisations achieve their goals and objectives.

Other authors report that employee empowerment increases workers' feelings of control, leading to ownership of their jobs, as employees feel more responsible, show more initiative, feel more satisfied, and have increased levels of self-efficacy and self-esteem (Conger and Kanungo, 1988; Thomas and Velthouse, 1990; Ivancevich and Matteson, 1993; Spreitzer, 1995). Hence, sometimes employees' feelings of control are significantly more important than feelings of competence.

Psychological empowerment is weighted more heavily as it is now seen as a protective factor for 'burnout' among workers exposed to work-related stressors (Laschinger et al., 2009; Boudrias et al., 2012); a problem which is also faced by social workers.

Wilson (2004) discusses the strength of Maslow's (1943) theory – that it supports management practices which can lead to employee autonomy and personal growth. Maslow's (1943) conceptualisation of the hierarchy of human needs starts from basic needs such as physiological and safety needs to personal development and growth needs, namely, self-esteem and self-actualisation needs.

> *Even if all these (lower order needs) are satisfied, we may still often (if not always) expect that a new discontent and restlessness will soon develop, unless the individual is doing what he is fitted for. A musician must make music, an artist must paint, a poet must write, if he is to be ultimately at peace with himself. What a man can be, he must be. This need we may call self-actualisation. (Maslow, 1954: 91)*

Wilson (2004) discusses the strength of Maslow's (1943) theory that it supports management practices which can lead to employee autonomy and personal growth. These have the potential to enable employees to satisfy their self-efficacy and self-esteem needs as well. Within the discourse of SHRM theory, it is important for management to pay attention to the argument that some people are motivated by higher level intrinsic needs (Conger and Kanungo, 1988). In line with this, one of the constructs of employee empowerment put forward by Conger and Kanungo (1988: 472) is the 'motivational construct'. This refers to the person's intrinsic need for power, achievement, self-determination and their self-efficacy beliefs (Bandura, 1986) to enable them to feel powerful and confident in doing their tasks. Furthermore, Bernstein (2003: 75) implies that when intrinsic rewards such as 'feedback, mastery or self-knowledge' are valued more than extrinsic rewards such as 'money, status, promotion', people are thought to be more 'empowered'.

Related to the motivational aspect of employee empowerment, Seibert et al. (2004: 346) conclude from their study that employee empowerment can be both an 'effective and efficient approach' with regards to motivating employees, as illustrated:

> *This study provides support for the notion that empowerment … can be considered both an effective and efficient approach to employee motivation and performance.*

It is also noted by Rosenthal et al. (1998: 170) that in a contemporary enterprising culture: 'the values of self-actualisation, freedom and "respect for the individual"' need to be given significant importance, which has resonance with the higher motivational needs of individuals (Maslow, 1943). It is also to be noted that self-empowerment is viewed with great importance, especially in the social work and psychology literatures where it is seen to be an essential part of individual empowerment; something which is missing in the management literature in the context of employee empowerment. This is noted by Pastor (1996: 5) who highlights that the idea of personal or self-empowerment has been a 'neglected issue' and is not widely connected with employee empowerment in the management literature. He goes on to explain that self-empowerment is one of two dimensions of empowerment: the first dimension is: 'that which individuals are responsible for doing themselves in order to feel empowered in their lives regardless of circumstances'; while the second dimension 'has to do with the way in which we work with others to nurture their sense of self-esteem, autonomy and growth' – this can make an individual strong with regards to psychological empowerment.

Clearly, psychological empowerment is important and potentially it can be achieved through the themes I have discussed emanating from the management and social work literatures, Huq's Models A and B. This stems from the argument that power-sharing, participative decision-making, devolution of responsibility, people-oriented leadership style (Model A) and access to information, collaboration and enablement (Model B) are viewed as having positive outcomes on an individual's motivation and psychological empowerment. Hence, organisational strategies, which strengthen employees' internal locus of control, are considered to be empowering and enabling.

The reason why attention to internal locus of control, self-efficacy and self-esteem of individuals is advocated, is that these help to shape how individuals view themselves in relation to their work environments and their perceptions of their own capabilities. Thomas and Velthouse (1990) agree that tasks become intrinsically motivating when employees derive positively valued experiences directly from a completed task. So, it is understandable that managerial strategies which strengthen employees' self-efficacy beliefs will make them feel powerful while strategies that weaken employees' self-efficacy beliefs will result in feelings of powerlessness. Hence, by creating conditions that will increase motivation, organisations can enable people in accomplishing their tasks and building a strong sense of self-efficacy. As previously discussed, Bandura's (1977, 1986) theory of self-efficacy explains how it influences individual feelings of empowerment. Through these arguments it is evident that psychological empowerment plays an important role in the practice of employee empowerment in organisations.

It is abundantly clear that just by telling people they are empowered does not automatically mean that employees are going to feel empowered. For organisations, it is important to note employee empowerment can be an individual and personal experience. Lashley (1994) explains how people's perceptions, experiences and feelings play a major part in employee empowerment:

> Whatever the intentions of managers, the effectiveness of empowerment as an employment strategy will be determined by the perceptions, experiences and feelings of the 'empowered'. Fundamentally, these feelings will be rooted in a sense of personal worth and ability to effect outcomes of having the 'power' to make a difference. (Lashley, 1994: 2)

It is worth noting, again, that this is about empowerment 'coming from within' as one office administrator in Large Organisation explains:

> I had a particularly strong minded manager … EP enabled me to say to him – 'I really believe what I think is the right way … let me try and move along, and then I will try your way'. And, I've been able to say – 'I want to do this because I think it's right, and I'm just not going to do what you tell me to do without thinking about it!'. (Office Administrator)

A study by Zhang and Bartol (2010) concluded that empowering leadership positively affects psychological empowerment and this in turn influences both intrinsic motivation and stimulates creative behaviours in employees. In this sense, it is critical to identify conditions that may foster a sense of powerlessness and disempowerment in an organisation, so that those factors that contribute to the lowering of personal power among organisational members can be effectively removed (Block, 1987; Conger and Kanungo, 1988; Peters, 1994; Corsun and Enz, 1999). As the self-efficacy of organisational members grow, the groups' collective efficacy grows as well (Bandura, 1986), which has resonance with the social work discipline. In social work, empowering users and clients means not only that they learn to resolve their own life problems and difficulties, but also that they become strong and are able to help others, thus contributing to the well-being of the community and society.

In a similar vein, Corsun and Enz (1999: 218) give great importance to the environmental conditions and suggest that 'an environment in which good organisational citizenship is present contributes to psychological empowerment … We suggest that if an organisation seeks to empower employees and can do only one thing, management should facilitate the creation of an environment in which workers are encouraged to assist others and take positive action beyond the limits of their prescribed roles', which also has resonance with social work discipline. Hence, the argument, *psychological empowerment is the glue that has a chance to hold the employee programme together, strategies alone will not do.*

Conclusion

It is evident that psychological empowerment is necessary for employees to be able to support employee empowerment initiatives in organisations. When people believe in their own ability, make assessments and judgements regarding their own tasks and *believe* they can do it, they become psychologically empowered.

On an individual level, psychological empowerment gives people self-confidence. It also encourages them to use their own initiative and motivates them to be innovative and creative. When organisations encourage innovative and creative behaviours, it is viewed as empowering. Furthermore, empowered employees are more likely to engage in such behaviours, rather than those who are 'tightly controlled'. Feelings of being in control of their work, high self-efficacy and self-esteem enable psychological empowerment in employees.

Clearly, there is evidence from a number of studies and several authors agree from the psychological perspective that there are benefits in empowering employees, with regards to acquiring positive locus of control, raised self-efficacy and self-esteem leading to self-confidence in individuals. Research demonstrates that employees feel and perform better when perceived locus of control, self-efficacy and self-esteem is high. Perceived control appears to enhance confidence, make tasks less stressful and more intrinsically rewarding. Hence, employee empowerment is viewed by several authors as part of best management practice for the optimum utilisation of people's talents in organisations.

It is already noted from the management literature which confirms that there is a considerable gap between the rhetoric and practice of employee empowerment in organisations (Huq, 2010). There is also significant concern about the lack of research with regards to the psychological implications of employee empowerment, namely, locus of control, self-efficacy and self-esteem of individuals, as these can help or hinder the employee empowerment process.

Several studies have demonstrated, as already discussed, that organisations need employees who are willing, able, self-efficacious and have a high level of psychological empowerment to accomplish tasks in an effective manner for employee empowerment to flourish.

> *Nevertheless, conceptualising empowerment as a set of organisational variables, a complex psychological state and a series of behaviours is worthwhile. In order for one to act empowered, one needs to perceive that he or she is empowered. (Siegall and Gardner, 2000: 715)*

An important outcome of strong, positive psychological empowerment on an individual level may result in collective self-efficacy amongst organisational members, leading to a strong efficacious workforce in organisations, which in turn helps to maintain a respectful relationship within members (internally) and customers (externally). This is particularly essential for front-line workers, social workers, and health and hospital workers.

Thus, all efforts must be carried out by organisational leaders to reduce and eradicate psychological disempowerment amongst employees, including people from management and non-management positions. Ongoing learning becomes necessary, as people from management and non-management positions develop skills and respond to the themes of employee empowerment in the management and social work literatures, namely, power-sharing, participative decision-making, devolution of responsibility and people-oriented leadership style (Huq's Model A); and access to information, collaboration and enablement (Huq's Model B), respectively.

In a competitive global environment, in which organisations are expected to provide faster and efficient service and be the best, employee empowerment is viewed as the answer to provide these in the best possible way. Questions such as how to empower employees are important, but equally, if not more, important, is to ask the questions, what is the purpose of empowerment and who to empower? Structures and strategies for employee empowerment alone will not do the job, organisations need to enable employees to develop a high level of psychological empowerment to be able to embrace the structures and strategies with regards to employee empowerment and deliver them to customers and deal with customers' needs in a confident manner. Psychologically empowered employees enable organisations to maintain consistency and sustain organisations' employee empowerment programmes. They must be viewed as assets for organisations who are sources of value creation.

PART IV
From Boardroom to Factory Floor:
'Let the Data Speak!'

Chapter 7

Employee Empowerment: Experiences of Two Organisations

Introduction

Qualitative interviewing helped me to gather vital information about the experiences of employees in both Large and Small Organisations with regards to employee empowerment, which can be used by organisations as 'lessons learnt'; taking into consideration Patton's (1987: 136) point: 'The primary data of in-depth, open-ended interviews are quotations. What people say, what they think, how they feel, what they have done, and what they know – these are the things that one can learn from talking to people, from interviewing them.'

In this section, the views of management and non-management personnel from both organisations have been accessed via quotations.

Interview questions were broadly based with regards to the following questions:

- What does employee empowerment mean to employees in the case study organisations?

- What is their perception and understanding of this term?

- How did the organisations address the seven themes of employee empowerment, namely, power-sharing; participative decision-making; devolution of responsibility; people-oriented leadership style (Huq's Model A) and access to information; collaboration and enablement (Huq's Model B)?

By providing relevant quotes, the findings are further strengthened by giving interviewees a platform for their 'voice' to be heard (Bowen and Lawler III, 1992; Morgaine, 1993; Clement, 1994; Rubin and Rubin, 1995; Denzin and Lincoln, 1998b; Strauss and Corbin, 1998; Bird, 1999; Greenberg and Baron, 2000). According to Denzin and Lincoln (1998c: 332): 'A critical text thus creates a space for multiple voices to speak; those who are oppressed are asked to articulate their definitions of their situations.' Excerpts from the interviews are quoted throughout this section, as and when needed, 'letting the voices of the interviewees come through at appropriate moments' (Rubin and Rubin, 1995: 257).

Large Organisation

BACKGROUND OF LARGE ORGANISATION

At Large Organisation, the CEO decided to initiate employee empowerment as a strategy in response to changes and threats perceived to emanate from the external environment.

This employee empowerment strategy was to be implemented through a planned formal programme, referred to in this book as 'Employee Programme' (EP)[1] and it was to be rolled out in all departments in Large Organisation.

Large Organisation was seeking to achieve the following through EP:

• Enhancement of the company's business.

• Creation of a better and more fulfilling life for customers and employees.

A substantial amount of company literature was produced by the organisation outlining the aims and objectives of EP.

The whole principle of EP … was all about empowering people, giving them accountability, and giving them responsibility, and allowing them to take considered risks. (Middle Manager, Large Organisation)

---

1   It should be noted that Employee Programme (EP) is a name given by the author to preserve the anonymity of the employee empowerment programme in Large Organisation.

At Large Organisation the aim was to 'empower all employees' in all its sites. This was quite a grand and ambitious company-wide strategy of the CEO! The culture of the company was to change from a 'command and control' type of organisation to a more relaxed one, where employees would have the freedom to take decisions and to act on them. In line with this thought, it was emphasised that leaders and managers would have to change their behaviour styles to a more 'directing, coaching and supporting' style.

As far as the CEO was concerned, the focus of EP was employee empowerment, which was defined as 'everyone understanding their role in the organisation, feeling ownership of the organisation and having a "just do it" approach to work'. The CEO was seeking to achieve a change in the culture of the organisation via employee empowerment, to move away from the autocratic style of management towards one which allowed people to feel 'committed and empowered'. It was assumed that management would delegate responsibility and authority downward.

PERCEPTION AND UNDERSTANDING OF EMPLOYEE EMPOWERMENT AT LARGE ORGANISATION

Participants from senior and middle management positions

It is interesting to note that people in senior and middle management positions at Large Organisation understood employee empowerment to mean different things. Senior managers described it as the ability of subordinates to get on with their jobs, 'to take the initiative and get things done' and not having to ask for 'permissions' or 'get authority' from management. They described it as giving employees the 'freedom' to take decisions at work. However, a number of middle managers felt confused and admitted that they had problems understanding what the word 'employee empowerment' meant, or how it was defined by the organisation. Their main worry was how can 'freedom' be given to employees where there were a number of rules and regulations and compliance to be followed by the organisation? This ambiguity and fear with regards to employee empowerment has strong resonance with the management literature.

> This (empowerment) is a funny word, sometimes I don't really know what empowerment specifically is. (Middle Manager)

In theory, senior managers' conceptualisation and understanding of employee empowerment echoed the rationale behind giving employees flexibility and freedom to take decisions at work, with regards to their Employee Empowerment Programme (EP) as illustrated:

> *We have always been giving instruction and monitoring progress until a task has been successfully completed, but the idea was to get away from this command and control style of organisation where people were slotted into their respective roles and controlled in all the aspects of what they did during their working day. So the thinking behind (empowerment) was that we are all individuals in our own right, we all make big decisions at home ... for example, we buy cars, buy houses, rear families, make decisions on their education and so on ... so why can't that be allowed for people to carry through their working life? Why can't people be given the authority or the freedom ... or the flexibility to be able to get on and do the job without being controlled and given commands on a daily basis? (Senior Manager)*

But, there is evidence of a significant mismatch between senior management's conceptualisation of 'giving employees freedom' with regard to empowering employees and the implementation of this in practice. The findings reveal that employees felt that they were not given the freedom as espoused by senior management, on the contrary, it is interesting to note that according to non-management personnel if employees took decisions they got 'hammered for it' by their managers, as explained by a non-management personnel:

> *We went through the motions of (empowerment), but at the end of the day, nothing really changed, as far as we can see, if you owned, took decisions and did it, you got hammered for it! (Office Administrator)*

This behaviour of managers was is in sharp contrast to the behaviours described by the CEO.

However, it is interesting to note that with regards to the conceptualisation and meaning of employee empowerment both by senior and middle management, certain themes emerged, for example, the most frequently mentioned themes were participative decision-making and devolution of responsibility; less frequently mentioned themes were power-sharing and a people-oriented leadership style.

Participants from non-management positions

At Large Organisation, non-managerial employees include engineers, office administrators and call centre operators. Similar to senior and middle management, non-managerial employees also had different interpretations of employee empowerment, ranging from 'culture change', to having the freedom to 'take decisions' on their own, without asking for permission from management.

Interestingly, several people from non-management positions made reference to 'decision-making' as their view of employee empowerment:

> *The decision-making is key (to) empowerment. We make decisions ourselves rather than (management) upstairs. (Call Centre Operator)*

A number of employees were in favour of 'culture' change or 'rules and regulations' that could enable them to take decisions. The concept of 'enablement' and 'having control' over work decisions has resonance with the social work literature, where users are empowered and enabled to take decisions in order to have control over their lives and situations. The ability to take decisions gave employees control over their tasks and hence they felt 'empowered':

> *I work in customer complaints, and sometimes I just have to go by what I feel to satisfy the customer … I feel I can decide … I feel empowered to make a decision. (Office Administrator)*

'Feeling empowered' also has resonance with social work, where people need to 'feel' psychologically empowered to have control over their lives, particularly because, with respect to decision-making, it gives people choices regarding decisions, which leads to high locus of control, self-efficacy and self-esteem. It should be noted that several participants from non-management positions made references to improvement in their self-efficacy, self-esteem and self-confidence, in the context of being able to take decisions with regards to the organisation's Employee Empowerment Programme (EP).

One of the problems was that nobody from management explained to people in non-management positions that EP was directly about empowering employees. This was largely due to the lack of a company-wide strategy for the dissemination of information about the aims and objectives of EP to everyone in a consistent manner.

TO WHAT EXTENT DID LARGE ORGANISATION ADDRESS THEMES OF EMPLOYEE EMPOWERMENT EMANATING FROM THE MANAGEMENT LITERATURE (HUQ'S MODEL A)?

This section reports the findings concerning to what extent (if at all) Large Organisation addressed the themes of employee empowerment emanating from the management literature, namely, power-sharing, participative decision-making, devolution of responsibility and people-oriented leadership style (Huq's Model A).

Power-sharing

In practice, there was little evidence of any significant power-sharing at Large Organisation. Furthermore, there was a considerable mismatch in perceptions between management and non-management personnel regarding the sharing of power, where the former claimed that there was no difficulty in this area, and the latter felt that, in reality, management still held onto their power. It is interesting to note that, in principle, senior managers acknowledged and understood that they had to change from the 'command and control' style of management and give people more power and allow them to do things without asking for permission.

> We had a management style, which was very much command and control. It was about telling people what to do, how to do it and when to do it ... We weren't allowing people basically to do something that they felt was appropriate for themselves. (Senior Manager)

Interestingly, although there was high consensus amongst senior managers that they did not have any difficulty with power-sharing, this view was not shared by middle managers. According to middle managers there was evidence that senior management still liked to control and hold onto their power. One middle manager described how senior managers still preferred 'to control and organise, and keep a firm grip on decision making!' Another middle manager explained that senior managers were feeling insecure and frightened to let go of their power.

> I think it's older, more set in their ways managers that are frightened, or maybe they like to just have the power and hold on to decision-making, when we as a company, should allow our people to take decisions, that's what EP was meant to be! (Middle Manager)

It should be noted that it was difficult for some managers in the beginning to 'let go' of power, as one manager candidly confessed:

> *Personally I have no difficulty with it (power-sharing) at all. The downside (is) … it does mean that you don't quite have your finger on every aspect of the job you used to have. But that's a good thing because it means that now I know I didn't have to have my fingers on every aspect of the job. I think you'll probably find this in all tiers of management, that it's very difficult to let go. (Middle Manager)*

Interestingly, middle managers appeared to be keener to change their behaviours and outlook than senior managers were, as they felt there were benefits in power-sharing since it freed up some of their time.

> *I've found it (power-sharing) has freed a bit of my time … certainly I don't find myself now making the detailed minute arrangements. I more or less handle things, do the bit of initial research myself and basically hand it over to others to carry on. So I don't get into the nitty, gritty of things. (Middle Manager)*

One of the aims was to change the 'command and control' behaviour of managers, however despite the principles of EP and the continuous enthusiasm of the CEO, in practice this area of power-sharing still remained problematic for management.

Participative decision-making

The majority of employees did not think EP had anything to do with decision-making. However, from Large Organisation's EP documents, it should be noted that participative decision-making was an essential part of EP, with the aim of empowering people and improving employee confidence, as explained by one middle manager:

> *As I see it the main aims and objectives of EP was to empower people, to give non-management people empowerment to make decisions by themselves, by owning issues or problems within their sphere, and by giving them the freedom to go ahead and resolving it for themselves. The idea was that they would become their own decision-makers … rather than have to refer problems to their manager. (Middle Manager)*

There was high consensus amongst people in management which was in keeping with EP principles; that the reasons for devolving decision-making were to move away from a 'command and control' culture and give people freedom to take decisions. This was based on the argument that people take a number of important decisions in their personal lives, so why should they not be allowed to take decisions at work? But several middle managers felt that senior managers were not committed to this way of thinking. In fact they felt that, in reality, many senior managers still adhered to the old culture of 'command and control' and found it difficult to let go, as they were keen to protect their territory with regards to decision-making.

> *Still very much the tier twos and above, that is senior management, who like to control and organise, and keep a firm grip on decision making! (Middle Manager)*

The key elements of participative decision-making were to allow people to own responsibility for the area of their business and make decisions:

> *we will allow people to own responsibility for the area of business, they could make decisions and they could take risks where there was a business justification, where we didn't break the rules that we've got to live by, such as regulation and compliance, and then they could go ahead and do, put their action plans in place and deliver what they had decided they wanted to do. (Senior Manager)*

A number of managers encouraged decision-making and felt that employees should not be strictly regimented.

> *I think the biggest benefit is a lot of people ... are making decisions for themselves now that would not have done before because they would have felt they were restricted and not empowered to do so. (Middle Manager)*

However, it was wrong to assume that all managers would encourage decision-making, as illustrated:

> *EP, decision-making and risk-taking ... actually if your manager didn't buy into that you could still get hammered for it. I know people who made a decision and their manager came down on them like a ton of bricks. (Office Administrator)*

Some managers, who were authoritative, were worried taking decisions could mean risk-taking and they did not trust their employees that they would necessarily take the best decisions. But, other managers who were interested in empowering employees remarked that employees needed to be explained what risk-taking entailed. By risk-taking it is meant that employees should not just take 'risks' but 'considered risks', as illustrated:

> *People should feel able to take considered risks to delight the customer, and not fear censure. Taking considered risks is not about being careless or reckless – it's about thinking through the cost and consequences of the risk paying off or otherwise, and selecting the most appropriate course of action. (Senior Manager)*

As far as the benefits of EP were concerned, a number of senior managers felt that they were 'patchy' and 'short lived' and they were worried that not all managers were pursuing the principles of EP and encouraging participative decision-making.

> *I do believe EP is too patchy, it just isn't going on all the time. I'm not convinced even within my own team that we keep it going ... it depends on the individual managers, some do, and some do not. (Senior Manager)*

In order for employees to 'take the initiative and get things done', participative decision-making was seen as an essential part of employee empowerment.

A study by Greasley et al. (2005: 363) revealed that 'if decision-making opportunities are facilitated, the employees argue that productivity is improved as they can make the most efficient decisions. However, when they feel unable to influence a particular decision, a sense of frustration can occur as they feel that they know a better way but because of their position they are unable to decide the best course of action'.

Nurturing these 'frustrated' feelings in employees can be damaging for organisations going down the empowerment route, as they tend to create 'them and us' attitude.

Generally, the findings of the interviews demonstrate that participative decision-making did have the most positive impact for a number of people. Psychologically, those employees who were able to take decisions felt good;

there was a strong indication that it resulted in high levels of self-esteem and self-confidence and in some cases it also made them feel valued.

It is important to note the existence of tension between employee empowerment and the need to adhere to rules and compliance issues. Several middle managers complained that it was difficult, and at times impossible, for employees to maintain a balance between adhering to rules and compliance and at the same time to follow the principles of EP and take decisions freely.

> *An observation I would make is that, our people are very aware of regulations and compliance issues in the company and because of that I do feel it makes people, not reluctant, but people are not confident enough at times to take decisions, because they feel that they might be going against the rule by doing this. (Middle Manager)*

Generally middle managers at Large Organisation found it difficult to adopt a culture of 'freedom and flexibility' when the organisation was riddled with so much compliance and rules. It was not always easy for them to just go ahead and take decisions. The difficulty was getting the balance right.

> *It's getting the balance – between EP and compliance. (Middle Manager)*

Clearly, there were mixed opinions about decision-making amongst non-management personnel. Although for some employees it helped to raise their confidence to take decisions, others did not feel free to take decisions without fear of being 'hammered' for it. It is also interesting to note that some individuals welcomed the greater scope for participative decision-making while others resented it. This has resonance with the management literature, which suggests that not everyone wants to take decisions or extra responsibility. It could be argued that this demonstrates that employee empowerment is easier and more feasible in practice in some situations/environments than in others.

Devolution of responsibility

Senior managers explained that devolution of responsibility was part of the ethos of EP, as it would give people the opportunity to be responsible for their own area of business. However, several senior managers agreed that although decision-making and taking responsibility were encouraged by the organisation, it was important for employees to take on board that they were still bound by regulation and compliance, therefore, decisions would have to be undertaken in a responsible way:

we will allow people to own responsibility for their area of business, they could make decisions and they could take risks where there was a business justification, where we didn't break the rules. (Senior Manager)

On the whole, the majority of managers felt that there was a change in their management style as a direct result of devolving responsibility. However, one middle manager admitted it was not easy to begin with:

Before (EP) I would have delegated, but, I would have always kept the issue on a long rope to make sure I could pull it in to see if it was going alright. Now I am much happier and more relaxed to devolve total responsibility ... So I think it has helped my management style in terms of that, made me more willing to do that. (Middle Manager)

Interestingly, there was high consensus amongst non-management personnel that due to the competitive nature of the industry, it was important that employees should be allowed to make decisions and take the responsibility to respond to customers without waiting for things to 'go up a chain and down a chain'.

Partly the benefits of making us a more flexible company was everybody in the company could make decisions quicker, take a bit more responsibility, rather than wait for it to go up a chain and down a chain, and everybody was able to respond to customers. (Office Administrator)

There was consensus amongst middle management that due to the command and control culture and a lack of trust, people were not always given the opportunity to take full responsibility for their jobs even though they were capable of doing so, because management kept a strict eye on them. But since EP had opened up this opportunity, this was seen as a significant culture change in the organisation.

I think it's a mixture of empowerment and responsibility. We've got a very highly skilled, trained work force, perhaps in the past we didn't give them freedom to make decisions that they are well capable in making, so that certainly opened the possibility to them. (Middle Manager)

Apart from job satisfaction, middle managers noticed some employees were enjoying other benefits as well, such as taking responsibility to build up their PDP (Personal Development Plan) and making suggestions for going to training and development courses of their own choice. This was perceived as having a tremendous positive impact on employees' self-esteem and self-efficacy. Prior to EP, managers always told people which training courses they should attend.

> *I think the shared responsibility for people's development has been an easing of my responsibility. Before (EP) I had to sit down and decide what I thought personally was the best road for someone to take to develop themselves. Now it's a very much more open format ... people put forward suggestions for his or her development. (Middle Manager)*

However, this was not consistent throughout the organisation. Again, it was found that a number of non-management personnel did not know what the aims and objectives of EP were, so several employees did not realise that they had an opportunity to develop their own PDP.

People-oriented leadership style

The CEO strongly believed that the leadership style needed to change from the 'command and control' style to a more supporting and coaching style in order to empower employees. There should be a relaxed management structure where employees did not feel afraid to take decisions on their own. Hence, the emphasis regarding leadership style was to move away from 'cops to coaches' via directing, coaching and supporting employees. The leadership style advocated was one of: 'development, coaching, training, fulfilment, communication, all the good things that allow us to harness the energy of people' (CEO).

Some of the senior managers did attempt to change their leadership style from the control and constant checking to a more flexible one:

> *I would work ... to make certain that I am not adopting the control style, so I will tend to give projects and jobs out to people and let them get on with it and not call daily meetings to check how they are doing. (Senior Manager)*

However, there was inconsistency in practice, as several employees felt that if they took decisions on their own, they got 'hammered for it'. It was noted earlier that compliance and regulations were perceived as a hindrance for some managers in allowing freedom and flexibility to employees with regards to decision-making. They felt that they needed to have a control style of management, as a number of managers explained that sometimes it was difficult to let go of the 'command' style, and this was mainly due to the compliance and 'regulatory environment' of the organisation.

> *For some aspects of the business that we're in, it has been quite difficult, because … we are operating in a regulatory environment we cannot allow our people to be flexible in certain areas … There will always be areas where we have got to fit within the rules and in our case it's regulatory and compliance. (Senior Manager)*

Another senior manager was afraid that total freedom and employee empowerment might lead to 'anarchy' in the workplace:

> *you could have anarchy, in that people would just be doing 'well I think that is the way it should be done' … There is a standard which we have to meet. (Senior Manager, Large Organisation)*

In many instances, people in management and non-management positions at Large Organisation felt that the organisation was paying 'lip service' and they feared that it was going back to the old 'command and control' culture. Furthermore, there was hardly any evidence of the management behaviour as described by the CEO, namely, directing, coaching and supporting. One explanation of why the CEO's enthusiasm may not have been shared by all managers could be, as Fenton-O'Creevy (2001) suggests, that when change has the effect of overloading managers, they may fall back on the command and control approach rather than supporting new initiatives.

As mentioned elsewhere, employee empowerment does not happen by just declaring that the organisation wants to empower its employees, or by slogans or exhortations.

Although in theory, Large Organisation addressed the theme of people-oriented leadership style with regards to the EP, in practice, it was difficult for several managers to change and adopt the aforementioned styles of behaviour. As one office administrator pointed out, the behaviours of some of the managers did not really change: 'We went through the motions (of EP), but at the end of the day, nothing really changed' (Office Administrator).

An essential point to note is that there was also a lack of training and educating of managers to develop the desired behavioural styles, namely, directing, coaching and supporting. An issue often overlooked is that senior managers need training in these areas too.

TO WHAT EXTENT DID LARGE ORGANISATION ADDRESS THEMES OF EMPLOYEE EMPOWERMENT EMANATING FROM THE SOCIAL WORK LITERATURE (HUQ'S MODEL B)?

This section reports the findings concerning to what extent (if at all) Large Organisation addressed the themes of employee empowerment emanating from the social work literature, namely, access to information, collaboration and enablement (Huq's Model B).

Access to information

The CEO of Large Organisation felt it was essential that employees should have access to information. There was a significant attempt by the organisation to facilitate this via EP, through several games, puzzles and challenges:

> The challenges were issued by internet. We wanted to get them internet literate, so we challenged them over the internet, by fax and on their hand-held terminals which they see when they go out into the field. (CEO)

The use of the internet and company intranet was also encouraged to increase employees' literacy and knowledge in the use of IT (Information Technology). Several employees in non-management positions readily embraced the use of IT:

> We have access to internet. There are lots of things we can find out ourselves. Everybody has internet and intranet access and email addresses. The chain of communication is improving all the time, and the speed of information that gets to people is improving all the time. (Call Centre Operator)

Several non-managerial employees agreed that there had been a gradual change, and that employees could now get certain information and updates:

> All that's gradually changing now. If we get to a situation where a decision affects us ... then at least we are getting updates on that to date and where the information is stored, which never used to be the case before. (Office Administrator)

Many employees at Large Organisation viewed the access to information via the internet and the intranet as a significant step forward, where previously they had no idea what was going on, as they had had to depend on their managers for information. However, there was one significant drawback to this, which was that most of the EP games and challenges and the use of internet and intranet, was not associated with employee empowerment by employees. This was largely due to the lack of a company-wide strategy for communicating the aims and objectives of EP.

Most employees in non-management positions had no idea EP had anything to do with employee empowerment. Even the CEO admitted her fears that some managers (including senior and middle managers) may not have cascaded the information about EP properly down to the non-management employees whom they were responsible for. Hence employees would not necessarily associate access to the internet and intranet with employee empowerment. Some of the CEO's fears did turn out to be well founded – a significant number of non-managerial employees were not aware of the aims and objectives of EP, this was largely due to lack of access to appropriate information.

Collaboration

In the social work literature, collaboration is about working together to achieve common goals, in other words to collaborate means to 'work jointly'.

The CEO of Large Organisation had openly admitted that there was no collaboration or joint work with employees, particularly at non-management level with regards to the introduction of EP. The original intention had been first to introduce EP to the management team and then the anticipation was that managers who attended EP workshops would then introduce it to their teams; it would then be cascaded down eventually to the non-management levels.

It is evident from the interviews that at Large Organisation there was a total lack of collaboration with non-management employees about the implementation of EP. A consequence of this was there was considerable confusion with regards to the understanding of the aims and objectives of EP. As discussed elsewhere, there was a lack of information; a large number of non-managerial employees were not aware that EP had anything to do with employee empowerment.

Interestingly, the findings of the interviews reveal there was also a lack of collaboration at the management level as well, as not everybody in management was informed about EP prior to its introduction and hence, at this level too, management did not work collaboratively. The CEO admitted openly and with great candidness that several people in management positions did not 'buy' into EP, and this fear proved to be correct. The evidence of a mismatch between senior management's expectations and perceptions with regards to employee empowerment, and those of middle managers and non-managerial personnel, stems from the lack of collaboration, as one call centre operator remarked: 'Nobody really knows what EP is supposed to be.'

Considering the definition of collaboration offered by *The Blackwell Encyclopaedia of Social Work* (2000: 67): '*Collaboration* refers to working together to achieve common goals', it is clear that there was a significant lack of collaboration with employees at Large Organisation. This was a serious omission, as Large Organisation incurred a considerable amount of expense to carry out EP, but did not get the returns it expected.

Enablement

At Large Organisation, the CEO's goal was to empower all employees:

> *I decided we should have this programme EP, which is fundamentally about empowerment. It's about making sure that every individual in the organisation understands their role utterly and completely. They feel that they own that bit of their job, that it's theirs, nobody else knows better than they do about it, and they are expected to deliver it. So, by giving them ownership and accountability, we then said: OK well the job is yours, so it's only right that you are responsible and you make the decisions. (CEO)*

In theory, the emphasis regarding the management style in EP was that of enablement. The CEO expected managers to move away from 'cops to coaches' so that they could enable their employees, particularly with regards to participative decision-making and devolution of responsibility, via the styles of behaviours of directing, coaching and supporting.

Although these styles of behaviours were not viewed as 'enablement' by managers or employees, the CEO had hoped that through the practice of the aforementioned styles of behaviour, managers would be able to enable employees to be empowered.

Clearly, the CEO at Large Organisation did not put much thought into the strategies for enabling employees to achieve the aims and objectives of EP. The document regarding the styles of management behaviour also stated that support was available for managers to develop these behaviours, but the majority of managers did not receive any training with regards to how these behaviours could be adopted. Furthermore, several managers expressed that they had had difficulty with facilitating enablement, due to strict compliance and rules that the company had to follow (mentioned elsewhere). After years of the 'command and control' style of management, several managers found it difficult to abandon these behaviours. So, although it was the CEO's intention to address the theme 'enablement', in practice it did not materialise.

SUMMARY

There is evidence of a significant mismatch between senior management's conceptualisation of employee empowerment and those of middle management and non-management personnel. Senior management proclaimed that employee empowerment was about taking the initiative and getting things done and most importantly they remarked that employees should have the freedom and be able to take decisions without asking for permission from their managers. In contrast, middle managers felt that it was difficult to practise these principles of EP, as the organisation was steeped in compliance and rules. They found it difficult to be flexible and at the same time in control.

With regards to the themes of employee empowerment emanating from the management literature (Huq's Model A), two themes, namely, participative decision-making and devolution of responsibility, were addressed to a certain extent, however, it should be noted that power-sharing and people-oriented leadership style were least addressed. There were significant difficulties for a number of senior management with regards to power-sharing. Many of them were reluctant to share power; some mature managers could not change their behaviours, as they were used to a command and control style of management.

Although, in theory, Large Organisation addressed the theme of people-oriented leadership style with regards to its empowerment programme (EP), in practice, it was difficult for several managers to change and adopt the aforementioned styles of behaviour. As one office administrator pointed out, the behaviours of some of the managers did not really change: 'We went through the motions (of EP), but at the end of the day, nothing really changed' (Office Administrator).

With regards to the empowerment themes emanating from the social work literature (Huq's Model B), only one theme, namely, access to information, was consciously addressed. The rest of the themes of collaboration and enablement were not consciously addressed.

A large number of employees reported they have not noted any significant change in the dominant management style. These perceptions are, of course, very different to those expressed by the CEO and, to a lesser extent, by senior management. While some senior managers, in particular, understood the philosophy and principles underlying the EP programme at a cognitive level, nevertheless at the affective level, they feared that too much empowerment could adversely affect day-to-day operations; one senior manager referred to a 'descent into anarchy', revealing an interesting difference between espoused theory and theory in use.

Thus, following the discussions of the merits and demerits of the formal approach to employee empowerment (EP) at Large Organisation, the findings regarding the informal approach to employee empowerment adopted by Small Organisation are discussed next.

Small Organisation

BACKGROUND OF SMALL ORGANISATION

Although there was no formal employee empowerment programme at Small Organisation, nonetheless the owner insisted that the concept of employee empowerment be introduced, even if it was only to key middle managers. It was made clear that none of the non-managerial employees was included in this.

It is also pertinent to revisit senior management's conception of employee empowerment at this stage, which gives a clear indication of what Small Organisation was seeking to achieve:

- Devolution of authority, responsibility and decision-making from the owner to key middle managers, and, to a lesser extent, to all team leaders, including those on the factory floor.

- Employee responsibility for work-related small decisions, but in consultation with team leaders or managers for bigger decisions.

- Open communications and information sharing through team briefings, weekly performance meetings, company newsletter, including the 'open door' policy of the owner.

- Forums (committees and fortnightly meetings) for dealing with health and safety, and welfare issues.

- Bonus, reward and recognition for employees engaging in desired behaviours.

PERCEPTION AND UNDERSTANDING OF EMPLOYEE EMPOWERMENT AT SMALL ORGANISATION

Participants from senior- and middle-management positions

As indicated above, the owner explained at the outset that the word 'empowerment' was used at management level only and not formally throughout the organisation. In this context, the owner had already forewarned that non-managerial employees such as office administrators and factory operatives would not have heard of employee empowerment.

> They don't understand the word (empowerment) … The majority of people want to go to work to do an honest day's work for an honest day's pay. (Owner)

This proved to be true, when non-management employees were asked if they had heard of the word empowerment, or what their understanding of empowerment was, there were unanimous replies from them, particularly factory operatives, that they had never heard the word before, or that they did not know what it meant. However, senior managers and middle managers were aware of employee empowerment and they described their understanding of it as 'giving people responsibility' and 'letting people make decisions', as illustrated below:

> [Empowerment means] giving people more responsibility and letting them have more of a say in how the company is run, not just telling them what they have to do, but letting them contribute as well to decisions that are made within the company. (Managing Director)

Middle managers at Small Organisation were keen to take on the challenge of employee empowerment, and gave a robust view of how they perceived it, ranging from 'having authority' and 'taking responsibility', to 'taking ownership':

To me empowerment would mean people feel as if they can make a change, people feel as if they have an input into the company and where the company is going, and they are not just A, B, and C in the company, but they actually feel part of the company and feel empowered to make changes that affect them. (Middle Manager)

To me empowerment is the ability to get on with your job, with authority and responsibility. (Middle Manager)

A number of responses by middle managers matched with senior management's understanding of employee empowerment, especially with regards to 'devolution of responsibility', which is presented as one of the themes of employee empowerment in the management literature (Huq's Model A).

To me empowerment means giving a certain level of authority, to carry out your duties and responsibilities under the umbrella of your department. (Middle Manager)

I would assume that empowerment would mean that everybody has their own responsibilities to develop the company as a whole ... senior management and middle management they are there as a guide, but, everybody has their own ability, the ability is there to develop yourself and to develop the company. (Middle Manager)

Middle managers also described their understanding of employee empowerment as being able to take decisions without constantly asking for permission and being able to air their views without fear.

Empowerment to me would be freedom to make a decision and stand by it, without having to ... ask for permission to do this, and permission to do that. (Middle Manager)

Being encouraged to act on decisions that you make without having to necessarily go up and speak to a manager, and being allowed to speak up and air your views, that's what I think empowerment is about. (Middle Manager)

Interestingly, these matched the views held by a number of people in management and non-management positions at Large Organisation too.

Participants from non-management positions

At Small Organisation, non-management employees include office administrators, factory operatives and the office cleaner.

As already explained, it was stated by the owner that at the non-management level, including the factory floor, the word 'empowerment' was not used. The following demonstrates the nature of the responses when non-managerial employees were asked if they had heard about empowerment. There were unanimous replies that they had never heard of the word, which matched the owner's prediction.

Q: Have you heard of the word empowerment being used here?

Examples of Responses:

'No'.
'It has never really been mentioned'.
'No, I haven't heard the word used here'.

Employees in non-management positions had not heard of 'empowerment' being used or practised in Small Organisation.

TO WHAT EXTENT DID SMALL ORGANISATION ADDRESS THEMES OF EMPLOYEE EMPOWERMENT EMANATING FROM THE MANAGEMENT LITERATURE (HUQ'S MODEL A)?

This section reports the findings concerning to what extent (if at all) Small Organisation addressed the themes of employee empowerment emanating from the management literature, namely, power-sharing, participative decision-making, devolution of responsibility and people-oriented leadership style (Huq's Model A).

Power-sharing

The owner explained clearly that power was not shared with non-managerial employees in the office or operatives on the factory floor. As mentioned elsewhere, non-management employees, including factory operatives, were encouraged with regards to participative decision-making and devolution of responsibility, but the scope of this was limited and had to be relevant to their jobs. The owner had promoted a number of experienced factory operatives into middle management and team leader positions and handed decision-making and responsibility down to them. Some of these middle managers were team leaders and they were largely responsible for managing the factory floor. The owner also explained that a number of key middle managers in the office were empowered, and he was happy to share power with them, but he was reluctant to hand power down to lower level employees.

The owner stated that, as far as he was concerned, he was happy sharing power, it meant that he did not have to be involved with day-to-day operational decisions. It also freed up some of his time to look at other things, such as strategic issues.

> It allows me to look to the future, I don't have to be involved on a day to day basis. (Owner)

A number of middle managers confirmed that power was shared and more responsibilities were given to them from the top.

> X has handed more power and responsibility over to managers (and to) certain people now on the factory floor. (Middle Manager)

> [Senior management] has really little to do with day to day productions at the moment, it seems middle management really do that themselves. (Middle Manager)

However, a significant point is that people often have problems letting go of their power. One middle manager confessed that, at the beginning, he had problems 'letting go of certain things' and it would take time to engage in the new behaviour of power-sharing with his subordinates, such as team leaders and factory managers on the floor.

> I would have a slight problem letting go of certain things, but I would say the majority of things I have … but, there are one or two things that I am still undecided whether I should hang on to it or whether I should let it go, and, it will only be through time that will decide whether that is going to happen. (Middle Manager)

Key middle managers explained that the whole idea of empowering them was to give them power to take decisions in the daily affairs of running the organisation, and this leads to ownership. This aspect of ownership was something that was missing at Large Organisation, where although there was a formal programme, many people felt detached from the ethos of EP.

> I think it [empowerment] is giving the power to take decisions necessary to run the company … [to] feel the ownership of the company, that it is our company … I feel X is confident to let us do it and I think a lot of empowerment flows from that, the fact that it is our company. Probably one stage in empowerment is actually feeling the ownership. (Middle Manager)

This is to do with empowerment 'coming from within', which has resonance with the social work literature, where the importance of feeling empowered from within is viewed to be essential. Interestingly, as the owner remarked, although the word 'empowerment' is not used in the organisation, a considerable amount of decision-making power was handed to key managers on whom a lot of trust was also placed.

> I'd say the word empowerment wouldn't be used as such, but, there is a certain amount of power handed to certain individuals. They [senior management] are not afraid to give power and they trust employees to carry [out] … tasks. (Middle Manager)

Participative decision-making

At Small Organisation, participative decision-making was seen to be extremely important and it was a company-wide practice. Senior and middle management described how everyone in the organisation, including management and non-management employees, were always encouraged to take decisions and put forward ideas and suggestions. Generally, the majority of managers were left to get on with their jobs and make decisions accordingly, without intervention from senior management. The owner purposely handed over the responsibility for decision-making to a number of managers and they were also accountable for the decisions they made. But, this privilege was only extended to a few, and not all, managers.

As far as risk-taking was concerned, management explained that risk-taking was not related to any drastic actions that would be expected from employees, but that it would be 'managed' risk. However, the culture of this organisation was that people did not take high risk on their own, as a senior manager explained that people would always talk with other people, ask for advice and feedback, which lessened the impact of any risks.

Several team leaders proudly remarked on the success of the company on winning the EFQM Excellence Award and they attributed this to the participative decision-making process where everyone has an 'input' into decision-making:

> *what makes this company successful is ... we are always involving everyone on the factory floor. We get the input from all over the factory floor not just management and senior management; everybody has to have their say. So, all year round there are meetings every week, fortnightly and monthly ... What is so good about X is the fact that he involves us in the decisions that affect the company. (Middle Manager, Factory Floor)*

But, it is important to note that not everyone was happy about decision-making. A number of managers were worried about the implications of taking the wrong decisions.

> *What happens if I make a decision that is bad for the company, that would probably be my own concern, who takes responsibility for that and all the implications that has. (Middle Manager)*

Furthermore, the extent of people's decision-making and responsibility appeared to be unclear; especially newly appointed team leaders on the factory floor felt limited in their decision-making powers. They felt they could take small decisions but not any major ones.

It seemed that not all team leaders had the same kind of decision-making powers, for some of them it was restricted to factory floor decisions only. Generally, most non-managerial employees felt that they could take decisions and were left to get on with their jobs as long as they achieved the desired results. However, they also added that their jobs did not need any major decisions anyway.

> *I'm just basically left to do my job, as long as I get the result at the end. A lot of the jobs that I do, I would know, I just do it my own way ... it's not a big decision-making job. (Office Administrator)*

Participative decision-making seemed to be limited within the boundaries of the jobs that non-managerial employees were responsible for, as a number of factory operatives agreed that most of their decisions were limited to activities on the factory floor. Basically, operatives just got on with their work on the floor and worked within their job boundaries; they knew what had to be done and did not hang around waiting for decisions. An interesting feature is most of them had the confidence to just go ahead and take a decision without fear if they had to, though within limited boundaries:

> *if nobody is here to make a decision ... we have to make it ourselves.*
> *(Factory Operative)*

> *We have a lot more freedom ... we can make our own decisions.*
> *(Factory Operative)*

However, a number of factory operatives, especially moulders, pointed out that even if they wanted to make decisions, there simply was not any scope to do so, as the criteria for specifications needed to be followed.

> *We have a rule book and the mould has a set mould, set diameter, set*
> *specifications and we can't go outside it. We can use our common sense*
> *if something goes wrong, but as far as decision making (is concerned),*
> *no, we don't make a decision. (Factory Operative)*

As far as risk-taking was concerned, there was agreement amongst factory floor operatives, that they would not be involved in any risk-taking related to strategic decisions, 'because management would take those sorts of decisions'.

> *We never take a risk. We always speak to our team leader or production*
> *manager ... he knows what we can do. (Factory Operative)*

By way of example, risk-taking was described by a middle manager as follows with regards to customer credit limits:

> *The credit limits are crucial! So, I would say that the management*
> *team would talk to each other for things like that ... they would take*
> *some risks, but not obviously what I would call 'silly' risks. (Middle*
> *Manager, Small Organisation)*

The important thing here is nobody would go ahead and take risks with regards to a making a decision without discussing with management, or their team leader.

Non-management employees had mixed feelings about decision-making. Most employees were confident to just go ahead and do what needed to be done; a small number of employees, however, were unsure. As far as their self-confidence to take decisions was concerned, it seemed to depend on the personality of managers, whether they encouraged people to take decisions or not (similar to Large Organisation).

Devolution of responsibility

At Small Organisation, giving people responsibility was seen as an important part of enabling them to be empowered, especially key middle managers. Senior managers described empowerment as 'giving people more responsibility'.

> Giving people more responsibility and letting them have more of a say in how the company is run, not just telling them what they have to do, but letting them contribute as well to decisions that are made within the company. (Managing Director)

Senior managers certainly attempted to hand over more responsibility to the management team, even to team leaders on the factory floor, and interestingly, unlike Large Organisation, responsibility was also tied to a bonus system.

> I try and give them more responsibility to get on with their job and look after their team of people. The management team would be responsible for most of the cost of the business, so their bonus is dependent on how they make the business work, and if they can improve on profit, they get bonus. They are responsible really for an awful lot that happens on the factory floor. They are responsible for their five critical success factors (CSF) every week and their weekly bonus. (Managing Director; the CSFs are: output, quality, waste, housekeeping and safety)

A number of middle managers noticed how team leaders were being given more responsibility than ever before.

> We have team leaders now in place. Whenever I started ... we had one team leader on night shift, now we have got two team leaders on each shift. There's more of an emphasis on team leaders taking responsibility on the factory floor and for managers to take a more back seat. (Middle Manager)

This probably led to team leaders being keen on taking responsibility seriously.

An awful lot [of] responsibility is thrown onto me. I'd say I put an awful lot more effort in, because I feel responsible, and I feel ownership with the company. (Middle Manager)

In fact, it is worth noting that most managers viewed 'responsibility' positively and felt it was a motivation for coming to work. Equally, team leaders also seemed to enjoy taking on responsibility.

If you have more responsibility you feel you have a purpose coming to work and you feel quite responsible! (Middle Manager)

I enjoy the responsibility, I feel more involved and feel more a part of it. (Middle Manager, Factory Floor)

As stated above, Small Organisation has applied for and won a number of prestigious quality awards. However, it became apparent that applying for awards generally can create anxiety and pressure for some employees. Team leaders reported that the responsibility for winning awards created a certain amount of pressure on the factory floor, as people felt that senior management's expectations were now a lot higher.

X expects a lot now, his expectation is a lot higher ... A lot more work is involved in it now which is a good thing ... But pressure is a lot higher, and the team leaders now are given a lot more responsibility, because of that it's a lot more intensive now. (Middle Manager, Factory Floor)

A number of managers described 'empowerment' in terms of 'devolution of responsibility', which is one of the themes of employee empowerment (Huq's Model A), emanating from the management literature.

I would suggest that it (empowerment) probably means that people are given more responsibility, they are responsible more for their own actions. (Middle Manager)

The majority of managers were keen to take responsibility and they seemed to have the confidence to carry it out and their perception of 'responsibility' was seen as a motivating factor at work and therefore was beneficial to the company.

There was high consensus amongst team leaders who were promoted from factory operatives to middle management positions, that being given responsibility has resulted in high self-esteem and it has also given them a feeling of being valued as a person.

> *A bit of responsibility gives me authority as well and a bit of respect ... they (management) are speaking to you like a person now. (Team Leader, Factory Floor, Small Organisation)*

Psychologically, there was a positive impact of vesting more responsibility amongst the key middle managers.

> *Because of total responsibility for my job, and there's nobody standing over and saying 'no, you can't do that, you have to do this', I have a role and responsibility and asked to get on with it ... if I make a mess, I know to hold my hand up and say, 'I've made a mess' and if I do well, I get rewarded for it. (Middle Manager, Small Organisation)*

> *It (empowerment) gives me more confidence. I think I have more confidence to actually implement some of the ideas and things that I am meant to do, and I go and discuss it with people, as to what ways it is going to assist the company, how it is going to improve quality and how it is going to empower people. (Middle Manager, Small Organisation)*

Interestingly, the majority of factory operatives also took responsibility seriously, and felt that looking after quality and any faults regarding products was everybody's responsibility. There was a sense of collective responsibility, which has resonance with the social work literature:

> *any faults in moulds or faults in paint ... is my responsibility and everybody's generally through the factory ... moulding and painting is everybody's responsibility. (Factory Operative)*

An important point made by one of the team leaders was that people on the factory floor should be rewarded appropriately for doing a good job, otherwise there would be a negative impact on their self-esteem and self-confidence.

There was an awareness of the economic implications if people did not take responsibility for customer satisfaction and quality, then the organisation would lose orders and this would have implications for profits and jobs.

> *Well everybody feels very responsible for customer satisfaction. The biggest reason is if we achieve quality ... we are going to get that bonus,*

and if customers out there are getting the goods, and they are happy
with them, and the quality is good, then they will order more ... So that
will have that knock on effect which can only be good for the business,
which is the bottom line. (Factory Operative)

Factory floor operatives also pointed out the importance of taking collective responsibility for quality and customer satisfaction and this led to an attitude that, irrespective of who makes mistakes, everyone looked out for faulty goods before they left the factory, it was described as 'team responsibility'; similar to 'collective responsibility' in social work.

However, it is true to say that not everybody wanted more responsibility. Interestingly, those who did not, were aware of their own limitations, and were not keen to take on any responsibility beyond their capacity.

People-oriented leadership style

Unlike Large Organisation, where there was conviction by the CEO that the leadership style needed to change from the 'command and control' style to more directing, coaching and supporting style; the owner of Small Organisation felt that there should always be an 'element of control' from the top. Moreover, he believed that leadership styles should be different with regards to management and non-management employees. With regards to non-management employees, the leadership style should be more about 'telling people' what to do rather than giving people 'freedom' to do what they liked. In his view: 'it's much easier telling people to do ... '. He also believed that, 'people in general like to be led'.

Not surprisingly, this way of thinking, as demonstrated from the findings, led the owner of Small Organisation to pursue more of an employee involvement programme rather than an employee empowerment one, certainly at factory floor level. Furthermore, the owner strongly believed that non-management employees and factory operatives would not understand what the word 'empowerment' meant. However, he believed in a different approach to leadership style with regards to the empowered key middle managers. It is interesting to note that in relation to these key middle managers, the owner was very keen that they should be empowered. He wanted them to be empowered to take decisions and carry out their responsibilities without constantly seeking permission from him, because it would 'free' him up to do other things, as he remarked: 'I don't have to be involved on a day to day basis.'

Having a flexible and supportive leadership style is an important theme in employee empowerment in the management literature. From that point of view, Small Organisation allowed freedom and flexibility towards some of the key middle managers, but retained a 'command and control' style of management with regards to employees in non-management positions.

TO WHAT EXTENT DID SMALL ORGANISATION ADDRESS THEMES OF EMPLOYEE EMPOWERMENT EMANATING FROM THE SOCIAL WORK LITERATURE (HUQ'S MODEL B)?

This section reports the findings concerning to what extent (if at all) Small Organisation addressed the themes of employee empowerment emanating from the social work literature, namely, access to information, collaboration and enablement (Huq's Model B).

Access to information

Although Small Organisation did not have a formal employee empowerment programme, access to information was open, even on the factory floor, for example, through newsletters, employee suggestions, discussion forums, and weekly, fortnightly and monthly meetings with employees. Furthermore, the owner personally had an 'open door' policy where any one of his employees could see him, even factory operatives, if they wished to do so.

Generally, factory operatives felt that if they had any problems, they could approach the owner about them.

> It feels like we can approach him, we can talk to him if we have any problems. (Factory Operative)

Management generally viewed the weekly, fortnightly and monthly meetings, including the newsletters, as forums for keeping employees informed, as one middle manager explained: 'We try to keep people informed as much as possible.' Another method of keeping employees informed was also to give constant feedback and the owner saw this as being essential:

> We have to continue to give feedback … if we don't do it and don't give people feedback how they are doing, then definitely we will slip! (Middle Manager)

Keeping people 'informed' was viewed as a key issue and one middle manager explained how it worked:

> *We inform people as much as possible, again in team briefs people are informed of the customer side of things, sales side of things, new customers coming on board, and if there are any hiccups from prospective customers. We try to keep people informed as much as possible. (Middle Manager)*

At the management level, the owner made sure the key managers whom he had empowered had access to information. These key managers also assisted the management team to complete the submission for the EFQM Excellence Award at Small Organisation. However, it is worth noting that the owner did not consciously practise open access to information as part of his employee empowerment strategy, as far as the non-management employees were concerned.

Collaboration

Interestingly, at Small Organisation, senior management were keen to collaborate with key middle managers and 'work jointly' with them in order to achieve the common goals of the organisation. Senior management collaborated with middle managers, particularly as middle managers were responsible for applying for the quality awards and writing up the submissions for the awards, in the main. But, as explained elsewhere, the owner had made it clear that he did not have any intentions to empower non-managerial employees. So, from this point of view, collaboration with non-managerial employees with regards to employee empowerment was not applicable. However, as explained elsewhere, as far as non-managerial employees were concerned, the owner was in favour of two themes of employee empowerment (Huq's Model A), namely, participative decision-making and devolution of responsibility.

As Small Organisation was a winner of various quality awards, including the EFQM Excellence Award, management was very attentive to the issue of quality. With regards to improving quality, management collaborated with middle managers and team leaders, including factory floor team leaders, with regards to quality award submissions. But, it could not be said that there was collaboration with non-management employees with a view to empowering them.

Enablement

At Small Organisation, the owner did not empower all employees, as explained before, only key managers were empowered. The question here is was the theme 'enablement' addressed with regards to these key managers?

One of the ways the owner tried to enable these key managers was by purposely sharing some power. One middle manager highlighted some of the benefits of sharing power; it meant that he was able to free up his time at the weekends and did not have to work longer hours.

> *[Power-sharing] has reduced my working hours ... because my working hours were quite long and involved late nights and weekends and I have already seen benefits in this in terms of not having to work weekends or late nights. (Middle Manager)*

The above manager further pointed out that people should not just be handed power, they also need to be trained in order to understand how their new responsibility and role fits in with the organisation:

> *[people need to be trained in] the basic elements and functions of the job, and understand the role as it fits into the whole unit.*

In the main, middle managers enjoyed having power and responsibility, and one respondent explained that she felt more 'in control' and confident to introduce new ideas and suggestions, while another manager remarked that it freed him to do other tasks. This aspect of feeling 'in control' has resonance with enablement, in social work.

> *I think I feel more in control, don't feel dictated to. I am given enough scope to do my own thing and to introduce any new ideas ... X will give direction but I feel as if we are given a lot of scope in our job. (Middle Manager)*

Senior management genuinely felt that all necessary steps were taken in their view, to enable these key managers to carry out their tasks. The owner believed that, 'Empowering people is to give them what they need to do'; this has resonance with the facilitation part of enablement. In this respect, key middle managers who were empowered agreed that they were given power and decision-making authority to enable them to carry out their tasks. There was provision of resources to attend training courses, and this was viewed as enabling by them. One middle manager pointed out how he felt enabled to do his job by being able to go on training courses:

> *Each individual person has a PDP and if I want to go on courses, I find this company very helpful that way. If we need improvement on certain aspects they'll put us on a course. (Middle Manager)*

A noteworthy point made by the owner was that in his experience people should be empowered within their ability. Clearly it would be unwise to empower employees without giving due consideration to people's abilities and skills. Training and coaching people were rightfully regarded as being vital in employee empowerment, which is to do with 'enablement'; this has resonance with the social work literature.

> *I think it goes back to what I said in the beginning. It's to empower people within their ability. If you empower people, or if you just delegate and empower people, and don't lead them and don't give them coaching, and don't help them, you can only expect failure, and that's what happens in lots of places. They just give it lip service. They empower people and then they wonder why (it failed) because nobody ever taught them anything. (Owner)*

Some team leaders on the factory floor also remarked that they were encouraged and supported by senior management with regards to participative decision-making. This gave them a feeling of control at work, which also has resonance with regards to enablement in the social work literature.

SUMMARY

Evidence from the interviews reveal that Small Organisation was practising employee involvement at factory floor level, but at the management level, the owner had endeavoured to empower some of his key middle managers.

Interestingly, with regards to the understanding of employee empowerment, there was agreement that power-sharing and devolution of responsibility were important aspects of employee empowerment, by both senior and middle managers. However, the owner made sure that power-sharing and employee empowerment only extended to some of his key middle managers and not throughout the organisation. Curiously, at Small Organisation, despite the fact that the company was a winner of the EFQM Excellence Award, aspects of 'command and control' were still there. Geary (2003: 347–8) points out that this should not come as a surprise, because, in the UK, 'the dynamics of change are not such that we have moved from a model of control and rigidity to one of empowerment and flexibility'.

At Small Organisation, the owner empowered some of his key middle managers, but with regards to other employees, including factory floor operatives, responsibility for small work-related decision may have been allowed, but for 'bigger decisions' they had to consult with team leaders or managers. With regards to this, a number of middle managers were unhappy about employee empowerment not being extended to other management and non-management personnel.

As far as non-management personnel were concerned, the emphasis was more on participative decision-making and devolution of responsibility. But, the findings of the interviews suggest that a number of factory floor operatives did not feel that they could take decisions, contrary to what the owner wanted to achieve. Furthermore, several factory operatives expressed that they would have liked to take more responsibility, but were not given the opportunity to do so, which led to disappointment and low feelings of self-efficacy and self-esteem amongst them; this has resonance with agency workers at Large Organisation.

However, despite this situation, there was little evidence from the interviews at Small Organisation that employees believed themselves to be working under a draconian regime. Most of the concerns expressed by employees about their work situation were not about power-sharing, participative decision-making or devolution of responsibility, but centred almost exclusively on basic issues, such as cleanliness of washrooms, excessive dust in the environment and the perceived unfair bonus system. On a psychological level, this created low self-esteem, loss of control and the feeling of being devalued by the organisation, which meant that other efforts made by management were undermined.

With regards to the themes of employee empowerment emanating from the management literature (Huq's Model A), it is also interesting to note that similar to Large Organisation, at Small Organisation power-sharing was the least addressed theme; other themes were moderately addressed at Small Organisation, namely, participative decision-making and devolution of responsibility. Interestingly, at Large Organisation most of these themes were addressed more at the theoretical level than at the practice level.

As far as the themes emanating from the social work literature are concerned (Huq's Model B), access to information and collaboration was practised to a large extent through open team briefings, weekly performance meetings, company newsletter, including an open door policy of the owner. However, as the owner had a two-tiered approach to employee empowerment, there was more information-sharing and collaboration with key middle managers whom he wished to empower than with non-managerial employees; particularly on the factory floor.

It is worth revisiting the two important elements associated with enablement in the social work literature; one is equipping people to exercise control over their lives and the other is facilitating this process so that they can achieve their goals effectively. Although neither of the organisations were practising 'enablement' in a conscious manner, nevertheless 'enablement' was considered important by respondents at both Small and Large Organisation.

Conclusion

It is interesting to note the two different (formal and informal) approaches to employee empowerment, in both Large and Small Organisation respectively.

In practice, Small Organisation adopted an informal approach to employee empowerment. It did not engage in any formal programme, such as EP at Large Organisation. In contrast to Large Organisation, employee empowerment had not been identified as an issue requiring particular attention, but was being addressed as a consequence of the company's submission for the EFQM Excellence Award. It was decided by the owner that key middle managers ought to be empowered, but not necessarily everybody in the organisation. The owner felt that lower level employees, such as non-managerial employees and factory operatives, would not be interested in empowerment, as he assumed that they just want to 'do an honest day's work for an honest day's pay'. However, not all middle managers agreed with this policy, some of them felt all employees should be empowered, including non-management personnel and factory operatives.

In order to compete in the global market and to respond to customer needs speedily, the transfer of decision-making authority is vital, especially to customer-facing workers, and recognising the importance of this Strategic Human Resource Management (SHRM) theory also suggests that in order to survive in global competitive markets, organisations need to empower employees. However, a study of employee empowerment by Ashness and Lashley (1995) carried out in the catering industry shows that although employees were able to take some lower level decisions, significant decisions still tended to be taken by the team manager at unit level. There are inconsistencies in organisations regarding the degree to which employees are allowed to input into decision-making. Cunningham et al. (1996) point out that those organisations which allow decision-making do so only to a limited extent. Another problem concerns the inadequacies where employees take the wrong decisions – will they be penalised or lose their jobs? If so, clearly they will be reluctant to be part of the decision-making process.

With regards to the themes of employee empowerment emanating from the management literature (Huq's Model A), it has already been noted that the two themes, namely, participative decision-making and devolution of responsibility, were addressed to a certain extent, however, power-sharing and people-oriented leadership style were least addressed. As far as empowerment themes emanating from the social work literature (Huq's Model B) are concerned, it was also noted that only one theme, namely, access to information, was addressed, but the rest of the themes, collaboration and enablement, were not really addressed.

Chapter 8

Psychological Impact:
Expectations and Outcomes

Introduction

There are strong arguments in the literature about the psychological implications of employee empowerment with regards to internal locus of control, self-efficacy and self-esteem of employees. These are viewed as significant and important, as employee empowerment can help achieve personal growth, by enhancing internal locus of control, self-efficacy and self-esteem.

Drawing on research and studies (as discussed in Part III), it is clear that employee empowerment has a direct influence on individuals' locus of control, self-efficacy and self-esteem beliefs. Hence, the argument is that employee empowerment strategies that strengthen these aforementioned beliefs will make individuals feel more powerful; in contrast, any strategies that weaken these beliefs will result in an increase in the individual's feelings of depression and powerlessness, thus leading to feelings of oppression (Freire, 1972; Friedmann, 1992). It is essential to pay attention to the psychological impact with regards to employee empowerment as an organisational strategy. It also helps in the evaluation of employee empowerment programmes (which is important for organisations).

In this chapter, the psychological impact with regards to employee empowerment as an organisational strategy for both Large and Small Organisations is discussed.

Large Organisation. Psychological Implications: Expectations and Outcomes

At Large Organisation, the CEO's vision was to create a culture where people felt valued: 'to create a working style where people feel valued, they feel important and they feel involved, and that their contribution makes a difference and is welcome.' However, even the CEO expressed doubts whether the employee empowerment programme really achieved these and admitted there were weaknesses in the implementation of it: 'If there is a weakness [it is that] we didn't spend sufficient time getting the message to all managers exactly what it was we are trying to achieve.'

In Large Organisation, the CEO assumed that most employees including people in management and non-management positions would 'buy' into the vision and the aims of EP, which was not the case. Clearly, there is evidence of a mismatch between senior management's expectations and perceptions in relation to employee empowerment, and those of middle managers and non-management personnel. Undoubtedly, one of the significant consequences of this is that Large Organisation did not achieve what it expected to achieve. The divergence between the widespread rhetoric of empowerment and the limited reality of empowerment programmes can lead to significant conflict and tension in organisations (Hales, 2000; Huq, 2010). Hence, despite strong arguments for employee empowerment in the management literature, several authors raise concern with regards to the complexities and problems surrounding it.

The evidence from the interviews clearly reveal that there was inconsistency in practice, and this led to Large Organisation achieving only some short-term success with regards to its aims and objectives. There was lack of evidence of any significant change in culture 'via relaxation of rigid rules and procedures', or 'change in management style from policing to coaching'. Although there was some short-term relaxation of rigid rules and procedures at the beginning of the introduction of EP, later on, there was fear amongst middle managers that the organisation was going back to a 'command and control' style:

> I've been running some focus groups in a number of units … and I've heard in the last few months some comments about managers moving back to old management style. Certainly, feedback and comments from people tell me that we are going back towards more command and control. (Middle Manager)

In a similar vein, a number of middle managers were concerned about whether EP really enabled all employees to deliver 'customer satisfaction', which was supposed to be an important aspect of it.

> *I'm still not convinced that we are seeing any perceived improvement [in customer satisfaction]. I'm just a bit concerned. (Middle Manager)*

This led to serious doubts about whether EP was an economic benefit at all, for example, one middle manager expressed concern with regards to the 'money and effort' that was incurred, as a result of running EP.

> *I don't think that the benefits are sufficient to justify what is being spent … I think I would be looking for a better return for my money. (Middle Manager)*

One middle manager at Large Organisation was worried about creating unrealistic expectations amongst employees and remarked: 'we just don't want to raise expectations', as he felt that there was a danger the organisation might not be able to meet employee expectations. In fact, EP did create expectations, where employees were led to believe that they could take decisions on their own, without asking for permission. And, the fears of the aforementioned middle manager did have substance, as one office administrator angrily noted, that if they took decisions, they got 'hammered for it!'

Interestingly, one of the areas where there was strongest agreement between both management and non-management personnel was that EP did deliver considerable benefits with regards to the positive psychological impact, such as self-efficacy and self-esteem of individuals, where they were able to take decisions. This tied in 'heavily with self-confidence' and in some cases 'enabled' employees to 'feel more empowered', which has resonance with the social work literature.

> *I think EP tied in very heavily with self-confidence, that helped me feel more empowered. (Middle Manager)*

> *It [EP] makes our job a lot easier, because now we are actually deciding what we are doing. We are not being told what to do; we decide how to handle a certain customer, a certain situation, so it makes our job a lot easier. (Call Centre Operator)*

However, several employees believed that the 'potential to deliver' the espoused aims and objectives of EP was thwarted due to lack of any follow up or reinforcement of EP values, as one office administrator remarked: 'I don't think EP has made any impact as expected! It was a very short-term thing.' This was also echoed by a middle manager:

> *Perhaps EP needed a little bit more follow up. Culture change and changing the way people feel about the place they work, the way they manage ... and the way they are managed isn't something that you change in three weeks or three months. (Middle Manager)*

Clearly, what Large Organisation was seeking to achieve was to move away from a 'command and control' culture to one that gave people 'freedom and flexibility'. This ethos of EP was well supported by the CEO, who was extremely passionate about EP and felt that the current 'management style was out of date'.

> *It was all about trying to create an environment where people felt empowered, and it was born partly out of sheer frustration ... that everybody seemed to ask permission all the time, rather than take the initiative and get things done. (CEO)*

However, evidence from the interviews indicate that there is a considerable mismatch between senior management's expectations and perceptions in relation to employee empowerment and those of middle managers and non-management personnel. There are significant consequences of this, because it is 'disabling' Large Organisation to achieve what it set out to achieve. A danger is that Large Organisation is reverting back to the 'command and control' style of management which is in total contrast to the aims of EP.

From the motivational perspective, Large Organisation did not pay attention to the psychological implications of employee empowerment with regards to the self-efficacy and self-esteem of employees. In order to respond to customers' needs in a timely and effective manner, it is essential for employees at all levels to be free to take decisions without the 'constant intervention of supervisors and the incessant surveillance of controllers' (Gandz, 1990: 74). In Large Organisation, one operator remarked that the pressure from being watched by managers constantly was too much and this resulted in a lot of stress amongst operators.

> *I think that's why there is more stress-related illness in operator services ... more so. Not physical supervision, but supervision as far as looking at what time you are on in the morning and what time you pick up your job, how long you spend on each job, that type of supervision has increased a lot ... it has become a lot more important to managers. Every time they are talking to you it is statistics. (Call Centre Operator)*

It is worth noting that this description of tight surveillance and supervision is contrary to the perception held by senior management.

Clearly, management had failed to 'enable' a large number of employees, to equip them with the necessary skills to carry out decision-making and take responsibility with confidence and, more importantly, without fear.

There was a significant lack of training and communication regarding how employees were expected to carry out the principles of EP. This demonstrates that just by telling people they are empowered, or forcing them to be empowered, does not necessarily achieve results; people have to have the desire to be empowered. This goes back to the argument in the management and social work literatures, that employee empowerment needs to come 'from within'.

It is not necessary that psychological empowerment means people have more power in the political sense, as in having more power, but rather that people feel powerful and confident *within*, as in feeling more powerful. For example, at Large Organisation, call centre operators in one of the sites where they were given power, did not actually view themselves as 'having more power'; but they did view themselves as 'feeling more powerful', which in turn raised their self-efficacy and self-esteem:

> *We manage our own work. We manage when we want to work, we can arrange swaps and that's really left to us, the operators. At the end of the day, if I decide I want to go on night duties for a week I can do that ... I don't have to ask a manager, I sort it myself. (Call Centre Operator)*

Interestingly, a number of office administrators explained that putting the onus on them to take decisions, which they had never had to take before, made them uncomfortable, as they felt some managers were 'offloading' this responsibility onto them. These employees argued that 'one day away' was not sufficient as far as training in this area of decision-making was concerned.

I think they put more onus on us regarding decision-making ... they are quite keen to offload that on us. But I don't see really, we got any much more training or anything because of EP. (Office Administrator)

One significant concern was the failure of management to include agency workers in EP. Senior managers had not given much thought to this important issue, as pointed out by one middle manager:

with the huge numbers of agency people that we employ, we have high turnover rates, and therefore there are a number of agency people in the centre who didn't even go through the (EP) in the first place. So, while I was excited about EP, I think it had good aims, good objectives, it was good fun, I am not convinced that I have seen manifest back in the workplace all the good benefits we would have liked to have seen, and that disappoints me. (Middle Manager)

An issue that has emerged from my study is the isolation of agency workers; they were not included in EP. The majority of agency workers felt extremely angry, disappointed and let down by the organisation because they felt that they were treated like 'outcasts' with regard to EP. Agency workers felt that they were of no value (Hill and Huq, 2004).

Within the different sites of Large Organisation, there was considerable variation in the perceptions of the impact of EP, including positive and negative.

At some sites, call centre operators felt EP had a negative impact on their lives at work because shortly after being given the authority and empowerment to reimburse customers in the event of service failure, the authority to take this action was suddenly withdrawn from operators. In one site, operators felt 'devalued' and 'humiliated', 'being treated like children' by such actions from management. This obviously resulted in feelings of low self-efficacy and low self-esteem amongst them, so their experience of employee empowerment was tinged with bitterness.

In contrast, in another site, call centre operators felt the impact of EP was extremely positive, as they were given the freedom and flexibility to manage their shifts and arrange their work time without consulting their managers. This gave them a 'feeling' of being empowered, because prior to EP they were not allowed to do this, and they remarked they had felt regimented and closely supervised. Hence, psychologically, operators in this site developed a high internal locus of control, self-efficacy and self-esteem.

Overall, there were mixed reactions and inconsistencies in the different sites at Large Organisation with regards to the impact of EP. A number of employees remarked 'no impact' because they felt that the changes that were happening in their organisation were not the result of EP but simply due to 'the changing environment'.

> *I don't believe it (the changes) has much to do with EP. This is due to the nature of the call centre and the changing environment ... the company culture in here is continually changing and it evolves from one campaign to another ... so it is part and parcel of our normal job. It just happens to tie in with EP, but I wouldn't necessarily think that was generated from it. (Call Centre Operator)*

For senior management, EP was seen as 'people growth' and with this in mind one senior manager pointed out that it was important that people were treated as 'mature adults who can take a project on and run it to completion, without being watched and supervised all the way ... I see clear evidence all the time where people feel that they have got more freedom and they feel they have got more empowerment, that they can go and do their job without somebody watching them over their shoulder'. Ideally, this should have been the case. But, this was vehemently contradicted by a number of employees who thought that there was more supervision and constant checking by management, particularly in call centres where there was continuous pressure to answer calls within certain time limits:

> *We have more checks than we've ever had before! (Call Centre Operator)*

Clearly, at the non-management level, there were high levels of mixed feelings amongst employees regarding decision-making. For example, some non-management personnel agreed that EP did help them to raise their self-efficacy and self-confidence because they felt they were given the 'freedom' to take decisions. But, there were others who felt that they were not encouraged to take decisions at all. It is worth noting that some parts of the call centres were so structured and steeped in guidelines, it was impossible to take any decisions and this resulted in some people having low self-efficacy and low self-esteem:

> *We have very strict guidelines in operator services, and we are not allowed to use our brain very much. We are not allowed to own a problem or take a decision. (Call Centre Operator)*

A number of employees at the non-management level were annoyed because participative decision-making depended on the personality of managers. Some employees felt that they were allowed to take decisions, while others, including operators and office administrators, felt that they were regimented and strictly controlled by their managers. This was detrimental to their psychological well-being, as they felt their decisions had no value. Again, this concerns the problem of raising employees' expectations and not meeting them.

This is a particular issue where some employees see others being empowered and allowed to take decisions, while they are not.

> We went through the motions (of EP), but at the end of the day, nothing really changed. As far as we can see if we took ownership of a problem and took any decisions, we got hammered for it! (Office Administrator)

Employees who were not able to take decisions clearly felt out of the loop which led to a feeling of low self-efficacy and low self-esteem.

> It is not that we have more confidence in our managers, we have more confidence in ourselves in serving customers ... the whole aspects of dealing with complaints. (Call Centre Operator)

An interesting feature is that a number of employees, who were strong enough and not afraid to stand up to management, were able to challenge the ethos of EP. They realised they had the right to use their 'voices' and they faced up to their managers and defended their decisions and actions. For some people this was extremely challenging, especially for those who had never voiced their opinions before. Some employees realised their potential for the first time, as one call centre operator who had previously never taken any decisions remarked with great enthusiasm: 'I didn't realise I could do this.' One of the benefits of challenging management was that it certainly helped a number of people psychologically to develop their self-efficacy and self-esteem, leading to self-confidence.

However, employee empowerment programme at Large Organisation was not a complete failure; it did have some short-term benefits for the organisation and its people. For some employees, they had learnt some new behaviours that helped them to develop their confidence which led to psychological empowerment. For these employees, this has been immensely beneficial because these are life-long skills and they will be able to use them wherever they go in the future.

Small Organisation. Psychological Implications: Expectations and Outcomes

At Small Organisation there was no formal employee empowerment programme. The owner decided to practise employee empowerment in an informal way, by empowering only a few key middle managers. As already explained, non-management employees on the factory floor were not included in this programme and they were not familiar with 'employee empowerment' on the factory floor.

The owner's perception of employee empowerment was mainly devolution of authority, responsibility and decision-making to these key middle managers and to a lesser extent to team leaders. Going down the hierarchy he wanted to retain control, hence factory floor employees (referred to as factory operatives in this book) had least authority and decision-making powers.

From the outset, the owner made it clear that employee empowerment did not include non-management employees in the organisation. However, it was possible to gather enough information from the key managers by asking questions about the themes of employee empowerment, namely, power-sharing; participative decision-making; devolution of responsibility; people-oriented leadership (Huq's Model A) and access to information; collaboration and enablement (Huq's Model B).

There was a considerable mismatch between senior management and middle management's perceptions with regards to empowering employees. It is worth noting that unlike senior management, some middle managers felt strongly that all employees, including factory operatives, should be empowered to take decisions that are necessary to run the organisation. Their argument was that sharing power leads to a feeling of ownership, and that this is vital for factory operatives as well. An important point stressed by middle managers was that sharing power and participative decision-making should not stop at middle management only, it needs to permeate right down the line through to the factory floor (something that did not match senior management's expectations and perceptions of employee empowerment).

> It means you can delegate right down through the company, that it's not just one person who makes the decision, it's the whole team ... it goes right the way down through the factory. (Middle Manager)

Although middle managers agreed that not everybody wants to be empowered or take on extra responsibility, the point they were trying to stress was that the opportunity in the organisation must be there for those employees who wish to do so:

> there are certain people … [they] just want to come in and do a day's work and go home and they are quite happy to do that, which is fine, there is nothing wrong with that. You cannot force people to be or do something they do not want to do, or be. The thing is, as long as you have the opportunity and the channels, that if people wish to go down that [empowerment] route, then they can. (Middle Manager)

There was certainly a feeling amongst the majority of factory operatives that they had the 'freedom' to take decisions, and they were able to take decisions without constantly seeking permission from their managers or team leaders.

> I don't want to run to the team leader every time something goes wrong, I have to try and work it out myself there and then. If a machine breaks down and if I can fix it, fair enough, I will go ahead and fix it. (Factory Operative)

Those factory operatives who were confident also felt that their managers trusted them and this had a positive effect on their self-efficacy and self-esteem, as illustrated:

> I think they put trust in us. We do our work, they just come down and hand us a schedule and that's it for the rest of the day … they know the work's going to be done. (Factory Operative)

An important point was made by a number of operatives that decision-making depended on the personality of the managers. Some of the managers encouraged employees to take decisions, while others wanted to control all aspects of their work, as illustrated below. It is worth noting that this also matched the responses made by a number of non-management personnel at Large Organisation. This kind of discouragement from some managers had significant psychological implications, it led to low self-esteem and frustration in a number of people at Small Organisation, especially those who felt that they would like to take decisions, but were not encouraged in any way.

> I'm not supposed to take decisions. [I get a feeling] it's not my place to decide. (Factory Operative)

Greasley et al. (2005: 363) conclude from their studies: 'if decision-making opportunities are facilitated, the employees argue that productivity is improved as they can make the most efficient decisions. However, when they feel unable to influence a particular decision, a sense of frustration can occur as they feel that they know a better way but because of their position they are unable to decide the best course of action.' Related to this, a number of non-management employees at Small Organisation on the factory floor commented that they felt a rise in their self-efficacy, self-esteem and self-confidence when they were able to take decisions and get on with their jobs without constantly seeking approval and asking permission from their managers or team leaders. With regards to human potential, one middle manager in Large Organisation summed up in his remark: 'If you don't push people, then they never get anywhere!'

Conclusion

Employee empowerment is about change. Any change in organisations is not without problems and difficulties, this was further compounded by the lack of knowledge of what employee empowerment is and its implementation with regards to both Large and Small Organisation.

In terms of what Large Organisation achieved as a result of EP is difficult to assess, since no metric had been put in place to measure its effectiveness and, at the time my research was carried out, no review of EP had taken place. Despite allocating a significant amount of resources to it, Large Organisation did not have any plans for evaluating EP. The result was that nobody in the organisation, not even the CEO, was able to say whether or not EP was delivering its aims and objectives. Given the extensive resources the company had committed to EP in terms of dedicated financial budgets and employees' time spent away from their job, these omissions seem somewhat cavalier. Perhaps the lack of measurement itself meant that some people did not take EP as seriously as they should have. There is a management maxim that 'people do what managers measure.'

The curious situation at Small Organisation, where there seemed to be a two-tiered approach to employee empowerment, was that there was only a small number of key middle managers who were empowered at the management level. With regards to this, a number of middle managers were unhappy about employee empowerment not being extended to other management and non-management personnel. This kind of contrary view has the potential to create conflict. As far as non-management personnel were concerned, the emphasis was more on participative decision-making and devolution of responsibility. Furthermore, several factory operatives expressed that they would have liked to take more responsibility, but were not given the opportunity to do so, which led to disappointment and low feelings of self-efficacy and self-esteem amongst them. Interestingly, this has resonance with agency workers at Large Organisation.

The owner at Small Organisation was keen to empower some of the key middle managers, though not all of them. In such a case, clearly there is evidence to suggest that Small Organisation did not adopt a company-wide employee empowerment policy, rather, employee empowerment at Small Organisation was partial at best. It should be highlighted here that there are possible dangers in empowering some employees and not others. A stark example of this is the situation of the disempowered agency workers at Large Organisation and the negative impact this had on them psychologically, such as lowered internal locus of control, self-efficacy and self-esteem.

The overall aim of my research questions was to gain a deeper understanding of what employee empowerment means in practice. Hence, in this section (Part IV) direct quotes from participants were presented, which certainly 'lets the data speak!'

My research findings based on empirical evidence indicates that the psychological implications of employee empowerment have been largely neglected by Large and Small Organisations. But, it is also true to say that the organisations simply did not realise that there would be any, hence, both organisations failed to create the psychological conditions that were necessary for employee empowerment to take place.

The argument is that by creating conditions that will increase motivation, organisations can enable people in accomplishing their tasks and build a strong sense of self-efficacy. It is easy for the disempowered to feel disenfranchised, hence Peters (1994: 87) emphasises that the 'central ethical issue in the workplace should be protection and support for people who are not empowered, especially the frontline worker'. Employee empowerment can be enhanced if organisations remove all impediments that lead to a sense of powerlessness, such as unnecessary rules and regulations and limited participation. But, it is surprising how many of the aforementioned impediments still remain in the workplace. As Pearlstein (1991) notes, many organisations are so bureaucratic that even routine actions need some form of approval.

Generally, the findings of the interviews from both organisations, Large and Small, demonstrate that participative decision-making did have the most positive impact for a number of people. Psychologically, those employees who were able to take decisions felt good; there was a strong indication that it resulted in high levels of self-esteem and self-confidence and in some cases it also made them feel valued.

On the whole, there appear to have been some benefits in relation to both participative decision-making and devolution of responsibility, especially on a psychological level, with regards to enhancing internal locus of control, raising self-esteem and self-efficacy amongst non-management personnel.

It is accepted that in many cases, people like taking on responsibility because they feel work becomes more meaningful, which leads to a 'feel good factor' and motivates employees. Ashness and Lashley (1995: 31) note from their study that several employees gained a great deal through the devolution of responsibilities, making them feel more involved and more trusted: 'in the main they (employees) enjoy the responsibilities which have been given to them'. It is noted in the management literature that employee empowerment increases workers' ownership of their jobs, as employees feel more responsible, show more initiative, feel more satisfied, and have increased levels of self-efficacy and self-esteem (Conger and Kanungo, 1988; Thomas and Velthouse, 1990; Ivancevich and Matteson, 1993).

It is interesting to note that neither of the above participants, at Large or Small Organisation, gained any political control or power, but as Kieffer's (1984: 32) study concludes, they too saw themselves becoming more 'efficacious participants', particularly in decision-making in their own specific area.

Viewed in this way, the process of empowerment is seen as not only helping people to believe in themselves, it also enables them to gain self-confidence, self-esteem and self-belief. As noted from social work literature, when service users experience low self-confidence and low self-esteem, it is difficult for them to have choice and control in their lives.

Similarly, at Small Organisation, several factory floor employees did not view themselves as 'having more power', but they too viewed themselves as 'feeling more powerful', which also raised their self-efficacy and self-esteem:

We have a lot more freedom ... we can make our own decisions.

Furthermore, from the psychological point of view, devolving responsibility can also be a mechanism for helping employees to be self-confident (Hellriegel et al., 1989; Kondo, 1997). It is also argued, for example, that the positive effects of self-efficacy and self-esteem can enable employees to cope with the extra responsibilities that employee empowerment brings.

Although there is considerable agreement in the management literature that employee empowerment refers to the enhancement of the capacity of some employees to take decisions, Hales (2000: 503) argues that there is ambiguity regarding what this 'capacity' refers to, in what way it is 'enhanced' and to which 'decisions' and 'agents' it applies. Furthermore, Hales (2000: 503) points out that it is unclear 'whether this capacity refers to *responsibility* for decisions (or outcomes) or the *power* to discharge that responsibility'.

As already discussed, critical theorists view power as domination. One of the ways for empowerment to be able to provide the means to 'combat the sources of domination', emphasised by Hardy and Leiba-O'Sullivan (1998: 475), is through sharing power with employees 'to transform those without power into equitable positions' (Denham Lincoln et al., 2002: 273).

However, it is worth noting Wilkinson's (1998) point that there is a broad range of initiatives that are looked upon as employee empowerment programmes with varying degrees of power held by employees, but most of them follow a strict management agenda, and they do not actually allow people to play a significant role in decision-making. A study of employee empowerment by Ashness and Lashley (1995) carried out in the catering industry shows that although employees were able to take some lower level decisions, significant decisions still tended to be taken by the team manager at unit level. There are inconsistencies in organisations regarding the degree to which employees are allowed input into decision-making. Cunningham et al. (1996) point out that those organisations which allow decision-making do so only to a limited extent.

In many instances, instead of gaining greater power, employees just assume higher levels of accountability together with unwanted responsibility or responsibilities; in which case employees could end up in a worse position than before. Thus, although employee empowerment offers a means of shifting the balance of power in organisations, the fact remains that sometimes the redistribution of power is not management's real concern. Interestingly, with regards to what organisations seek to achieve via employee empowerment, responses from non-management employees from both Large and Small

Organisations reveal that their expectations were quite modest. There was high consensus from people in non-management position from both organisations that they did not desire more power in the political sense, but more discretion and responsibility for decision-making within their own work situation and greater scope for utilising their capabilities (Hill and Huq, 2004). This has resonance with the social work literature. In this context, it is worth noting that the theme of enablement from the social work literature was viewed to be extremely important from the point of view of employees, but not by management, at Large Organisation.

The concepts of 'feeling in control' and 'enablement' are important aspects of employee empowerment, and this has resonance with the social work literature, where empowerment is about enabling people to improve the quality of their lives. It is equally important to note that most non-managerial employees at Large Organisation who viewed employee empowerment positively, remarked that EP provided enormous benefits (though short-term) with regards to raising their self-efficacy, self-esteem and self-confidence which has resonance with the social work literature, that is when people feel they are in control over their lives or situations, they acquire high self-efficacy, self-esteem and self-confidence and that when people are enabled they feel psychologically empowered and vice versa.

PART V
Does it Deliver?

Chapter 9
The Story Unfolded

Introduction

By questioning participants of both organisations, Large and Small, with regards to their perceptions, understanding and experiences of employee empowerment, the story begins to unfold.

Leavy (1994: 111) states:

> *Over time what tends to become evident is the recurrence of some central themes and conceptual obsessions around which the researcher's intellectual curiosity begins to converge in the ongoing attempt to draw some insight out of the data and make some holistic sense of it.*

Thus, to draw *insight out of the data* it was useful to carry out a cross-case comparison to get an understanding of the common problems and an account of people's first-hand experiences of employee empowerment, across the two case organisations, Large and Small.

Cross-case comparison can offer greater potential for explanation (Gable, 1994; Rubin and Rubin, 1995; Denzin and Lincoln, 1998a; Johnson and Duberley, 2000; Patton, 2002). Johnson and Duberley (2000) argue that cross-case analysis or comparison helps to search for common patterns within cases, thereby confirming or disconfirming views in the literature.

Responses by participants from both organisations, Large and Small, are reported in this section.

Discussion of Complexities and Difficulties Faced by Both Large and Small Organisations

PERCEPTION AND UNDERSTANDING OF EMPLOYEE EMPOWERMENT OF PEOPLE FROM SENIOR AND MIDDLE MANAGEMENT POSITIONS

It is interesting to note that there were some shared perceptions and understandings of employee empowerment, despite the contrasting (formal and informal) approaches adopted by Large and Small Organisations, respectively. For example, senior and middle managers in both organisations described employee empowerment as 'the ability of employees to get on with their jobs', 'giving people responsibility' and 'letting people make decisions'. Interestingly, in both organisations, employee empowerment was viewed by the majority of managers as trying to 'devolve decision-making' and 'responsibility down the line' to subordinates, in order for managers to be free to do other things:

> I am trying to get team leaders to become more responsible for some of my tasks, to allow me to become more responsible for some other tasks. (Middle Manager, Small Organisation)

In keeping with SHRM this helps achieve effective use of human resources at all levels.

A number of managers at Large and Small Organisations also linked employee empowerment with participative decision-making, and devolution of responsibility.

> The main aims and objectives of EP were to empower non-management people, give them some empowerment to make decisions for themselves by owning issues or problems within their sphere, and by giving them the freedom to go ahead and resolve it for themselves. The idea was that they would become their own decision makers, rather than have to refer problems to their manager. (Middle Manager, Large Organisation)

> [Empowerment means] giving people more responsibility and letting them have a say in how the company is run, not just telling them what they have to do, but letting them contribute as well to decisions that are made within the company. (Managing Director, Small Organisation)

This has resonance with the management literature, where participative decision-making and devolution of responsibility are two of the employee empowerment themes (Huq's Model A). At Small Organisation, middle managers also added that their understanding of employee empowerment was being able to take decisions without constantly asking for permission and being able to air their views without fear.

> *Empowerment to me would be freedom to make a decision and stand by it, without having to … ask for permission to do this, and permission to do that. (Middle Manager, Small Organisation)*

Although there was no formal employee empowerment programme at Small Organisation, senior management in this organisation described their perception of the company's approach to empowerment mainly in terms of devolution of authority, responsibility and decision-making. Non-management employees, particularly factory floor operatives, may be responsible for work-related small decisions, but not 'bigger decisions'. These matched the views held by a number of people in management positions at Large Organisation as well.

Interestingly, although participative decision-making and devolution of responsibility were two common themes that were strongly associated with employee empowerment by managers at Large and Small Organisations, it should be noted that the theme they associated least with employee empowerment was power-sharing.

PERCEPTION AND UNDERSTANDING OF EMPLOYEE EMPOWERMENT OF PEOPLE FROM NON-MANAGEMENT POSITIONS

At Small Organisation, as the non-management employees were not included in the employee empowerment programme, it was not meaningful to ask them questions about their understanding of it. As mentioned elsewhere, the owner explained that the word 'empowerment' is not used widely in the organisation at non-managerial level, particularly amongst factory operatives. During the interviews, when non-managerial employees were asked if they had heard about empowerment, there were unanimous replies that they never heard of the word, which matched the owner's prediction.

In contrast, Large Organisation had a formal employee empowerment strategy (EP), and the CEO's aim was to empower everyone in the organisation.

When non-management personnel were asked about their views with regards to the understanding of employee empowerment, their perception of employee empowerment ranged from 'culture change' to 'having the freedom to decide' and being able to take decisions 'without fear'. Most of them remarked that 'participative decision-making' gave them control over their tasks and actually enabled them to take decisions without asking permission from management, and for them that was 'employee empowerment'.

It is important to note, as mentioned in earlier chapters, that the concepts of 'feeling in control' and 'enablement' are important aspects of employee empowerment, and this has resonance with the social work literature, where empowerment is about enabling people to improve the quality of their lives.

It is equally important to note that most non-managerial employees at Large Organisation who viewed employee empowerment positively, remarked that EP provided enormous benefits (though short-term) with regards to raising their self-efficacy, self-esteem and self-confidence which has resonance with the social work literature, that is when people feel they are in control over their lives or situations, they acquire high self-efficacy, self-esteem and self-confidence.

Discussion of Themes of Employee Empowerment Addressed by Both Large and Small Organisations

THEMES FROM MANAGEMENT LITERATURE (HUQ'S MODEL A)

Power-sharing

At Small Organisation, senior management had already explained and admitted that direct power was not handed down to non-management employees. Even as far as management personnel were concerned, some power was shared, but only with a few key middle managers.

At Large Organisation, there was a significant mismatch in perceptions between management and non-management personnel regarding power-sharing, as management claimed that they had no problems sharing power, while non-managerial employees clearly felt that, in reality, management still 'held onto their power'. Even middle managers felt there was a lack of power-sharing, as they remarked that senior managers liked to keep a 'firm grip on decision-making!' One of the aims of EP at Large Organisation was to change the 'command and control' behaviour of managers. But, despite the principles of EP and the continuous enthusiasm of the CEO, in practice this area of power-sharing still remained problematic for management, particularly senior managers. Hence, Ford and Fottler (1995: 22) rightfully highlight the 'struggle' management face between 'the delicate balance in giving employees control over their own work processes without at the same time losing control over what employees do'.

A number of managers confessed that they found it difficult to share power, and felt a bit insecure because they did not have their 'finger on every aspect of the job', and in some ways they felt that this was disadvantageous and had the potential for conflict in the organisation. It is worth noting that one of the key themes in neo-modernism is that 'organisations need to be orderly human systems in which conflict needs to be carefully controlled' (McAuley et al., 2007: 106).

As mentioned before, power-sharing was a theme that Large and Small Organisations least addressed, which matches the arguments put forward by Denham Lincoln et al. (2002) that, in reality, the redistribution of power may not be management's real concern.

Participative decision-making

There were similarities in perceptions with regards to participative decision-making at Large and Small Organisations, not only amongst managers but also non-management employees. For example, a number of managers from both organisations felt that participative decision-making 'freed up' a lot of their time to do other things that they were not able to do previously, and that was perceived to be a benefit for them. Equally, the majority of non-managerial employees in both organisations remarked that participative decision-making had a positive impact, it helped to raise their self-esteem, self-efficacy and self-confidence, and enabled them to feel 'empowered'.

At Small Organisation, although in principle participative decision-making was encouraged amongst non-managerial employees, significant decisions were still taken by management, which matches other studies, by authors such as Ashness and Lashley (1995) and Cunningham et al. (1996). With respect to this theme, a significant drawback in both organisations was that a number of non-management employees still felt excluded from participative decision-making, and clearly this needs to be addressed.

Devolution of responsibility

Unlike Large Organisation where the CEO's aim was to initiate an 'employee empowerment strategy' throughout the organisation, the owner of the Small Organisation did not have a company-wide strategy to empower all employees. However, part of his informal approach was to empower a small number of key middle managers; they were given substantial responsibility to run the organisation and were empowered to take strategic decisions as well.

Senior and middle managers described their understanding of employee empowerment as 'giving people responsibility' and 'letting people make decisions'. Middle managers at Small Organisation were keen to take on the challenge of employee empowerment, and gave a robust view of how they perceived it, ranging from 'having authority' and 'taking responsibility', to 'taking ownership':

> To me empowerment would mean people feel as if they can make a change, people feel as if they have an input into the company and where the company is going, and they are not just A, B, and C in the company, they actually feel part of the company and feel empowered to make changes that affect them. (Middle Manager)

Clearly, a number of managers both at Large and Small Organisations linked employee empowerment with participative decision-making, and devolution of responsibility. Comparable to participative decision-making, there were similar perceptions at Large and Small Organisations amongst managers and non-managerial employees with regards to devolution of responsibility. For example, in both organisations, managers felt devolution of responsibility allowed them to concentrate on other aspects of their jobs, and non-managerial employees felt that it enhanced their self-confidence.

At Small Organisation, management was very attentive to the issue of quality, which they regarded as being everybody's responsibility. Key processes are managed in a team environment by the senior management team, and all processes are measurable. Each member of the team is given responsibility for managing and continuously improving the key processes.

Although there was no formal programme in Small Organisation to introduce the concept of employee empowerment, the EFQM Excellence Award played a major part.

However, it is interesting to note that the majority of non-managerial employees in both organisations felt the need to be remunerated for taking more decisions and responsibility, in other words, wages needed to match the level of responsibility people were asked to take. Interestingly, Small Organisation attempted to pay a lot more attention to this matter from the human resource perspective; this was lacking in Large Organisation.

> *I mean the structure is set up so that everybody can gain individually better through their personal development plan. Everybody has a team bonus of some sort with their colleagues working together as a team and everybody has some company bonus. (Senior Manager, Small Organisation)*

As in participative decision-making, the drawback with devolution of responsibility was that a number of non-managerial employees in Large and Small Organisations felt excluded from it, and so it needs to be addressed too.

People-oriented leadership style

It has been useful to compare the approach to people-oriented leadership style at the two case studies. As explained previously, the CEO at Large Organisation advocated the desired leadership styles to be 'Directing, Coaching, Supporting and Counselling'; whereas at Small Organisation, the owner decided to have a two-tier approach to his leadership style, where he empowered some of his key middle managers but none of the employees in non-management positions.

His belief was that non-management employees do not understand the word 'empowerment' and it would be dangerous to empower employees in such a situation. For him it was important to 'empower people within their ability', and with this perception, he took the steps to empower the most senior and experienced managers. The owner of Small Organisation did not actually consciously address the issue of people-oriented leadership style. Although he empowered his key middle managers, there was no evidence to suggest that he was particularly involved in coaching, supporting or directing them. However, he encouraged people to approach him if they had any problems and he was perceived by the majority of his employees as 'approachable'.

In contrast, at Large Organisation, the four desired styles of behaviour, namely, 'Directing, Coaching, Supporting and Counselling', were integral to the empowerment programme (EP). It was realised that employees should be treated as adults and they should have the freedom to get on with their jobs without having to ask permission to do things. This was echoed by a middle manager who explained that, in theory, the management style in EP was about 'treating people like adults, letting them make their own decisions without having to come constantly asking for permission to do things'.

The SHRM literature advocates that in order to empower employees, management should treat them as mature adults who can take decisions on their own. However, it is interesting to note that the findings from both case studies demonstrate that not all managers treated people like 'mature adults' who can take decisions, rather in many cases adult employees were told what to do and how to do it:

> it's much easier telling people to do ... (Owner, Small Organisation)

It is also vital to give due regard to coaching and supporting leaders and managers, as demonstrated at Large Organisation, where lack of training and appropriate support resulted in several managers retaining the old command and control behaviours. Several employees remarked that management style did not change, as they still felt they 'got hammered' for taking decisions, without managers' permission. A number of employees also commented that they did not feel managers had changed from 'cops to coaches'; instead they felt the culture was still strict, highly regimented and policed. In such cases it was not possible for employees to *feel* empowered. A point worth noting with regards to Large Organisation is that the CEO was extremely enthusiastic and fired up with the idea of EP and she wanted all her managers to adopt the new culture of employee empowerment with equal eagerness. Perhaps she expected this to happen too quickly, as the owner of Small Organisation cautions: 'one of the down sides of empowerment is when you empower too much too soon ... people don't have the management skills or the actual experience'.

The next section compares and contrasts the findings concerning the extent to which (if at all) Large and Small Organisations addressed the themes of empowerment emanating from the social work literature, namely, access to information, collaboration and enablement (Huq's Model B).

Discussion of Themes of Employee Empowerment Addressed by Both Large and Small Organisations

THEMES FROM SOCIAL WORK LITERATURE (HUQ'S MODEL B)

Access to information

Both Large and Small Organisations facilitated access to information in different ways. Large Organisation made available its internet and intranet facilities to employees, while Small Organisation used other means, such as newsletters, weekly, fortnightly and monthly meetings, and so on. A significant point worth noting with regards to this theme is that respondents at Large and Small Organisations felt access to information made employees self-reliant, confident and empowered. Respondents in both organisations agreed they were able to voice their opinions and views and access information on their own, without always relying on managers, as one call centre operator in Large Organisation enthusiastically remarked: 'there are lots of things we can find out ourselves'.

Some employees realised that they had the right to use their voices and faced up to their managers and defended their decisions and actions. For some people this was extremely challenging, especially for those who had never voiced their opinions before.

> *Those who were a little more shy and retiring, it was a change for them.*
> *(Office Administrator)*

Certainly, at Large Organisation the use of IT encouraged several employees to take IT courses to further their knowledge and become more computer literate. However, as mentioned previously, a major drawback with regards to the use of the internet and intranet was that it was not associated with employee empowerment by employees. This was largely due to the lack of a company-wide strategy to communicate to employees that enhancing and learning computer skills was supposed to be part of the employee empowerment programme. The fact that employees had information at their fingertips, through the press of a button, 'which never used to be the case before' as remarked by one office administrator, seemed to increase their self-confidence and made them feel good that they could do this. Non-managerial employees acknowledged this was a brilliant change because previously information was difficult to get.

At Small Organisation, key middle managers had access to computer and internet facilities, but as far as factory operatives were concerned, the newsletter was an important vehicle for accessing company news, customer profiles, business targets and suggestions for improvements by employees and most importantly news about the organisation's quality awards. Employees were keen to read about suggestions that were made by other employees and teams.

However, it was difficult to know whether employees felt empowered, as non-management employees, especially factory operatives, were not included in the employee empowerment strategy at Small Organisation. But, certainly employees felt informed, involved and valued to have access to information about the organisation they worked for.

From the psychological perspective, it is worth noting that at both Large and Small Organisations, easy access to information had a positive impact on employees. A number of employees felt that they were able to accomplish tasks (due to availability of information) and develop their competence (computer literacy) leading to high self-efficacy and self-esteem; this included some middle managers as well.

Collaboration

It is surprising to note that there was a lack of collaboration (working together to achieve common goals) at both Large and Small Organisations. One would expect that at Large Organisation there would have been more robust collaboration because of the formal nature of the employee empowerment programme, which would necessitate the need to collaborate and work jointly with all employees in all sites. But, even between senior and middle management at Large Organisation, there was very little collaboration. EP was supposed to be cascaded down the line. Senior managers had direct meetings about EP with middle managers, who, in turn, were to cascade the information about EP and its various events and activities down the line to their teams and subordinates. Findings reveal that with regards to non-managerial employees, there was no collaboration on how to how to achieve the aims and objectives of EP.

Clearly, EP was a top-down management agenda, with little or no input from employees in non-management positions. Ironically, it was supposed to be an employee empowerment programme for everyone, including non-managerial employees. Several employees simply did not know what EP was about, and a number of them confused it with a 'fun day out' or 'charity work' for the community. There is a danger that a lack of collaboration can lead to different interpretations of employee empowerment (Denham Lincoln et al., 2002) and therefore different expectations, again creating the potential for conflict.

At Small Organisation, the owner had already explained that non-management employees, including factory operatives, were not empowered. Hence, it is obvious that there was no collaboration with them with regards to employee empowerment. However, it can be said that there was collaboration with the key middle managers who were empowered. Nevertheless, as far as Large and Small Organisations were concerned, neither organisation consciously addressed the collaboration theme.

Enablement

With regards to enablement, at Large Organisation, the CEO felt that managers needed to develop particular behaviours, such as 'Directing, Coaching, Supporting and Counselling', to enable their subordinates to achieve EP aims and objectives. In principle, she understood that enablement of employees was necessary, and in this respect she felt managers' role was to facilitate employees so that they were able to work within EP principles. Hence, the management behaviours advocated were: 'development, coaching, training, fulfilment, communication, all the good things that allow us to harness the energy of people' (company document). However, a fundamental flaw was that most managers were not equipped with these skills and no resources were set aside to provide training for managers to develop them. It was assumed that managers would simply become coaches and facilitators overnight.

In contrast, at Small Organisation, although only key middle managers were empowered, the owner did make provisions for training these managers in their relevant areas, be it finance, sales or customer services.

> If you empower people and don't lead them and don't give them coaching, and don't help them, you can only expect failure, and that's what happens in lots of places. They just give it lip service. They empower people and then they wonder why [it did not work], because nobody ever taught them anything. (Owner, Small Organisation)

In this case, he was enabling middle managers to be empowered to take decisions and responsibility, which led to high self-esteem and self-confidence amongst the key middle managers who were empowered. However, there was no training provided for them to be coaches or facilitators.

Conclusion

By cross-case comparison, comparing and contrasting, more information was gathered about people's perceptions and experiences of employee empowerment including the themes in Huq's Models A and B.

Several authors in the management literature agree that there is significant diversity regarding the conceptualisation and understanding of employee empowerment. This was found to be true as far as the case organisations were concerned, where management and non-management personnel described employee empowerment in different ways. At Large Organisation, senior and middle management described employee empowerment in a number of ways, ranging from 'participative decision-making'; 'devolution of responsibility'; 'not having to ask for permission' or 'get authority' – to moving away from the 'command and control culture' to one that gave people 'freedom and flexibility'. At Small Organisation, the word empowerment was used in the context of 'the EFQM Excellence Award' criteria and senior and middle managers strongly associated it with 'participative decision-making' and 'devolution of responsibility'.

It is accepted that in many cases, people like taking on responsibilities because they feel work becomes more meaningful. Ashness and Lashley (1995: 31) note in their study that several employees gained a great deal through the devolution of responsibilities, making them feel more involved and more trusted: 'in the main they (employees) enjoy the responsibilities which have been given to them'.

Out of the four management themes of employee empowerment, namely, power-sharing, participative decision-making, devolution of responsibility and people-oriented leadership style (Huq's Model A), the themes that were most strongly addressed at Large and Small Organisations were the following: participative decision-making and devolution of responsibility. Interestingly, power-sharing was least addressed by both organisations. However, it is important to note that instead of power in the political sense, it is evident from this study that the majority of employees at both Large and Small Organisations desired more power and control over their working lives. In this respect, it is useful to note Beresford and Croft's (1993: 50) definition of empowerment in the social work literature, which is 'making it possible for people to exercise power and have more control over their lives'. It should also be noted from the empirical findings of this study that this kind of power, having control over one's work and being able to take work-related decisions, was considered important by employees, which interestingly has resonance with the social work literature. It was also perceived by employees to have a positive effect on their internal locus of control, self-efficacy and self-esteem, which made employees feel confident to perform their tasks and take decisions in their work situations.

From the psychological perspective, where employees were able to take decisions, they experienced an increase in their self-esteem and self-confidence, in contrast to those employees whose managers did not allow participative decision-making.

Chapter 10
What Does it Actually Deliver?

Introduction

The introduction of any change has an impact on organisations and it also creates expectations amongst people. Organisations fail to take these two important aspects into consideration, that is, the impact and expectations of the implementation of any changes, small or radical.

It was important to find out what impact if any employee empowerment had on people from management and non-management positions. Employee empowerment did create expectations in people from different levels and departments in both Large and Small Organisations. This was something that was overlooked in both the case study organisations.

Large Organisation invested considerable resources and this is a pertinent question raised in this section – what did it achieve from its employee empowerment programme? Likewise, even though Small Organisation did not invest a formal employee empowerment programme, nevertheless this question also applies, that is, what did Small Organisation achieve by empowering its key managers? Another question is also relevant, that is, what does employee empowerment actually deliver? The impact and expectations of employee empowerment are discussed in this section with regards to both organisations, Large and Small.

Impact and Expectations of Employee Empowerment

It cannot be said that there was no impact or expectations of 'employee empowerment' at both Large and Small Organisations. It is evident from the interviewees' responses that there were both positive and negative impact and, in some cases, unmet expectations.

People in management positions in Large Organisation made clear reference to the psychological implications of employee empowerment, with regards to internal locus of control and having self-confidence; these were deemed to be important in employee empowerment, together with 'learning and growing'.

> I think it [empowerment] is about helping people to learn and grow so that they can make their own decisions, and have more control of the things around them. Also they don't have to ask permission or get authority for things that are clearly within their control because they are actually the 'experts'. (Middle Manager)

A number of middle managers at Large Organisation did make reference to positive psychological benefits, such as how EP had raised their self-confidence and helped them to feel 'more empowered' as illustrated:

> I think empowerment tied in very heavily with the self-confidence that helped me feel a bit more empowered. I possibly would be more inclined to take a risk [because of empowerment] ... it is self-confidence. (Middle Manager)

A significant number of non-management personnel (including office administrators, engineers and call centre operators) at Large Organisation acknowledged that decision-making in EP had a positive impact with regard to their self-efficacy and self-esteem, leading to self-confidence. They felt that they could make decisions relating to their tasks, without seeking permission from management all the time.

> It [empowerment] means just within yourself, you know you can do it. (Call Centre Operator)

However, this was not the view throughout Large Organisation, particularly with regards to agency workers who felt powerless to take any decisions and severely suffered a lack of control over their work situations (Hill and Huq, 2001, 2004). There was concern by a number of middle managers with regards to the failure of senior management to include agency workers in EP programmes, as they observed how it made them (agency workers) isolated and furthermore it divided the workforce. Senior management had obviously not given much thought to this important issue:

> *with the huge number of agency people that we employ, we have high*
> *turnovers, and therefore there are probably a number of people in the*
> *centre who didn't even go through the EP programme. (Middle Manager)*

Although the aim was to empower everyone in the organisation, not everyone in non-management positions understood or was even aware of this; which led to significant mismatch between senior management's expectations and perceptions in relation to employee empowerment and those of middle managers and non-management personnel. For example, even the CEO of Large Organisation admitted that employees would not associate all the changes that were happening with employee empowerment because she feared there were weaknesses in communicating to employees what EP was about. There were negative results from this, because some employees felt EP did not have any impact or effect on them, as one call centre operator remarked: 'I don't think EP has affected us. There has been changes in the few years, but I don't think it has been connected to EP.'

A number of call centre operators felt frustrated because they were not able to make full use of their abilities, talents and knowledge, simply because a number of managers did not live up to EP principles. There were feelings of hopelessness amongst people as they felt disappointed by managers' negative attitudes at the workplace, and this resulted in anger and frustration:

> *I think one of the problems is that managers don't realise that we*
> *actually were in previous jobs before we came in here. We have different*
> *abilities, talents and knowledge. (Call Centre Operator)*

In order to empower employees and promote freedom and flexibility at the workplace, any feelings of fear and oppression must be eradicated. Senior managers had alluded to this in their responses:

> *When you walk into the office or when you walk into a team meeting,*
> *is there a feeling of oppression, a feeling of 'I better sit here I can't say*
> *a word', or is there a wide open atmosphere where people can input no*
> *matter what job they do.*

Many people did not feel that there was an 'open atmosphere' to voice their opinions, as they raised concerns about their fear to talk openly and honestly in front of management.

*It would be much nicer if we could speak out and give an honest and open
view on things, but we are still afraid to do that. (Office Administrator)*

A number of factors contributed to these fears, such as downsizing and
redundancies, and therefore it was not surprising that people were suffering
from low morale. Lack of job security added to their fears, resulting in 'silence'
in front of management. Under such circumstances, it is hardly surprising
that it becomes difficult for employees to believe in management or buy into
any change programmes.

Despite a promise of culture change through EP, in reality a number of
people in non-management positions felt 'nothing changed'. This highlights
the danger of raising people's expectations and not meeting them.

With regards to the impact of EP, there were mixed responses; as several
employees felt 'no impact' because they could not associate any of the changes
that were happening at Large Organisation with EP, rather they felt these were
due to 'market changes'.

In a strange way, parallel to this (although at Small Organisation
only key middle managers were empowered), a number of people from
non-management positions including factory operatives felt a positive
impact due to the changes brought about by winning the 'EFQM' quality
award – but obviously none of these changes could be attributed to employee
empowerment on the factory floor. Anyway, the owner of Small Organisation
had already explained that employee empowerment was only for key
middle managers so impact and expectations with regards to employee
empowerment on factory operatives were not applicable.

However, for key middle managers the informal employee empowerment
had a positive impact. They enjoyed the challenge of 'having authority',
'responsibility' and 'taking ownership'.

*To me empowerment is the ability to get on with your job, with authority
and responsibility. (Middle Manager)*

The fact that these key middle managers had the authority to take
decisions without asking for permission raised their self-esteem and
they felt psychologically empowered, which was a positive impact of
employee empowerment.

An area not given much consideration in the management literature is the danger of raising employees' expectations and then being unable to meet them (Claydon and Doyle, 1996; Hardy and Leiba-O'Sullivan, 1998; Appelbaum et al., 1999; Greasley et al., 2005).

Related to this, at Large Organisation, one middle manager was concerned about raising employees' expectations, particularly if managers had to revert back to command and control mode, this would collapse employees' hopes of any empowerment.

> While you can raise people's expectations ... I have concerns that one day we might have to close the door a little bit and say hold on, we have to have control as well. So I have those concerns, I just don't want to raise [employees'] expectations. (Middle Manager, Large Organisation)

Claydon and Doyle (1996) conclude from their study that unmet expectations created frustration in employees who felt that they were not given much direction but were required to find their own routes. Parallel examples are also seen in the case of Large Organisation, where employees were led to believe that they had freedom to take decisions, but they felt 'frustrated' when they were unable to take decisions without constantly referring to their managers. An important point in social work, highlighted by Zastrow (2003: 126), is that because service users have an 'internal understanding' of the problem, they are able to help each other.

Hence, it is in the interest of organisations not to create unrealistic expectations amongst their employees, as unmet expectations have the potential to create misunderstanding and conflict, leading to disempowerment rather than empowerment of employees.

This scenario is evident as one middle manager at Large Organisation was worried about creating unrealistic expectations amongst employees and remarked: 'we just don't want to raise expectations' as he felt that there was a danger the organisation might not be able to meet employee expectations. In fact, EP did create expectations where employees were led to believe that they could take decisions on their own, without asking for permission. And, the fears of the aforementioned middle manager did have substance, as one office administrator angrily noted, that if they took decisions they got 'hammered for it!'

The failure to communicate the aims and objectives of employee empowerment effectively can have significant consequences, because there is a danger that inevitably employees will create their own definitions and perceptions of employee empowerment, which in turn can negatively influence expectations and perceived outcomes (Cunningham et al., 1996; Denham et al., 1997; Morrell and Wilkinson, 2002).

Although Large Organisation had a formal employee empowerment strategy, there is evidence to suggest that a significant number of employees in non-management positions did not 'feel empowered' because they felt they were not allowed the 'freedom' to take decisions. The expectations of this group of employees were that they should be given the 'freedom' to take decisions and accomplish their tasks, but their expectations did not materialise.

At Small Organisation, although employee empowerment was not practised on the factory floor, operatives were encouraged to take minor decisions. However, a number of factory operatives remarked that although they were asked to take decisions and furthermore responsibility was given to them, on several occasions, management would still check on them. This undermined their confidence which resulted in low self-esteem. Factory operatives developed a perception that management did not trust them.

> *They [management] tell us to make decisions and then when we do make decisions, they are coming down on the floor and checking, which is sort of undermining us straight away. (Factory Operative, Small Organisation)*

The undermining of the decisions taken by operatives on the factory floor sometimes created a negative impact on their self-esteem and self-efficacy – thus leading to a feeling of 'oppression' and 'disempowerment' (created by management's attitudes towards them).

However, not all managers undermined their decisions, there were those who encouraged it and that helped them to maintain their self-esteem and self-efficacy. Furthermore, as there was a good team spirit amongst factory operatives and most of them were 'good friends' or 'mates' outside of work, this helped them to get on with their work by their inner circle of 'comradeship'. This has resonance with social work as mentioned earlier, with regards to Zastrow's (2003: 126) reference: 'service users have an "internal understanding" of the problem, they are able to help each other.'

What Does Employee Empowerment Actually Deliver?

If we review the situation at Small Organisation, the EFQM Excellence Award was a significant motivator with regards to the adoption of an employee empowerment strategy in the organisation. However, this strategy was restricted to a small number of key managers, where this particular group of managers did feel that they were empowered to take decisions and 'get on with their job' and enjoyed a high level of self-efficacy and self-esteem.

Although employee empowerment was not cascaded down to the factory floor in a formal strategy, in an informal way some non-management employees and factory operatives did feel that when they were able to take work-related small decisions, it enabled them psychologically to attain self-efficacy and self-esteem.

An important aspect of giving people extra responsibility also meant that some of the factory operatives were promoted to middle management positions as team leaders, and furthermore their new position was also linked to an increase in wages, and this had enormous positive psychological benefit to the people concerned.

There was a unanimous feeling amongst these newly promoted team leaders that they were pleased to be able to take decisions and they did not feel that they were 'just a number' in the organisation. It was important to be able to have an input into the decision-making process of the organisation, as one team leader from the factory floor aptly explained:

> It makes us on the factory floor feel … we are not just a number, we are part of a team, we are part of what is going on … and I think if we feel that we are not just coming in doing our job and going home, we feel part of something. We have a bit more pride in what we are doing. (Team Leader, Factory Floor, Small Organisation)

A number of factory floor operatives developed a sense of pride and belonging, which led to high self-esteem and self-confidence amongst them to take decisions and they felt that they were able to do things without always being told what to do.

> I don't want to run to the team leader every time something goes wrong, we have to try and work it out ourselves there and then. If a

> *machine breaks down if we can fix it, fair enough, we go ahead and fix it. (Factory Operative, Small Organisation)*

> *It's no use standing and waiting for the boss to tell you what to do all the time. I mean you don't want somebody in charge walking behind you all the time. (Factory Operative, Small Organisation)*

Psychologically, it seemed that there was a positive impact of vesting more responsibility in people. A number of team leaders, including managers on the factory floor, remarked that employees now had an opportunity to put forward ideas and suggestions and that they were encouraged by managers and leaders to do so. However, they also emphasised an important point that factory operatives should be rewarded appropriately for doing a good job, otherwise, the consequences of that would lead to negative implications on their self-esteem and self-confidence.

> *If a person does a job well, there has to be some sort of an appreciation, he can't stay in the same job all his life and not be appreciated, so he has to move up, there has to be that sort of ... reward. Nobody wants to sit there and do the same job in and out, and not have any chance to move up further. (Team Leader, Factory Floor, Small Organisation)*

Team leaders who were promoted from factory operatives to middle management positions felt a rise in their self-esteem and it also gave them a feeling of being valued as a person.

> *With a bit of responsibility, I suppose that gives me authority as well, and a bit of respect ... they [management] are speaking to me like a person now. (Team Leader, Factory Floor, Small Organisation)*

Middle managers were also of similar opinion, that being allowed to basically run the factory had given them self-confidence and raised their self-esteem, and this was noticeable in their confident body language and tone of voice.

> *Senior management is more than happy to let us manage the factory and basically we've got the responsibility to just get on with it. (Middle Manager, Small Organisation)*

This was to do with psychological empowerment – a feeling of being able to do that 'comes from within', where managers felt confident that they 'can do' the task.

However, on the factory floor there were certain issues that created unhappiness amongst operatives, which were important for management to be aware of, such as the bonus system, poor hygiene and household factors (dust and heat and washroom facilities), which led to low self-esteem amongst a majority of people on the factory floor. One important point emerged from the interviews – that some factory operatives remarked that the work was not challenging enough, and this has the potential for people to develop low self-esteem.

> I would say the money is not bad, the job's terrible, and you can leave your brains at home. (Factory Operative, Small Organisation)

Surprisingly, despite these problems, a number of factory operatives described themselves as 'happy' at work and there were various reasons put forward for this, ranging from being able to 'get on with people', 'good team work' and 'good fun with mates'.

> My opinion would be it is heavy work, hard work, but its good fun at the same time. All the lads get on with one another, it's good fun. (Factory Operative, Small Organisation)

> We are a very close team and there's an opportunity to have a good laugh and a carry on without being told off and I think that's the main thing about enjoying your work. There's nothing worse than coming in … and doing the same repetitive thing all the time. (Team Leader, Factory Floor, Small Organisation)

There were other factors that contributed to 'feeling good'. Open communication and suggestions for improvements on the factory floor at Small Organisation were encouraged, and information was shared through team briefings, weekly performance meetings and the company newsletter; the owner also had an 'open door' policy. However, the motivation behind providing these aforementioned policies at the factory floor level was mainly to fulfil the criteria of the EFQM award requirements, rather than empowering factory floor operatives. The owner of Small Organisation was satisfied with the enhancement of the psychological motivation through involving factory floor operatives at this level, and his key middle managers at the higher level of decision-making and responsibilities. This is what Small Organisation was seeking to achieve anyway.

In contrast, at Large Organisation, there was definitely a commitment from the CEO to empower all employees. As far as she was concerned, the focus of EP was employee empowerment. Her aim was to move away from the autocratic 'command and control' style of management towards one in which all employees felt 'empowered'.

There was lack of evidence of any significant long-term change in culture 'via relaxation of rigid rules and procedures', or 'change in management style from policing to coaching'. Although there was some short-term relaxation of rigid rules and procedures at the beginning of the introduction of EP, later on, there was fear amongst middle managers and non-management employees that the organisation was going back to the 'command and control' culture.

It is important to note that the concepts of 'feeling in control' and 'enablement' are important aspects of employee empowerment, and this has resonance with the social work literature, where empowerment is about enabling people to improve the quality of their lives. It is equally important to note that most non-managerial employees at Large Organisation who viewed employee empowerment positively, remarked that EP provided enormous benefits (though short-term) with regards to raising their self-efficacy, self-esteem and self-confidence which has resonance with the social work literature, that is when people feel they are in control over their lives or situations, they acquire high self-efficacy, self-esteem and self-confidence. However, as agency workers were not included in EP, it left them feeling devalued and contributed towards low self-efficacy and low self-esteem amongst this group of employees.

A number of call centre operators expressed empathy for their agency worker colleagues, and described that they (agency workers) felt unwanted and at the bottom of the heap.

> Agency workers were not involved in EP. There were new ideas by agency staff, but they were told you can't take part, because you are agency workers, you are not staff, which I think is ridiculous! (Call Centre Operator, Large Organisation)

From the psychological perspective, it is worth noting that both at Large and Small Organisations, psychologically, people felt good about being able to take decisions. There were strong indications that participative decision-making resulted in high self-esteem amongst employees, as it made them feel 'valued':

> *I think decision-making was good, in that it made everybody feel a valued member of the company. (Office Administrator)*

Furthermore, in Large Organisation, another positive example of psychological outcome is that if employees made mistakes, some of them were not afraid to talk about them, whereas, before the introduction of EP, they felt they could not.

> *If they [managers] say 'you have done this totally wrong', but you haven't, you can stand for your actions and say you had a reason for doing it. But, before [EP] they would have told you off, 'you shouldn't have done it'. Well, now you stick up for your actions all the way ... [and say] 'you gave me empowerment'. We actually have a better way of expressing. (Call Centre Operator, Large Organisation)*

Access to information also had a positive impact on employees. A number of employees felt that they were able to accomplish tasks (due to availability of information) and develop their competence (computer literacy) leading to high self-efficacy and self-esteem, this included some middle managers as well.

The aims and objectives of EP reflected the CEO's thinking and Large Organisation was seeking to achieve enhancement of the company's business and creation of a better and more fulfilling life for customers and employees. The CEO was keen to change the culture of the organisation through relaxation of rigid rules and procedures via EP, and through the change in management style, from 'policing to coaching'. This sums up what Large Organisation was seeking to achieve, but despite the rhetoric of EP, it did not achieve fully what it set out to.

Conclusion

At Large Organisation, it was interesting to note that, similar to people in management positions, non-management personnel also had diverse understandings of employee empowerment, ranging from 'culture change', 'having the freedom to decide' and 'not asking for permission from management' to go ahead with tasks. Being enabled to take decisions and having control over their tasks was perceived by a number of non-management employees as creating a feeling of being empowered (Kieffer, 1984; Lashley, 1994). However, as agency workers were excluded from EP, this group of employees clearly felt devalued, demoralised and suffered disempowerment; similar to social workers as reported by Fook (2012: 130): 'When they felt powerless, they were often in situations where they were in an unfamiliar environment and/or felt devalued by others.'

However, it should be noted that several employees in non-management positions in Large and Small Organisations who reported that they felt confident did so whenever they were given responsibility and were able to take decisions and carry out a task to its end by themselves, which has resonance with what Lashley (1996: 335) describes as an 'inner state of empowerment'. This is aptly highlighted by one middle manager, at Small Organisation:

> *I would assume that empowerment would mean that everybody has their own responsibilities to develop the company as a whole … senior management and middle management they are there as a guide, but, everybody has their own ability, the ability is there to develop yourself and to develop the company. (Middle Manager, Small Organisation)*

Thus, there is evidence from both Large and Small Organisations that the notion of empowerment 'comes from within', when participants felt confident that they 'can do' the task.

> *It [empowerment] doesn't mean you are allowed to do this, it means within yourself you know you can do it. (Call Centre Operator, Large Organisation)*

However, this was not the case with regards to agency workers who could not take part in EP and were extremely angry, disappointed and felt let down by Large Organisation. It is worth noting that an issue that has emerged from my research is the situation of agency workers (Hill and Huq, 2001, 2004). Unknown to management, many of whom, as the evidence suggests, may be 'serious victims of disempowerment' (Hill and Huq, 2004).

It is worthwhile noting the psychological implications of locus of control, self-esteem and self-efficacy with regards to employee empowerment at both organisations, irrespective of whether it was via formal or informal methods. This is an enlightening outcome of the research that has come about due to the honest and open nature of the interview responses. From the literature review it is abundantly clear that there is a lack of research regarding the psychological implications of employee empowerment (Chiles and Zorn, 1995; Spreitzer, 1995, 1996; Siegall and Gardner, 2000). Spreitzer (1995: 1462) argues that 'the empirical study of psychological empowerment is in its infancy.' Hence it was deemed necessary to bring attention to this.

The cross-case comparison was extremely valuable – several common patterns emerged as a result of it, despite the contrasting formal and informal approaches to employee empowerment at Large and Small Organisation. It was interesting to note that a number of managers from both Large and Small Organisation were in agreement that power-sharing, giving people responsibility and devolving decision-making actually 'freed up' their time to perform other tasks.

Cross-case comparison was helpful not only in describing patterns and trends, but also in identifying differences. Although looking for common themes across cases is helpful, it is also useful to note that each case may be different (Gable, 1994; Rubin and Rubin, 1995; Johnson and Duberley, 2000) – a relevant point for this study, as the two cases were indeed different, not least because one adopted a formal employee empowerment strategy and the other an informal one.

The honest responses from participants highlight the practical problems that people in both management and non-management positions faced. Furthermore, by drawing upon both the literature reviews (management and social work) and identifying issues and patterns common to the case studies, Large and Small Organisations, it presents a holistic understanding of employee empowerment with regards to a number of issues which both organisations came across.

At Large Organisation, a number of employees felt there were positive benefits due to EP, particularly with regards to increasing their locus of control, self-efficacy and self-esteem, because of participative decision-making and devolution of responsibility. But there were others, such as agency workers, who clearly did not feel any benefits, as they were excluded from the EP programme. In this case, it is important to note that several agency workers experienced low self-esteem and low self-efficacy.

An important revelation that emerged from Large Organisation is the 'plight of agency workers', a number of whom felt that it was not fair that they were always left out of EP events. They described how they felt 'depersonalised' and denied of any status in the organisation. Since it was in the interest of Large Organisation for agency staff to be as productive as possible, then this practice of excluding them from EP was ill-advised and counter-productive.

At Large Organisation, it has already been established that there were major inconsistencies in the perception of EP, because of a lack of proper communication, leading to different interpretations and expectations.

At Small Organisation, as non-management employees, especially factory operatives, were not included in the employee empowerment strategy, even though they did hear about the word 'empowerment', it cannot be said that there were employee empowerment practices on the factory floor, but they certainly felt informed, involved and valued to have access to information about the organisation they worked for. Key middle managers felt empowered through participative decision-making and devolution of responsibility. Interestingly, these managers also remarked that they felt the owner did share power with them, including strategic decisions.

From the remarks of factory floor operatives it is clear that the hygiene factors and the bonus system in Small Organisation had a negative impact on the self-esteem and self-efficacy of employees.

Although there are robust arguments for employee empowerment in the management literature, a number of authors raise concern with regards to the complexities and problems surrounding it. Undoubtedly, there is a lot of tension and potential for conflict surrounding employee empowerment. In Claydon and Doyle's (1996: 23) view: 'Empowerment is therefore no magic bullet providing a unitarist "cure" for organisational "pathologies"', while Hales (2000: 501) expresses concern about 'the divergence between the widespread rhetoric of empowerment and the limited reality of empowerment programmes.' This could lead to significant conflict and tension in organisations. Under these circumstances what is actually achieved by employee empowerment as an organisational strategy? What do employees achieve (if anything)? The analysis of these questions can be 'lessons learned' for future generation of organisations who are keen to implement employee empowerment.

It is understandable that managerial strategies which strengthen employees' self-efficacy beliefs will make them feel powerful while strategies that weaken employees' self-efficacy beliefs will result in feelings of powerlessness.

Evidence from both organisations indicate that people need to be 'treated well' at work and be respected as adults, and not shouted at, as illustrated:

We don't like to be shouted at. (Call Centre Operator, Large Organisation)

If you treat employees well, they will then treat you well and do the work. (Factory Operative, Small Organisation)

Clearly, people are conscious as individuals they are not willing to tolerate oppressive management behaviour or control (Freire, 1972; Huczynski and Buchanan, 2001) or being humiliated or put down by management. There is a danger that professionals, experts or managers can often become obstacles to employee empowerment. The danger is that people who have more power can easily become oppressive.

A study of people conducted by Lord and Hutchinson (1993: 9) who had experienced extensive powerlessness in their lives identified (amongst other things) the importance of personal control and the relationship between empowerment and self-efficacy to be significant. They also point out that: 'No single factor or experience created a sense of powerlessness; rather, it was a build-up of factors and experiences that developed into a disempowering situation.' It is worth noting that feelings of powerlessness do not happen overnight. For people in non-management positions it may be an accumulation of factors and build-up of situations that organisations are often unaware of. Hence, one of the ways for them to engage with management is to create an opening for their views to be heard (Bowen and Lawler III, 1992; Morgaine, 1993; Clement, 1994; Foy, 1994; Collins, 1996a; Bird, 1999; Greenberg and Baron, 2000). From the psychological and motivational point of view, having an opportunity to have a 'voice' in determining how work is done is ranked high as a motivator, as is evident from my case studies.

Interestingly, Greenberg and Baron (2000: 148) conclude: 'When people are denied a voice they believe they should have, they respond negatively – even if the resulting decision is the *same* as it would have been if they had participated.'

Hence, it is important for people, such as agency workers in Large Organisation and factory floor employees in Small Organisation, that their 'voices' can be heard.

An essential point in employee empowerment is that the employees' 'voice' needs to be heard, and it must have an impact on organisational decision-making to enable greater equality of parties. One middle manager in Large Organisation indicated that employee empowerment gave some people a chance for their 'voice' to be heard, which led to an improvement in their self-esteem, self-efficacy and self-confidence.

> *Empowerment gives you more confidence. I think you have more confidence to actually implement some of the ideas and things that you are meant to do, and go and discuss it with people, as to what ways it is going to assist the company, where it is going to improve quality and where it is going to empower people. (Middle Manager, Large Organisation)*

In contrast, psychologically, there is a negative effect of powerlessness which leads people to view themselves as being incapable of having any control in their lives, or of being able to influence others.

There is strong agreement that empowered individuals are more likely to be creative because they feel less constrained in an empowered environment and less bound by rules and regulations (Thomas and Velthouse, 1990; Velthouse, 1990; Peters, 1994; Spreitzer, 1995; Pearson and Chatterjee, 1996). Interestingly, the Chief Executive in Large Organisation realised that a more 'dynamic, energetic approach to business' is needed to encourage innovation and creativity rather than a 'tightly process driven culture'.

Indeed, it was the pressure of global competition that drove Large Organisation to go down the route of encouraging people to come forward with innovative ideas, new and different ways of doing things, as illustrated below:

> *I have been in this organisation longer than most people round this table. I can see a big change, because 5 years or 10 years ago, we weren't encouraged to give ideas. We didn't have an opportunity to give feedback, and I think it is part of the culture here that they (management) now do encourage people to come up with new ideas and different ways of doing things. (Call Centre Operator, Large Organisation)*

However, it is difficult to comprehend what Large and Small Organisations actually achieved from their employee empowerment programmes, as there was a lack of measurement or metrics. Most of the evidence of any benefits is anecdotal evidence only. This is unfortunate, particularly for Large Organisation, as they had invested heavily in their EP programme. One middle manager was upset and angrily pointed out the lack of measurement. In his opinion, Large Organisation missed out on a great opportunity to develop their people and their human resource department.

> *To me [measurement is] what is needed. There is no measurement, no*
> *record, there isn't anything! (Middle Manager, Large Organisation)*

Clearly, both Large and Small Organisations faced complexities and difficulties during the process of employee empowerment. Undoubtedly, there were several issues that needed attention, but Chapters 9 and 10 also highlight some of the rewarding experiences of employee empowerment that employees have had through positive psychological empowerment leading to high locus of control, self-efficacy and self-esteem, in many instances, as expressed by participants themselves.

PART VI
Changing Role of Leaders

Chapter 11
De-Skilling and Re-Skilling

Introduction

One of the biggest challenges for empowered organisations concerns the role of leaders. There are crucial questions that need to be raised. What roles should leaders play? What kind of qualities do they need to have and how should they develop their skills? What are the strategic plans for leadership training in an empowered organisation?

It is generally agreed that there are problems in understanding what leadership is on a general level because leadership can mean different things to different people, and in the context of employee empowerment it is even more complex (Bennis, 1984; Graen and Uhl-Bien, 1995).

There are several unfounded assumptions, such as leaders are automatically empowered, they know what employee empowerment is about and they have ready-made skills to carry out their duties as leaders in an empowered organisation. A review of literature on leadership in the context of employee empowerment has been unsatisfactory. How should leaders lead and enable employees to be empowered? There is inadequate discussion and research in the management literature, yet leadership is critical; it can be the difference between success and failure in the practice of employee empowerment in organisations (Bennis, 1984: 16).

> If I have learned anything from my research, it is this: The factor that empowers the work force and ultimately determines which organisations succeed or fail is the leadership of those organisations.

Leadership is important in an empowered organisation and there is agreement in the management literature that exemplary leadership skills that are empowering include power-sharing, networking, coaching, negotiating, facilitating and enabling (Block, 1987; Conger and Kanungo, 1988; Conger,

1989; Hosking and Morley, 1991; Parker and Price, 1994; Peters, 1994; Staw et al., 1994; Keller and Dansereau, 1995; Honold, 1997; Corsun and Enz, 1999; Heslin, 1999; Koberg et al., 1999; Nesan and Holt, 2002; Cameron and Caza, 2005; Greasley et al., 2005; Ogden et al., 2006; Logan and Ganster, 2007; Joo and Shim, 2010; Silzer and Dowell, 2010; Hashemi et al., 2012; Burke et al., 2014).

The Power-Sharing Conflict

A fundamental problem with regards to employee empowerment is that, in management's view, sharing power with other employees will diminish their own power (Tjosvold et al., 1998). Management is therefore often reluctant to believe, or perhaps fail to understand, that the sharing of power helps to build dynamism and energy in organisations (Murrell, 1985; Morgan, 1986). For example, Murrell (1985: 36) explains: 'to empower is to create power.' Thus, by giving power to employees it does not mean leaders or managers have to lose power, a point that is further elaborated by Lorsch (1995: 109):

> *Power is zero-sum. This is a serious misconception.*
> *... one party (employees) can gain power without the other party (management) losing it.*

Burdett (1991: 23) offers a more pragmatic understanding of power by recognising that there are two primary sources:

> *power legitimately passed by the organisation to an individual, or a team, down the hierarchical chain, and power which employees take as a result of opportunity provided by the organisation or indeed take arbitrarily. The extent and nature of the second scenario lie ultimately with the scope of the opportunity at hand, and the degree to which individuals wish to exercise their option to utilise that power.*

The degree to which individuals in non-management positions 'wish to exercise power' is indeed an opportunity for them, because lower level employees are not entirely without power. The challenge for management is 'raising consciousness' and supporting people in non-management positions to develop their skills in this area. Hellriegel et al. (1989) argue that much of the discussion regarding power tends to focus on the top of hierarchical relationships; in other words the power of leaders over subordinates, but lower level employees also have power, although it may not be apparent.

Indeed, if this is recognised and allowed to flourish, there is enormous potential to unlock employees' energy, innovation and creativity.

Employees possess a great deal more power than is realised (Hellriegel et al., 1989; Neumann, 1992/3). It is therefore a myth to think that subordinates or people in lower level positions do not possess any power at all. Lower level employees may have interpersonal power, including expert power, or knowledge, and this may put them in a position to be able to actually influence their leaders. However, they may not always be aware of this or have the necessary skills to exercise and influence.

In an empowered organisation, leaders need to make sure that decisions regarding day-to-day operations are pushed lower and lower down the organisational hierarchy, and this process of delegating power from higher to lower level employees constitutes decentralisation (Greenberg and Baron, 2000). However, it is crucial that the sharing of power by leaders is not just rhetoric, as Lashley (2001: 160) argues, it is important employees feel that the distribution of power is genuine: 'Thus any attempt to understand empowerment both as a general concept its application in individual contexts, needs to consider the extent to which organisational power has, or has not, been redistributed.'

Hence, on a practical level, for leaders there are obvious difficulties and problems with power-sharing, such as how much power should be shared and with which employees. One of the ways for leaders to play a positive role is to provide the means to 'combat the sources of domination' identified by Hardy and Leiba-O'Sullivan (1998: 475) through sharing power with employees 'to transform those without power into equitable positions' (Denham Lincoln et al., 2002: 273). Many organisations may have contributed to feelings of powerlessness through rigid policies and mechanistic structures, despite the fact that several writers argue that the distribution of power is more important than the hoarding of power (Kanter, 1984; Block, 1987; Conger, 1989; Goski and Belfry, 1991; Martin and Vogt, 1992; Daft, 1999).

Wilkinson (1998) warns that there is a broad range of initiatives that are viewed as employee empowerment programmes with varying degrees of power held by employees, but most of them follow a strict management agenda, and they do not actually allow employees to play a significant role in decision-making. In fact, in many instances, instead of gaining greater power, employees just assume higher levels of accountability (Marchington, 1995; Claydon and Doyle, 1996), and in such cases employees could end up in a worse position than before. Thus, although employee empowerment offers a means of shifting the balance of power in organisations, the fact remains that the redistribution of power may not be leaders' real intention or concern (Denham Lincoln et al., 2002).

It is interesting to note that most leaders in both organisations, Large and Small, particularly Large Organisation, in my case study, struggled with power-sharing. Nevertheless, power-sharing is an important theme of employee empowerment and this is acknowledged in both the management and social work literatures. In the management literature, Lashley (2001: 160) emphasises that 'The power dimension is fundamental to understanding the concept of empowerment and variations in its form and application'. In the social work literature, it is emphasised that lack of power leads to 'disenfranchisement' and 'hopelessness' in individuals (Kieffer, 1984; Parsons, 1991; Breton, 1994; DuBois and Miley, 2005). Furthermore, in the social work literature, it is clearly stated that without the sharing of power there can be no empowerment, as Parsloe (1996: 56) points out: 'It is the conception of power that gives life to empowerment', because without the sharing of power, empowerment in social work is regarded as having no meaning. In this sense, there are implications for leaders and the role that they need to play in an empowered organisation.

However, power-sharing is not straightforward, it is not just handing power down. One of the ways leaders can do this is by removing conditions that foster powerlessness and implement policies and strategies that enable rather than disable employees to attain organisational goals, thus keeping in line with SHRM aims and objectives. There must be strategies to enable employees to be and feel empowered, 'finding creative ways of engaging with people so that empowerment has meaning, so that participants can believe that their values and interests are shaping events, without the stifling interference of elitist, hierarchical or other debilitating influences' (Beirne, 2006: 90).

As mentioned elsewhere, it is crucial that leaders relinquish some of their control over resources and decision-making to other employees, particularly if front-line employees are to be empowered. An essential point to remember is that power should be exercised responsibly at all levels by all people whether they are in management or non-management positions, otherwise the organisation could suffer.

Leadership in Social Work: What Can Be Learned?

In social work, empowerment is viewed to be 'central to social work theory and practice' (Adams, 1996: 3). This is the fundamental difference between empowerment in management and social work, whereby employee empowerment is not central to management theory and practice. Adams (1996: 3) states: 'without empowerment, it could be argued that something fundamental is missing from the social work being practised.'

In the social work literature, the ethos of empowerment is a 'bottom-up' approach, as explained by Kirst-Ashman (2003: 203):

> A 'grassroots, bottom-up approach' means that people at the bottom of the formal power structure, such as ordinary citizens, band together to establish a power base.

In contrast, from the review of the management literature and the findings of this study, it has been observed that employee empowerment is always a top-down management agenda. At Large Organisation, the CEO was passionate about employee empowerment and tried to implement this philosophy to management first, who were then asked to cascade the information down the line. Similarly, at Small Organisation, it was the owner who decided to empower some of his key team leaders, to satisfy the EFQM quality criteria. It is worth noting that collaborating and involving employees at 'grassroots' level, was largely missing in both case organisations of this study, particularly with regards to agency workers in Large Organisation (Hill and Huq, 2001, 2004) and factory operatives at Small Organisation.

Another significant difference is that in social work, the power-sharing theme is given much more importance in the practice of empowerment, than it is in management. Related to this, it is worth noting the theory of empowerment described in the *Dictionary of Social Work*:

> Theory concerned with how people may gain collective control over their lives, so as to achieve their interests as a group, and a method by which social workers seek to enhance the power of people who lack it. (Thomas and Pierson, 1995: 134)

Hence, without the sharing of power, empowerment in social work is viewed as having no meaning. Professionals and service providers in social care must share power with service users, who are at the bottom of the formal power structure, to help them to establish a power base. In this sense, this is considered to be a significant change as far as management and professionals related to the discipline of social work are concerned, whereby service providers share power with service users, as observed by Sheppard (1995: 7): 'giving users and carers greater power and control ... than was previously the case.' Attention to systems and methods to empower service users and to address their powerlessness, has re-emerged as a central theme in social work practice (Guterman and Bargal, 1996).

An important role of social worker is to enable. However, it is important to note from the social work literature, that there are two elements of enablement, one is giving people more control over their lives and the other is to help them exercise this control effectively.

Hence, social workers also have to take the role of facilitators (Kieffer, 1984). Related to this, Beresford and Croft (1993) highlight the need for training, education and support for social workers.

Empowerment in social work is not without problems. It is interesting to note that leaders in social workers also face difficulties and challenges with regards to empowerment. Barriers and resistance to change by different levels of management in social work is not uncommon, as noted by Braye and Preston-Shoot (1995: 111). These authors report that this stems from fear. Leaders and other professionals in social work might suffer fear of loss of status and power. Many professionals, including management, also experience fear of change and uncertainty about the future. Furthermore, top-down bureaucracy has been identified as another organisational constraint (Braye and Preston-Shoot, 1995: Shera and Page, 1995). Related to this, Shera and Page (1995) point out that sometimes the organisational structure in the form of bureaucracy can be a hindrance. This kind of top-down bureaucracy can lead to vulnerability and loss of control and helplessness, not only in employees, but sometimes in leaders as well, leading to powerlessness, which has negative implications for service users at the other end. This has resonance with the management literature where leaders often do not have the authority to share power or devolve decision-making down the line. Thus, leaders in social work may also suffer from powerlessness, and it is important to realise that they too need to be empowered (Stanton, 1990; Shera and Page, 1995; Guterman and Bargal, 1996; Parsloe, 1996).

An important point emphasised in social work is that in order to enable service users to have control over their lives and feel empowered, it is essential that social workers need to feel empowered themselves (Adams, 1996; Guterman and Bargal, 1996). In this sense, the argument is that social workers who feel empowered are more likely to possess the motivation and capacity to enable and help empower other individuals and groups.

It is instructive to note from the social work discipline that enabling is not only about equipping people with skills, but sometimes social workers also have to act as facilitators to help achieve this (Kieffer, 1984). Similarly, leaders in organisations may have to act as facilitators too. In some situations, leaders may need to develop trust and respect, to have faith in others and tolerate mistakes, accept the legitimacy of risk-taking, give responsibility coupled with authority and encourage others to learn (Schein, 1993; Hitt et al., 2006).

Hence, as previously noted, empowerment in social work is not just for service users, it must include everyone, namely employees, leaders, managers and social workers. Sometimes the organisational structure in social work itself can be a hindrance in the distribution of power, just as it is in management. Clearly, there are common problems and difficulties that both management and social work disciplines face.

Leaders Need to Pay Attention to Psychological Empowerment

It has been argued in both disciplines, namely, management and social work, that psychological empowerment of people is necessary. I am using the term 'people' here, because it must be 'psychological empowerment' of all people that work in the organisation and this includes people in management (CEOs, leaders, managers) as well as people in non-management positions.

It is easy to forget that it is not always the marginalised group that needs to be empowered – often the leader or the CEO may have power theoretically, but in practice may be disempowered to use it. By default a promotion to leadership has been made, but the individual may lack in areas of locus of control, self-efficacy and self-esteem. Hence, when in leadership positions, a self-evaluation of their own psychological empowerment is much needed for newly appointed leaders and CEOs. If the leader himself/herself feels disempowered, or does not know what employee empowerment means, then unknown to them the danger is that a disempowering culture and environment may develop. From the SHRM approach, it is important to pay due consideration to this issue, being aware of it and lending more support. Hence, it is important to pay attention to 'the disempowering experience of empowerment' (Fook, 2012: 59).

> *Being given power may not be experienced as empowering, but in fact may have disempowering effects. Despite the best intentions, our empowerment theory does not always translate well into practice. Sometimes, in the attempt to empower, a disempowering climate and culture is set up. (Fook, 2012: 59)*

It is not always recognised that from a psychological point of view, people in leadership and management positions can also suffer from low self-efficacy and self-esteem; just because they are in management or leadership positions does not necessarily mean that they can escape these feelings. Their traditional authority and practice is challenged when they need to achieve 'a loosening of control' over employees, otherwise it can adversely affect them (employees), especially in terms of their self-confidence, self-efficacy and self-esteem (Keller and Dansereau, 1995).

Authors such as Fincham and Rhodes (2005: 430) conclude that traditional organisational hierarchies are 'structures of deeply entrenched power, and this has also proved to be a major constraint on work humanization'. Often, people with power at the top, such as leaders or chief executives, are uncomfortable with changes, and feel so threatened by the fear of losing their control that projects can encounter great resistance, with the result that they are sometimes even dropped. Thus, psychologically: 'Empowerment programmes can be difficult to implement ... because they destroy hierarchies and upset the familiar balance of power' (Daft, 1999: 257).

Power-sharing is fundamental in both disciplines, social work and management. With regards to 'working in partnerships', this ethos of power-sharing is well argued in social work. 'Social workers value working in partnerships with both their clients and their colleagues' (DuBois and Miley, 2005: 6). In this sense, these authors argue that working in partnership psychologically encourages people to put forward their best efforts, as illustrated:

> *It's not likely that you'll do your best when you feel like you're a cog in a wheel, wondering if what you're doing truly matters. It's not likely that you'll contribute fully when you feel subservient, wondering if what you're doing will be judged to be inferior. It's more likely that you'll do your best when you feel appreciated and supported by those with whom*

you work … It's more likely that you'll commit to a project when you
view yourself as a partner in the process. (DuBois and Miley, 2005: 6)

Heslin's (1999: 61) point is valid that empowerment may not be for everyone, and this needs to be acknowledged, as illustrated:

However, empowerment is not for everyone. Staff need to have
developed the capability and self-assurance to assume the extra
responsibilities that empowerment bestows upon them. This often
requires training and the acquisition of relevant skills over time.
Even if staff have these attributes, some people are not interested in
being empowered. For instance, they could view it as an unwanted
source of stress or as a burden of extra work. Staff thus need to be
sufficiently willing able and self-efficacious for empowerment to be
appropriate. Similarly, [leaders or] managers need to have developed
an appropriate level of maturity in any number of areas before they
are able to effectively empower staff.

The problem is that leaders are not trained to facilitate and support their subordinates in relation to employee empowerment. The danger is that disempowered employees can begin to feel disenfranchised, hence Peters (1994: 87) emphasises that the 'central ethical issue in the workplace should be protection and support for people who are unempowered, especially the frontline worker.' Hence, it is imperative that employee empowerment needs to be supported by leaders. Providing resources and training to subordinates are also necessary, as from the social work literature it has been noted that these are also seen as enablers of the empowerment process in practice.

Although empowerment is advocated with regards to professionals, social workers, groups of people and/or communities, the growth of the individual is also considered essential (Rappaport, 1987; Adams, 1990). By providing training and development programmes for leaders they can learn to adopt new roles as coaches, mentors and facilitators. This can help to increase employees' psychological empowerment (Joo and Shim, 2010).

Clearly, at both Large and Small Organisations, several employees would have welcomed more opportunity to take decisions, but they felt that relevant support and opportunities were not created by their leaders to do so. At Large Organisation, many employees felt that when they returned to the workplace, nothing had changed, in reality there was little scope to apply what they had learned, to take decisions or be creative, particularly in the call centres.

Several employees at Large and Small Organisations agreed that empowerment to them meant an increase in self-esteem and self-confidence, because they felt enabled to take decisions and carry out their tasks without managerial approval, which resulted in a high internal locus of control. This resonates with Kieffer's (1984) argument that 'feeling more powerful' is more important than 'having more power' in the political sense. In the social work literature, it is stated that feeling more powerful is important for service users, as people need to gain control over factors whether they are social, political or psychological, which are critical to overcoming feelings of oppression, powerlessness and disempowerment (Rappaport, 1987; Adams, 1990; Breton, 1994). Thus, Sheppard (1995: 31) argues: 'The task of empowerment is to change the individual from their (current) empirical self – who is actually disempowered – to their potential self.' This resonates with Maslow's concept of self-actualisation and suggests that it is the responsibility of leaders to empower other employees to reach their potential so that the organisation achieves the maximum return on its investment in human resources. In other words, even if there is power-sharing, it is still important for leaders to enable employees to feel an inner 'state of empowerment' (Lashley, 1996: 335), whereby the notion of empowerment *comes from within*.

The Role of Leaders: People-Oriented Leadership Style

In Block's (1987) view, the traditional contract between employees and employers is patriarchal in nature and that means high control and submission to authority. In this kind of mindset, the assumption is that employees are not able to complete tasks without constant supervision and if employees are given authority it will be counter-productive for the organisation. Therefore the belief is that authority from the top must constantly be reinforced. Block (1987: 29) describes this as the 'pessimistic view of human nature'.

Clearly, traditional leadership roles need to be questioned and there is a need for clarity regarding the role of leaders in an empowered organisation. Leaders who have patriarchal attitudes and a passion for control will find it difficult to work in an empowered organisation (Block, 1987). An important point worth noting with regards to employee empowerment is that it is bound to have implications for the relationship between leaders and subordinates. Facilitating an employee empowerment culture may not be easy for leaders, particularly if they are coming from a bureaucratic organisation of which they were a part. In such cases, leaders need to learn new ways of behaviour that are compatible with an empowered organisation.

Long (1996: 5) observes: 'The traditionalist view of leadership [management] – that the follower waits to be directed by those in charge – is moribund. The new and most effective leader will be the one who establishes the objectives, clarifies the limits of authority and autonomy and enables individuals to take responsibility for the achievement of the objectives in their own area.'

In order to nurture the growth of the individual, it is vital that leaders adopt a people-oriented leadership style. Referring to the leadership role in social work, the literature review reveals that it may range from being an enabler, facilitator, teacher to resource provider or counsellor, thus they might need to adopt any or all of these roles. From the responses by participants in my case study, it is clear that people-oriented leadership style is desirable in an empowered organisation. It helps to build positive relationships at work, which is an extremely important part of the leader–subordinate relationship at work (Cameron and Caza, 2005).

The results of a study by Koberg et al. (1999) suggest that feelings of empowerment are more likely to be found in a work group with an approachable leader who encourages the worth of the group, that is, their self-esteem, and facilitates group effectiveness rather than a leader who does not. On a psychological level, leaders can boost the performance of their employees by supporting and helping to raise their self-efficacy. So, it is understandable that managerial strategies which strengthen employees' self-efficacy beliefs will make them feel powerful while strategies that weaken employees' self-efficacy beliefs will result in feelings of powerlessness.

There is a growing realisation that as pressures for survival increase, these have an impact on leaders' workload as well. On a psychological level, Heslin (1999) argues that more and more staff need to make decisions and take actions. Furthermore, empowering employees to take responsibility also frees up leaders to concentrate on other things.

It is not in an organisation's interest if leaders are spending excessive time and effort on operational issues rather than strategic ones. Relating to this, leaders need to work closely with the SHRM planning staff, in order to recruit the right talent.

Having people with relevant talent within the SHRM planning is essential (Silzer and Dowell, 2010), making sure people have the ability to work in an empowered organisation. Hammuda and Dulaimi (1997: 294) highlight the role of leaders as one of coach and as an 'Organisational Emancipator', the managerial role becomes one of coach and leader. Newly empowered employees require guidance and someone in a position to rally around them. In this new role, leaders need not make decisions for their employees, but they will provide the structure and framework within which the employees themselves can make 'good decisions'.

It is proposed by Pearlstein (1991) that leaders not only need help to develop their own skills and knowledge necessary for improving their leadership, but they must learn how to develop and encourage empowering behaviour in others. However, there is a lack of knowledge regarding the role that leaders need to play and how they should lead in an empowered organisation. There is a false assumption that all leaders have to do is let employees know that the organisation is going to empower them, and everything should follow, as in the misconception with regards to the case of Large Organisation in my study.

As noted from the review of the management literature, according to Hammer (in Gibson, 1997: 97), what is required is a model whereby employees 'at the front lines' are allocated considerable autonomy and responsibility for decision-making and problem-solving and management exists 'not to direct and control or to supervise, but rather to facilitate and enable'. It is also vital to give due regard to coaching and supporting leaders, as demonstrated at Large Organisation, where lack of training and appropriate support resulted in several team leaders retaining the old style of command and control behaviour. Several employees remarked that management style did not change; as they felt they 'got hammered' for taking decisions, without team leaders' permission. A number of employees also commented that they did not feel leaders had changed from 'cops to coaches'; instead they felt the culture was still strict, highly regimented and policed. In such cases, it was not possible for employees to feel empowered.

A point worth noting with regards to Large Organisation is that the CEO was extremely enthusiastic and fired up with the idea of EP and she wanted all her managers and team leaders to adopt the new culture of employee empowerment with equal eagerness. Perhaps she expected this to happen too quickly, as the owner of Small Organisation cautions: 'one of the downsides of empowerment is when you empower too much too soon ... people don't have the management skills or the actual experience.'

It is also agreed by several authors that these are some of the essential qualities for leaders in an empowered organisation, such as trusting employees and providing positive support (Conger, 1989; Staw et al., 1994; Heslin, 1999); networking, negotiating and enabling (Kouzes and Posner, 1987; Conger and Kanungo, 1988; Thomas and Velthouse, 1990; Hosking and Morley, 1991; Peters, 1994; Long, 1996; Heslin, 1999; Koberg et al., 1999; Lashley, 2001; Cameron and Caza, 2005; Greasley et al., 2005; Beirne, 2006; Logan and Ganster, 2007; McAuley et al., 2007). The argument is that through enabling employees, leaders can create conditions that are motivating, which help employees to be empowered, accomplish tasks and develop their individual competence. Greasley et al. (2005: 363) conclude from their studies: 'By enabling employees the opportunity to make decisions and to feel trusted, it is possible that they can feel empowered.' Through enabling employees, leaders can create conditions that are motivating, which help employees to be empowered, accomplish tasks and develop their individual competence.

Another essential quality for leaders to develop is to practice collaboration (which is viewed as important in social work) if organisations want to go for employee empowerment (Honold, 1997; Appelbaum et al., 1999). Leaders cannot achieve organisational success by themselves; they need to work in collaboration with all employees (management and non-management personnel), that is, 'work jointly' with them to achieve common goals (Sykes, 1976: 196). In such cases, a command and control culture is disempowering and disabling, and thus works against the practice of employee empowerment, as has frequently been seen in Large and Small Organisations in this study.

It is useful to note the meaning of the word 'collaboration' in the social work literature (stated in *The Blackwell Encyclopaedia of Social Work*) as this is another important aspect of empowerment in that discipline: '*Collaboration* refers to working together to achieve common goals' (Davies, 2000: 67). Thus, in social work, collaboration is seen as an active form of working together, 'Collaboration is an active process of partnership in action' (Whittington, 2003: 16). Referring to the importance of collaboration in social work practice, Weinstein et al. (2003: 7) also emphasise that 'collaboration between professionals and with service users and carers is essential to the successful delivery of care services.'

In the context of empowerment, in order to be an empowering leader, leaders need to collaborate with everyone in the organisation (management and non-management personnel) working together 'to achieve common goals'. This applies to managers and team leaders as well. Just by telling people that they are empowered, does not necessarily produce the desired results. In the interest of achieving common goals leaders must collaborate and work together with employees. However, in the management literature, the importance of collaboration has not been emphasised in the context of employee empowerment.

It is also crucial that leaders take a lead in fostering positive relationships at work. In order to do that they need to develop other skills as well, such as coaching, mentoring and providing rewards (Heslin, 1999; Houtzagers, 1999; Lashley, 2001). In this new role, leaders will not be making the decisions for their employees, but they will provide the structure and framework within which the employees themselves can make good decisions. In a similar vein, Wilson (2004: 167) states: 'Potentially empowerment can mean workers take more control over their jobs and working environments.'

Peters (1994) notes that leaders sometimes fail to understand that employee empowerment is not merely about doing things for employees, it is also about removing barriers, thereby enabling employees to empower themselves and this stimulates innovative and creative behaviours in employees. From the psychological point of view, being encouraged to be innovative and creative motivates people at work. It can help employees to get out their routine work and develop their innovative and creative side without fear of retribution; come up with new ideas and new ways of delivering customer satisfaction, thus creating a sustainable competitive advantage. The principal challenge for leaders is to empower people in the organisation so that they are able to take new initiatives and risks on a daily basis (Peters, 1987). 'With the intense pressure of global competition, sustaining market position has become a challenge for organisations' (Peters, 1987: 459).

But being innovative, creative and taking risks is not without its problems; mistakes are bound to happen. Hence, it is important for empowered organisations not only to provide an environment of risk-taking, but also to make sure that employees are encouraged to learn from their mistakes. People cannot be encouraged to take risks without management placing trust in them. Where there is risk involved, trust and confidence in people are vital (Murrell, 1985). Parameters and boundaries for decision-making and risk-taking should be made clear for all employees, including people from management and non-management in the context of direction and clear boundaries.

These arguments with regards to employee empowerment have strong resonance with the SHRM theory and neo-modernist organisation theory which challenges the 'place of the "human" in organisations' (McAuley et al., 2007: 101). Hence, Beirne (2006: 1) aptly argues:

The competitive challenges of thriving in global markets and harnessing rapidly changing technologies put a premium on responsiveness, flexibility and imagination throughout organisations, qualities that are stifled rather than cultivated by rigid job structures and the strict demarcation of tasks and responsibilities. From here, empowerment is a matter of straightforward economics, of acknowledging the potential value in untapped human resources.

Referring to my case study, participants from both Large and Small Organisations also mentioned other qualities of a leader, such as the importance of communication, planning, evaluation and feedback. These combined qualities have the potential of developing leaders who can support an empowering culture in an organisation. Empowering leadership also positively affects psychological empowerment, which in turn influences both intrinsic motivation and creative behaviours in employees (Zhang and Bartol, 2010); thus the growth of the individual is enhanced, the importance of which is strongly emphasised in the SHRM and neo-modernist thinking.

Conclusion

An important point to note is that a complex journey such as employee empowerment cannot be considered without appropriate leadership. In the management literature, although it is agreed that leaders play an extremely important role in empowering people, it does not clarify what kind of qualities or behaviour is expected of them. Hence, there is a lack of role model with regards to leadership in employee empowerment. One of the contributions of my research is that employees want a leader who is people-oriented; they possess skills such as supporting, collaborating and enabling.

Leadership has not been given much attention by either Large or Small Organisation during the employee empowerment initiatives. A noteworthy conclusion of this study is that, given the capitalist nature of organisations towards profit-making, employee empowerment undoubtedly poses a challenging practice for leaders. Those who advocate employee empowerment should not under-estimate the tremendous complexity that surrounds it. It is important to note that, to date, the research findings of this study suggest that employee empowerment may be a much more complex area than many suspect, and the ideology of 'putting people at the heart of the organisation' (McAuley et al., 2007: 101) remains a serious challenge for organisations.

As has already been noted, SHRM emphasises that leaders should pursue policies that increase employee commitment, motivation and flexibility, in place of control and standardisation (Rosenthal et al., 1998). Hence, a number of authors advocate employee empowerment because of its perceived positive psychological benefits for the individual, such as an increase in internal locus of control, an increase in self-efficacy and self-esteem. Furthermore, it is implied in the management literature that employees with high self-efficacy and self-esteem are able to take decisions and solve problems better than those who have low self-efficacy and low self-esteem, thereby freeing up leaders for other operational or strategic duties.

The complexities of employee empowerment have been largely under-estimated and it is clear that organisations struggle with regards to its implementation and practice. Leaders also tend to ignore the psychological implications on employees, which leads to anger and frustration in people. The lack of knowledge regarding what employee empowerment is, has been a fundamental concern in the management literature, and in this respect it is important that leaders are knowledgeable and understand the meaning of employee empowerment. Furthermore, the existence of confusion between employee empowerment and other management initiatives, such as employee involvement and employee participation, may also have contributed to the confusion regarding how to lead in empowered organisations. This book makes an important contribution by reporting the differences between the aforementioned management practices and putting arguments forward that employee empowerment is a construct in its own right with particular themes as in Huq's Model A and B.

The evidence-based findings of my studies also demonstrate that it is essential to have a supportive environment for employees to enable them to feel empowered within themselves, this was something that leaders in Large and Small Organisations were not aware of, and therefore they paid little attention to employees' feelings of self-efficacy, self-esteem and self-confidence. As has already been noted, SHRM emphasises that leaders should pursue policies that enable an increase in 'employee commitment; motivation and flexibility, in place of control and standardisation' (Rosenthal et al., 1998: 170).

The importance of leadership in an empowered organisation cannot be over-emphasised. Developing a people-oriented leadership style that supports employee empowerment is a significant part of the employee empowerment process.

PART VII
Huq's Model of
Employee Empowerment

Chapter 12

Call for a *'Corrective Response'*: Huq's Model of Employee Empowerment

Introduction

Clearly, there is high consensus in the management literature that employee empowerment is necessary for the survival and success of organisations. It is a management response to an increasingly complex and competitive external environment. 'Empowerment is critically important in enabling ... businesses and organisations to survive in this ever-expanding national and international marketplace' (Ripley and Ripley, 1993: 29). In a similar vein, Belasco (1989: 12) states: 'If we are to deal with the serious competitive problems facing our nation, we must change the way we do business. The only way to accomplish this needed change is to empower people to execute change ... The future of our country depends on our ability to become masters of empowerment.' Thus, it is extremely important that organisations seeking to move in that direction should ensure their conceptualisations of 'employee empowerment' at least deliver on these issues.

But, as already discussed there are serious concerns in the management literature with regards to considerable gaps in our knowledge and understanding of a range of issues with regards to employee empowerment; both at the conceptual and practice levels, which have been highlighted throughout this book. Recognising these concerns and guided by the *'kaleidoscope of themes'* (Huq's Model C), this chapter calls for a 'corrective response' to form a new employee empowerment model, which takes into account key themes of employee empowerment from both disciplines, that is, management and social work and furthermore incorporates the psychological implications of locus of control, self-efficacy and self-esteem, leading to psychological empowerment. I have named this new framework of employee empowerment Huq's Model of Employee Empowerment (Huq's Model D), explained in this chapter.

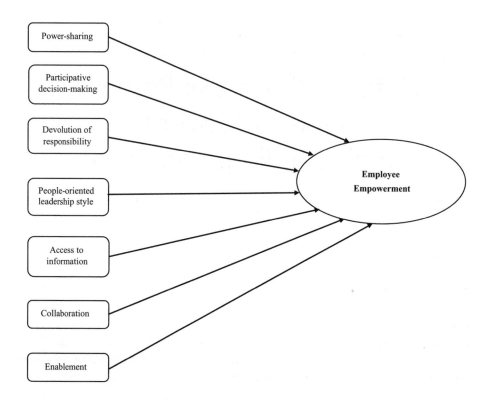

Figure 12.1 **Huq's Model C: a *'kaleidoscope of themes'* of employee empowerment**

Enlightenment: A *'Kaleidoscope of Themes'* (Huq's Model C)

Clearly, the knowledge from the management literature review proved unsatisfactory, hence as explained previously, it was deemed necessary to draw knowledge from another discipline, namely social work (Huq, 2008), where empowerment is an important construct. The perspective of empowerment in social work is different, empowerment is not only viewed as a 'goal for client groups' Frans (1993: 312), but also that 'the practice of empowerment is now a central paradigm' (Adams, 1996: xv). An extensive review of the social work literature on empowerment was highly illuminating, as already discussed in Part II.

Enlightened by the themes of employee empowerment in the management literature (Huq's Model A) and the social work literature (Huq's Model B), it made sense to combine these themes from both literatures, thus creating a synergy between the two disciplines; which I have termed in this book the *'kaleidoscope of themes'* of employee empowerment (Huq's Model C).

Thus, 'kaleidoscope of themes' of employee empowerment comprises the seven themes, namely, power-sharing, participative decision-making, devolution of responsibility, people-oriented leadership style, access to information, collaboration and enablement (Huq's Model C).

Huq's Model C summarises the 'holistic' nature of employee empowerment acquired from the knowledge derived from both management and social work literatures and the findings of my doctorate study. Each 'employee empowerment' theme in Model C has a role to play. It is useful to note Patton's (2002: 62) explanation of the 'holistic point' through an illustration of the story of 'nine blind people and the elephant': 'Each person touches only one part of the elephant and therefore knows only that part. The person touching the ears thinks an elephant is like a large, thin fan. The person touching the tail thinks the elephant is like a rope ... And so it goes. The holistic point is that one must put all of these perspectives together to get a full picture of what an elephant actually looks like.' And, so it is with the 'kaleidoscope of themes' of employee empowerment, Huq's Model C, one must put all of the themes together to get a full picture of what the *employee empowerment elephant* might actually mean at the conceptual and practice levels. Hence, by generating a 'holistic picture' of empowerment some progress can be made.

Thus, Huq's Model C is important, as it sheds light and highlights that the concept of employee empowerment requires a holistic approach and we need to understand employee empowerment through the 'kaleidoscope' of all the aforementioned seven themes.

Call for a '*Corrective Response*':
Huq's Model of Employee Empowerment (Huq's Model D)

In Part I, I tried to unravel the mystery of what employee empowerment is by observing the different ways it has been described in the literature, which was highly enlightening, leading to the 'kaleidoscope of themes' of employee empowerment (Huq's Model C). This multi-disciplinary approach has been extremely valuable, which led me to scope for a new model of employee empowerment and, together with the findings of my case studies, I felt that a 'corrective response' was now needed for an employee empowerment model, which must also take into account the psychological implications of locus of control, self-efficacy and self-esteem, leading to psychological empowerment. This I have named Huq's Model of Employee Empowerment (Huq's Model D), thus, helping to create a much needed platform for psychological empowerment as well.

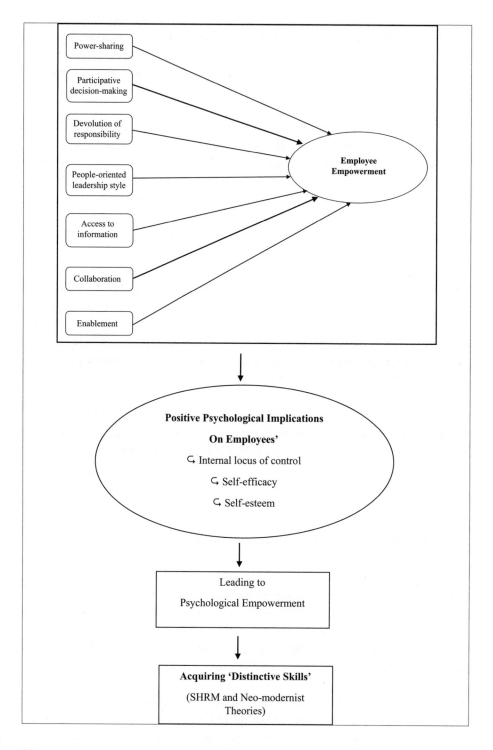

Figure 12.2   Huq's Model of Employee Empowerment (Huq's Model D)

Explanation of Huq's Model of Employee Empowerment (Huq's Model D)

Clearly, in the management literature, there is lack of clarity not only at the conceptual level with regards to the definition of employee empowerment; at the practice level too, concerns are due to lack of appropriate models or frameworks and guidance on how employee empowerment can be introduced and implemented in practice. These gaps need to be filled, as the danger is that organisations may attempt to implement employee empowerment without a clear understanding of what it means, how to implement it and the complexity that surrounds it; as already demonstrated by the examples of the two organisations in my case study, Large and Small.

In Chapter 1, the concern about the lack of appropriate models or frameworks by several authors in relation to how employee empowerment may be implemented and operationalised has been highlighted (Pastor, 1996; Pearson and Chatterjee, 1996; Hammuda and Dulaimi, 1997; Wilkinson, 1998; Siegall and Gardner, 2000; Denham Lincoln et al., 2002). The question is, if organisations want to implement employee empowerment, how do they start? It has been established that lack of knowledge with regards to employee empowerment has been the main barrier to its implementation. Hence, the 'kaleidoscope of themes' (Huq's Model C) is the starting point, if any understanding of employee empowerment is to take place. This comprises the seven themes, from both management and social work literatures, namely, power-sharing; participative decision-making; devolution of responsibility; people-oriented leadership style; access to information; collaboration; and enablement. These are the key characteristics of employee empowerment.

The entry point to employee empowerment can be made through any one (or more) of these themes, or all of the seven themes, according to the readiness, resources and commitment of the organisation's leaders, CEO and employees. There is no hierarchy to these themes, hence it is very user-friendly. Each theme can enable the organisation to get ready for the next theme. So, for example, if an organisation decides to start with the theme of 'participative decision-making' it may also want to enter into the theme of 'access to information' and so on.

Each theme has the potential to positively impact on employees' commitment, mood, performance and task. Furthermore, the aggregate impact of all the themes of employee empowerment as in the 'kaleidoscope of themes'

(Huq's Model C) has the potential to lead to psychological empowerment of people in management and non-management, including leaders.

It is important to look at the whole model that is Huq's Model of Employee Empowerment (Huq's Model D), and take into account the link between the themes of employee empowerment as in the *'kaleidoscope'* and how it influences the psychological implications of employees' locus of control, self-efficacy and self-esteem, leading to talents and 'distinctive skills' that are sought after by organisations as mentioned in SHRM and neo-modernist theories, taking on board the argument in the domain of SHRM (discussed in earlier chapters) that organisations pursuing an employee empowerment strategy actually enable their employees to build up 'distinctive skills' and 'competencies', such as decision-making, problem-solving, taking responsibility. These 'distinctive skills' (Walton, 1999) of employees in turn help the organisation to compete and cope with the changes in the marketplace.

In the neo-modernist paradigm, 'people' play an important role in organisations. Thus, neo-modernism challenges the 'place of the "human" in organisations' and is 'concerned with putting people at the heart of the organisation' (McAuley et al., 2007). Furthermore, from the human resource point of view, neo-modernist theory argues that 'people want to be empowered so they can take responsibility for themselves' (McAuley et al., 2007: 110). So, why should people be deprived of wanting to take responsibility at work and prove that they can add value to the organisation?

However, an important point to note, which is evident from the findings of my case studies, is that, just by introducing the themes as in Huq's Model C, that is the *'kaleidoscope of themes'*, employee empowerment may not necessarily be achieved; management need to be aware that attention to internal locus of control, self-efficacy and self-esteem of employees is also essential. Hence, Huq's Model of Employee Empowerment (Huq's Model D) is important, as it takes into account the aforementioned psychological aspects of employee empowerment. It is worth noting that people come to work not just to earn money, but also to use their skills and 'for a feeling of worth, a sense of dignity' (Wilson, 2004: 65). This has resonance with Maslow's (1943) conceptualisation of human needs in organisations, whereby people progress from basic needs to personal development and growth needs, namely, self-esteem and self-actualisation needs.

Gandz (1990: 78) states that, 'Most employees want to be empowered to contribute to their roles. The task of management is to develop the framework within which this process can occur.' But, the dangers of practising employee empowerment without an adequate knowledge base is unsafe; it is confusing for employees, both at the management and non-management level and counter-productive for organisations, as they do not achieve what they set out to achieve by going down the employee empowerment route. Hence, my argument, that *leaders need a framework within which the empowerment process can take place*. It is essential that whoever is responsible for the implementation of the employee empowerment programme in organisations has adequate knowledge and is willing to share this knowledge in order to build a planned strategy, with relevant team leaders, to be able to cascade down the information and strategic plan at all levels of the organisation to include everyone.

Thus, Huq's Model D is a holistic approach to empowering employees and an opportunity to engage people more closely with the concept of employee empowerment through the *'kaleidoscope of themes'* and enabling them to acquire psychological empowerment. In the post-modern world, it is hoped that Huq's Model of Employee Empowerment (Model D) will help organisations understand and implement employee empowerment with some success rather than trying to implement it without a model at all!

Creating a Platform for Psychological Empowerment

The philosophy behind Huq's Model of Employee Empowerment (Huq's Model D) is to create a platform where people's 'voice/s' can be heard, creating the path to psychological empowerment.

Based on the information with regards to employee empowerment provided by the two literatures (management and social work) and together with the evidence from my case studies, a positive impact on employees' locus of control, self-efficacy and self-esteem can lead to psychological empowerment, which is one of the desired results of employee empowerment.

Several participants during my interviews alluded to the importance of the psychological implications of employee empowerment; that is, locus of control, self-efficacy and self-esteem with regards to their lives at work. Participants explained that, in particular, when they were able to take decisions related to their task at work, they felt in control and a rise in their confidence, leading to high self-esteem, and vice versa. According to Snape and Spencer (2003: 14): 'If several reports confirm a statement then it can be considered true as a representation of a socially constructed reality.'

A number of authors are also of the opinion that attention to internal locus of control, self-efficacy and self-esteem of individuals is important, because these experiences help to shape how individuals view themselves in relation to their work environments (Spreitzer, 1995; Holt et al., 2000). In Holt et al.'s (2000: 48) view:

> *empowerment is not an act or physical incident. It is employees'*
> *perception that they believe in and (really do) control what happens*
> *to their work processes, and that they are capable of controlling those*
> *processes efficiently and effectively. Employees' cognitive growth controls*
> *their fundamental behaviour towards their work environment, so positive*
> *perception becomes an integral part of successful empowerment.*

It is interesting to note with regards to the power-sharing theme that instead of power in the political sense, the majority of employees at Large and Small Organisations desired more power and control over their working lives (Huq, 2010). In this sense, it is useful to highlight Beresford and Croft's (1993: 50) definition of empowerment in the social work literature, which is 'making it possible for people to exercise power and have more control over their lives.' It is enlightening from my case studies that this kind of power is about having control over one's work and being able to take work-related decisions, which was considered important; interestingly this has resonance with social work literature. It was also perceived by employees to have a positive effect on their locus of control, self-efficacy and self-esteem, which made employees feel confident to perform their tasks and take decisions in their work situations confidently.

Conger and Kanungo (1988) conclude from their studies that employee empowerment has positive implications on employees' internal locus of control. In this context, Wilson (2004: 167) notes: 'Potentially empowerment can mean workers take more control over their jobs and working environment. They should be able to enhance the contributions they make as individuals and members of a team and also seize opportunities for personal growth and fulfilment.'

The above arguments demonstrate that it would be instructive for management to pay attention to employees' internal locus of control, self-efficacy and self-esteem in the context of employee empowerment to enable them to develop their potential. This has resonance with SHRM and neo-modernist theories discussed in Chapter 1. Illustrated below is the point of view of neo-modernists:

> *The neo-modernists are interested in ways in which the values and beliefs*
> *of people shape and are shaped by their experience of organisational life.*
> *This leads to their interest in organisation culture, in the ways that*
> *organisations 'need' to be designed around people and in understanding*
> *processes of change. (McAuley et al., 2007: 101)*

However, it is important that employees must also be given the opportunity and support by management to use their skills effectively, otherwise this could have a negative impact on the internal locus of control, self-efficacy and self-esteem of individuals. For example, in Large Organisation, lack of opportunity and the conditions to use employees' skills and talents had a negative impact, as illustrated previously:

> *it really is vital, if we think that we can't take decisions and we really*
> *wanted to, do we really want to work for that kind of company? On*
> *a personal level if I wanted to do something, I think I really should*
> *be able to do it and then they [managers] say 'no, we don't want*
> *you to be doing that', well fair enough, you obviously don't want*
> *the talents that I have, so I will go and find [another employer] who*
> *might appreciate me and give me the opportunity to [take decisions].*
> *(Call Centre Operator)*

A number of employees in Large Organisation complained that they felt frustrated because they were not able to make full use of their abilities, talents and knowledge, simply because a number of managers did not adhere to the EP principles of allowing employees to take decisions and responsibility. Clearly, it is essential for management to create the conditions and opportunity to develop and enhance their talented employees, particularly those that are able and willing to use their own initiative to be creative, take responsibility and make suitable decisions.

What is highly interesting is that evidence from the interviews at Large and Small Organisations demonstrate that employees strongly felt the theme 'enablement' to be essential in employee empowerment (which is a theme drawn from the social work literature). Similarly, other studies have also shown that 'high levels of worker control over decision making are associated with high levels of psychological well-being and job satisfaction' (Parker and Price, 1994: 911). In the words of Conger (1989: 18): 'individuals believe themselves powerful when they feel they can adequately cope with environmental demands – that is, situations, events, and people they confront. They feel powerless when they are unable to cope with these demands.' In other words, the inner state of empowerment is about *feeling more powerful* rather than having more power in the political sense (Huq, 2010). This has implications from the psychological perspective on employees' internal locus of control, self-efficacy and self-esteem as Lashley (1994: 2) argues: 'the effectiveness of empowerment as an employment strategy will be determined by the perceptions, experiences and feelings of the "empowered". Fundamentally, these feelings will be rooted in a sense of personal worth and ability to effect outcomes: of having the "power" to make a difference.'

It is noteworthy to draw attention to the situation of agency workers who perceived themselves as victims of disempowerment and had no 'sense of personal worth', as highlighted at Large Organisation (Hill and Huq, 2001, 2004). There are potential dangers in empowering some employees and not others. Agency workers in Large Organisation, did not feel psychologically empowered, as they were suffering from a loss of self-efficacy and self-esteem because they were not allowed to take part in the EP employee empowerment programme. They felt extremely angry, disappointed and let down by the organisation because they were treated like 'outcasts'. This resulted in low self-confidence, self-efficacy and self-esteem amongst a number of them, who felt marginalised and of little value.

Clearly, agency workers felt a considerable loss of self-confidence and control at work. From the social work literature it has already been noted that people need to have some control over their lives, whether social, political or psychological, and this is critical to overcoming feelings of helplessness, powerlessness and disempowerment (Kieffer, 1984; Parsons, 1991; Breton, 1994). Agency workers represent a large category of workers globally, to which relatively little research attention has been paid – despite the fact that their services are widely used in industry and commerce. Thus, employee empowerment initiatives may not deliver the desired results, unless employees themselves feel empowered, 'you feel you can decide ... you feel empowered to make a decision' (Office Administrator, Large Organisation).

On a practice level, evidence from my case studies demonstrate that individuals or groups are not empowered unless they believe themselves to be so. Several participants reported that empowerment comes from within. This has resonance with Kieffer's (1984) study, where participants did not view themselves as having more power, but rather as feeling more powerful. There are other parallel examples of this in my case studies too. For example, at Large Organisation, call centre operators at one of the sites did not view themselves as 'having more power', but they did view themselves as 'feeling more powerful', which in turn raised their self-efficacy and self-esteem. This is aptly illustrated by Siegall and Gardner (2000: 705):

> *While one can change attitudes by first shaping behaviours, we believe that the true benefits of empowerment (however defined) will not be seen unless people first perceive themselves as being empowered. For example, if a person has the organisation's 'permission' to act autonomously but does not believe that she or he has the capability of acting effectively, then the autonomy will not result in improved outcomes for either the organisation or the person.*

The overriding goal of social work activity is to enable people to overcome conditions that hinder them from participating in order to better their lives. This may be on a social, political or psychological level, but is critical to overcome feelings of helplessness and disempowerment (Kieffer, 1984; Parsons, 1991; Breton, 1994).

Psychological empowerment not only paves the way for employees to develop their ability to empower themselves, enhance their locus of control, self-efficacy and self-esteem; it also needs to be highlighted that it has the potential to develop the abilities of leaders to reframe, de-skill and re-skill, enabling them to achieve psychological empowerment too, as there may be cases when leaders in organisation lack self-efficacy and self-esteem. Just because people are in management or leadership positions, it does not necessarily mean that they automatically feel psychologically empowered. Thus, Huq's Model D is an attempt to help create a much needed platform for psychological empowerment for everybody – whether they are in management or non-management positions.

Conclusion

In this book I have attempted to raise awareness that employee empowerment requires organisations to address a number of themes and related to this argument I have presented a *'kaleidoscope of themes'* (Huq's Model C), namely, power-sharing, participative decision-making, devolution of responsibility, people-oriented leadership style, access to information, collaboration and enablement, which led to creating the framework for employee empowerment which I have offered in this book called Huq's Model of Employee Empowerment (Huq's Model D).

I have discussed the extent to which Large and Small Organisations addressed these aforementioned themes of employee empowerment (or not), in their employee empowerment strategies and practices. In this summary report, below, is a re-visit to the themes of employee empowerment, as in the *'kaleidoscope of themes'* (Huq's Model C), namely, power-sharing, participative decision-making, devolution of responsibility, people-oriented leadership style, access to information, collaboration and enablement.

POWER-SHARING

Power-sharing was mere rhetoric in both Large and Small Organisations. In reality, power-sharing did not take place. At Large Organisation, senior management still liked to hold onto their power; while middle management grappled with how to share it, and how much to share. At Small Organisation, although the owner shared some power with key middle managers, those whom he chose to empower, he still retained power and control with regards to any strategic decisions affecting the organisation.

PARTICIPATIVE DECISION-MAKING

At Large Organisation, there was a genuine desire from senior management to devolve decision-making down the line, however, there was inconsistency in practice; for example, agency workers were not included. Furthermore, the extent of participative decision-making varied in different sites and depended on the attitudes and behaviours of managers concerned. At Small Organisation, the owner was keen to devolve decision-making to key middle managers and a few team leaders, but not to all employees, particularly factory operatives.

DEVOLUTION OF RESPONSIBILITY

At Large Organisation, there were efforts to devolve responsibility down the line, but the problem again was that it did not include all employees, and again it depended on the site and the attitudes and behaviours of managers concerned. At Small Organisation, responsibility was devolved to key middle managers and a few team leaders, but not to factory floor operators.

PEOPLE-ORIENTED LEADERSHIP STYLE

In theory, the CEO of Large Organisation wanted managers to adopt a people-oriented leadership style. The emphasis regarding management was that they must move away from 'enforcement and control' and from 'cops to coaches', via four styles of behaviour, namely 'Directing, Coaching, Supporting and Counselling'. But, not everybody embraced this; some managers simply did not want to change. So, in practice this remained rhetoric, far from being widely practised. At Small Organisation, the owner allowed freedom and flexibility only to key managers, but retained a command and control style of management with non-management employees.

ACCESS TO INFORMATION

At Large Organisation, through the use of the internet and intranet, access to information was encouraged. But, most employees did not equate this with EP. At Small Organisation, through the use of newsletters, regular weekly and fortnightly meetings and employee suggestion schemes, the owner tried to keep his employees informed and involved, but only key middle managers had open access to information, when they needed it.

COLLABORATION

The lack of collaboration in Large and Small Organisations has been surprising. Since both organisations were winners of the EFQM Excellence Award, at European and other levels, they would have had to address employee empowerment in a serious manner, as they would have been assessed in relation to it. Yet, there was strong evidence to demonstrate that there was little or no collaboration with non-management employees concerning employee empowerment. It is instructive to learn from the social work literature that the practice of empowerment in that context is largely based on collaboration between social workers and service users. But, collaboration in the context of employee empowerment was not found to be the case in Large and Small Organisation.

At Large Organisation, the CEO admitted there was very little collaboration with management, let alone employees in non-management positions, with regards to employee empowerment, prior to the implementation or during introduction of it in the organisation. Senior and some middle management were told about the employee empowerment (EP) programme, but that was hardly collaboration.

At Small Organisation, although the owner collaborated with his key middle managers with regards to the submission of the EFQM Award, there was no collaboration with other employees in management and particularly non-management employees, such as factory floor operatives, who had no idea that the organisation was practising employee empowerment at all or applying for the EFQM Quality Award.

ENABLEMENT

At Large Organisation, the espoused enabling behaviours, such as directing, coaching and supporting by leaders, were not evident in practice. On the contrary, most employees felt a lack of support and trust to get on with their jobs without seeking permission from their superiors. At Small Organisation, only a handful of key middle managers felt that they were enabled and supported and given freedom to carry out their tasks, but this was not felt by all employees in management and non-management positions.

It has already been noted that lack of knowledge about what employee empowerment is, has led to a significant gap with regards to information about how to implement it. Pearson and Chatterjee (1996: 17) highlight: 'Overall, a great deal of interest has been shown for how empowerment works rather than how to make it work.' Furthermore, management has not paid attention to the impact such a radical change as employee empowerment might have on employees and the organisation. Hence, in practice: 'its application in organisational settings is fraught with misunderstanding and tension' (Denham Lincoln et al., 2002: 271), leading to a frustration amongst managers (Ford and Fottler, 1995: 22). This is evident from my case studies. Lack of knowledge with regards to employee empowerment, what it means and how it should be implemented, created a considerable confusion between management and non-management personnel, particularly at Large Organisation.

There was a significant mismatch between senior management's expectations and perceptions in relation to employee empowerment, and those of management and non-management personnel, at Large Organisation. For example, middle managers complained that senior managers did not live up to their expectations, particularly with regards to their promises of power-sharing. In their view, senior managers still liked to hold on to their power. This is in sharp contrast to the perception of senior managers, who claimed that they had no problems sharing power with their subordinates. Non-managerial employees complained that despite the rhetoric of EP, Large Organisation was reverting back to the old ways of 'command and control', in contrast to the perception of senior managers, who claimed that there was 'flexibility and freedom' in the organisation. Related to this, a concern highlighted by Beirne (2006: 81) is that employee empowerment can sometimes 'offer an impression that progressive management is at work, yet fail seriously to challenge, or regularly slip back to, more conventional values and command structures.'

At Small Organisation, the owner adopted a severely constrained approach to employee empowerment, whereby he empowered some of the middle managers, but none of the non-managerial employees. As explained, factory floor operatives were not aware that the organisation was actually pursuing employee empowerment practices.

A consequence of the differing conceptualisations of employee empowerment is that the many definitions that flow from them, and which have differing foci and emphases, tend to add to the confusion and ambiguity with regards to the meaning of employee empowerment. In order to reduce the conceptual ambiguity of employee empowerment and its confusion with various management practices, theoretical development and a model for practical application of employee empowerment is important. It is hoped that my proposed framework, Huq's Model of Employee Empowerment (Huq's Model D) will provide a useful base and tool for the practical application of employee empowerment.

On a cautionary note, when organisations are contemplating the implementation of employee empowerment, leaders need to educate themselves appropriately and communicate definitions and explain meanings, otherwise employees will not only challenge the inevitable ambiguity but may also develop their own definitions of employee empowerment. Leaders need to educate other team leaders and managers in their organisation to cascade the knowledge and information to all departments.

Leaders in organisations thus have a responsibility to create a conducive environment that encourages and supports education and learning for everyone and fosters the ability and talents of people, leading to psychological empowerment. Individuals with high self-esteem, self-efficacy and self-confidence are valued resources for an organisation.

Epilogue

Within the context of intense global competition, it has been established that organisations are constantly seeking new sources of competitive advantage. In line with this argument, I have pointed out that employee empowerment came to prominence as a management response to rapid economic and technological change and an increasingly complex and competitive external environment. Increasing market competition and the need to comply with quality standards and award criteria, have forced organisations to think of ways to meet these demands. As discussed, one of the ways many organisations choose to do this is to empower their employees. However, I have pointed out the problem is that leaders in organisations are introducing employee empowerment without fully understanding what it means or what they are committing themselves to. Furthermore, in the absence of a 'framework', they also face difficulties with regards to implementing it.

This book has drawn attention to a number of significant points related to the topic of employee empowerment, which has been subjected to relatively little empirical investigation. In this book, I have shared the findings of the case studies of my research, which is highly interesting with regards to the two organisations, Large and Small, which took different approaches to employee empowerment; the former a formal one and the latter informal. Through an interpretive approach, qualitative interviewing allowed me to capture the richness of people's experiences of employee empowerment in their own words. It enabled me to gain deeper understanding of what it means to feel 'empowered' or 'disempowered'. Relevant quotes, and an 'interpretive approach', in Part IV, provided an opportunity for the 'voice' of interviewees to be heard.

The 'interpretive approach' with regards to organisational research has been gaining attention. The rationale for this is that social reality is something that is constructed and interpreted by people. Denscombe (2002: 18) argues:

> From the interpretivist's point of view the social world does not have the tangible, material qualities that allow it to be measured, touched or observed ... It is a social creation, constructed in the minds of people and

reinforced through the way people believe in it, relate to it and interpret it. And for this reason, interpretivists tend to focus their attention on the way people make sense of the world and how they create their social world through their actions and interpretations of the world.

In line with this, Banister et al.'s (1994: 74) point is instructive, that is, 'If our aim is to understand someone, then we must gain understanding from within that person, empathize with them, get to know their story, explore their social world through their frameworks.' Hence, as my study was concerned with people's personal experience of employee empowerment, qualitative methods were appropriate in order to 'capture the richness and diversity of human experience' (Sommer and Sommer, 2002: 221); thus purposely avoiding fitting people's experiences into any 'predetermined standardized categories' (Sommer and Sommer, 2002: 221).

The triangulation of data (perceptions of employee empowerment held by senior managers, middle managers and people in non-management positions) helped me to delve into people's experiences and feelings of employee empowerment from different perspectives, namely, senior management, middle management and non-management. As McLeod (2001: 2) states, the aim of qualitative research 'is to develop an understanding of how the world is constructed' and this notion implies that 'we inhabit a social, personal and relational world that is complex, layered and can be viewed from different perspectives' (McLeod, 2001: 2). It is worth remembering the rationale behind triangulation, which according to Smith (1996: 193) is that 'if you use a number of different methods or sources of information to tackle a question, the resulting answer is more likely to be accurate.'

An important point to note is that the actual experiences of employees should not be under-estimated, as reflected in D'Annunzio-Green and Macandrew's (1999: 277) conclusions from their studies: 'This company may not have arrived at their expected destination, but the value of the journey to get there should not be underestimated.' Both Large and Small Organisations derived considerable value from their attempts at employee empowerment, specifically with regards to the psychological implications, for example, increasing employees' internal locus of control, self-efficacy and self-esteem. These are noted to be paramount in the empowerment of both service users and social workers in the social work literature.

Indeed, for many employees it was a life-changing experience, especially for those who had never exercised their 'voice' before. This has strong resonance with the social work literature, where empowerment enables service users to have a 'voice' in the kinds of services that they believe meet their needs and not what 'experts' think the needs of service users should be (Breton, 1994; Mattaini et al., 1998; DuBois and Miley, 2005). Some employees realised their own potential for the first time, for example one call centre operator at Large Organisation who had never taken any decisions before, remarked with great enthusiasm: 'I didn't realise I could do this!' An important point to note is that people do have a 'voice' but they do not realise that they can use their 'voice'. In this respect, empowerment can enable people for their 'voice' to be heard and develop their ability to help themselves.

There were also attempts to remedy working conditions and improve motivation at work, at Large and Small Organisations. In this sense, another value of the employee empowerment journey is that 'Some remediation of problems in managing the employment relation is certainly better than nothing at all' (Wilkinson, 1998: 53). It is interesting to note the two different strategies pursued by the case study organisations. At Small Organisation, employee empowerment was an informal strategy that included a few key middle managers. Interestingly, not all of them agreed with the owner with regards to this method of excluding non-managerial employees and factory operatives from the employee empowerment strategy. This kind of situation where one group of employees is empowered, and others are not, can create doubt in the latter group about their capability to achieve their tasks, and hence disempowered employees can also easily become demoralised and demotivated (Heslin, 1999).

With regards to the formal employee empowerment programme, EP, at Large Organisation, there was a lack of communication in disseminating the information. The aims and objectives of EP, which was meant to be about empowering employees, were not communicated properly and, as reported, in some cases were not communicated at all. This created confusion and lack of understanding, as one middle manager pointed out: 'I think it [empowerment] is a very difficult word. Firstly, it is very difficult to define and secondly, everybody seems to define it in their own terms.' Most employees had their own interpretation of EP. They did not know what its aims and objectives were, as the CEO confessed: 'If there is a weakness – we didn't spend sufficient time getting it clear in the manager's head exactly what it was we are trying to achieve [through EP].' Even managers realised that there were significant problems in the implementation of EP, as illustrated:

> *I'm not sure that people always understand and appreciate why EP*
> *is being done and what's it all about. That may possibly be partly our*
> *fault of getting the message across. (Middle Manager)*

There is the danger that employee empowerment can be interpreted by employees in different ways, not only within but also across different hierarchical levels, which can lead to the danger of employees assuming a meaning of employee empowerment which is different to that intended by management. This has the potential to create confusion with regards to the boundaries of employees' decision-making authority and the potential for conflict. Hence, there is a need to set clear definitions and boundaries.

The lack of a shared understanding regarding employee empowerment was disabling Large Organisation, as it did not achieve what it could have potentially achieved via EP. Managers were supposed to cascade the programme, but it seems their temperament was *mercurial* in nature, as their enthusiasm with the EP programmes went up and down. For a short while, some managers allowed employees to take decision and then they took that power away. As one participant remarked, 'nothing really changed'.

This curious situation at Large Organisation may well be due to the *'laissez-faire'* approach to implementation, whereby senior managers only communicated the aims and objectives of EP to middle managers, who were then left to their own devices to implement it (or not). Undoubtedly, employee empowerment brings about enormous changes in organisations. In this sense, it is instructive to note the arguments put forward by Argyris (1998: 201), 'when change programmes are imposed without recognising the limitations of empowerment and when managers and employees are not helped to deal effectively and openly with them, the organisation ends up worse off than it was to begin with.'

There is general agreement in the management literature that the traditional management model, of the manager being in control and employees being controlled, is moribund. 'Command and control' methods are becoming unsustainable in organisations, particularly in the developed world, as they do not give employees a 'say' and 'control' over their own work situations. It is also agreed that organisational effectiveness derives from judicious utilisation of human resources (Siegall and Gardner, 2000). Hence, if leaders empower their employees, for example, to have more control over their work, take decisions and responsibility at the operational level, this will free leaders to take decisions and responsibilities at the strategic level, which in turn would lead to a more judicious utilisation of human resources at all levels. Furthermore, from the human resource point of view, neo-modernist theory argues that 'people want to be empowered so they can take responsibility for themselves' (McAuley et al., 2007: 110).

However, setting employee empowerment within the right context and through proper communication is important. Hammuda and Dulaimi (1997: 289) state: 'Any company that cannot deliver to its customers the product and service with better quality, and at a faster pace and a lower price than that of its global competitors may soon be out of business.'

There is a context in which employee empowerment operates, so individuals need to be aware that they just cannot say 'well, you told me that I was empowered, so I do not need to tell anyone what I am doing'. Hence, this is important for leaders in organisations to note that they need to teach and educate their employees to understand that employee empowerment requires employees to recognise where the limits are and to take responsibilities for their actions.

It is also essential to realise that just by saying employees are empowered or giving employees autonomy alone will not lead to a person feeling empowered. Employees need to feel they are capable, competent and psychologically empowered. The Model of Employee Empowerment, Huq's Model D, highlights the importance of the psychological implications of employees' locus of control, self-efficacy and self-esteem, leading to a platform for psychological empowerment. Related to this, the plight of agency workers is another significant contribution of my case study; this group of employees has been identified as not only being seriously disempowered, but also in danger of being exploited (Hill and Huq, 2001, 2004). If organisations employ agency workers and they are to derive an optimal output from them, they need to give due regard and include them in employee empowerment programmes. There are potential dangers in empowering some employees and not others, especially if they are keen to take on responsibility and decisions in organisations.

At Large Organisation, for example, agency workers suffered a significant amount of powerlessness, which has the potential for discrimination in organisations (Hill and Huq, 2001, 2004). Several agency workers genuinely wanted to take part in EP, but they were ignored. Agency workers felt devalued and suffered considerably from low self-efficacy and low self-esteem because they were not included in any EP activities. Indeed, agency workers may be serious victims of disempowerment and open to exploitation. Parallel to this, at Small Organisation, non-management employees and factory floor operatives were not even allowed a 'voice' to express their opinions about empowerment and so they too may be victims of disempowerment.

In fact, the disempowering effect comes from people's feelings when they feel change is impossible. It is worth noting Kieffer's (1984) point that when people feel powerless, they lose their sense of control. Ethically, Peters (1994: 87) emphasises that the 'central ethical issue in the workplace' should be protection and support for people who are unempowered, 'especially the frontline worker.' However, leaders should remind people that with power-sharing comes responsibility. Interestingly, from the social work literature review, with regard to responsibility, it is enlightening to know that an important aspect of social workers' responsibility in bringing about empowerment is to develop clients' potential so that they are able to get their needs met. This helps the process of self-help. Based on the concept of self-help, empowerment can enable people to work towards helping themselves and others to maximise the quality of their lives and to achieve their goals (Adams, 1990). Psychologically, people feel good when they do have power to take decisions that directly affect their jobs. For example, a key middle manager in Small Organisation highlighted the fact that they had the power to go ahead and take decisions made them feel that they were not 'just a number' in the organisation, which has resonance with DuBois and Miley's (2005) 'cog in a wheel' description.

It is also true to say that not everybody has the same motivation to be empowered, as Neumann (1992/3: 26) points out: 'While some employees welcome the job variety and opportunities for training implied by empowerment, many employees do not demonstrate a willingness to be empowered.' It is worth noting that there are likely to be differences among employees, as not all employees have the same need for power. Further, 'years of experience of being powerless' can lead to difficulties, as Lashley and McGoldrick (1994: 34) note: 'Employees who have years of experience of being powerless may have major difficulties in accepting the new responsibilities placed on them.'

An interesting point to note is that the owner at Small Organisation claimed that non-management factory operatives did not want to be empowered, 'They don't understand the word [empowerment] … The majority of people want to go to work to do an honest day's work for an honest day's pay.' However, Beirne (2006: 82) cautions:

While the expression 'we're only in it for the money' can regularly be heard from workers, there is evidence that it does not represent a full or decisive view, or provide a reliable guide to behaviour. It is, in some cases, a defence mechanism, an internalised way of dealing with regimes that treat them as little more than 'pairs of hands' with no worthwhile brains to support a creative contribution. Consequently, people can warm to initiatives when they feel it safe to take them seriously.

Hence, before organisations rush into empowering their employees it is worth paying heed to cautionary warnings such as 'they need to determine whether and how empowerment fits their situation' (Bowen and Lawler III, 1992: 39). Organisations also need to be aware of the tension and conflict that could be created by empowering some groups and not others.

SHRM theory states that organisational effectiveness derives from 'judicious utilisation' of all human resources; and all organisational members need to be engaged and active for a company to be successful (Siegall and Gardner, 2000). This was not the case in either Large or Small Organisations, by excluding a number of people from employee empowerment, the case organisations in this study did not 'judiciously utilise' their human resources effectively. In this case, it is instructive to note from the social work literature: 'Growing in confidence and becoming better informed are both powerful means to empowerment for people who have felt burdened and diminished' (Wilson, 1995: 85). It is also worth noting Kirst-Ashman's (2003: 203) point from the social work literature, that empowering people needs a 'bottom-up' approach and it also needs collaboration with the lowest levels of employees.

Another serious flaw was that no metrics were put in place, nor any evaluation carried out with regards to what impact employee empowerment might be having at Large and Small Organisations; this seems particularly remiss at Large Organisation, where significant resources had been allocated to EP.

Thus, lessons learned from the interview responses via evidence from the two case studies offer rich and practical examples of people and situations of what works and what does not, with regards to both formal and informal ways of employee empowerment. Related to this, Beirne (2006: 84) points out:

Post-mortem studies and accounts of schemes that have faltered or backfired are especially useful, marshalling evidence that can help practitioners to anticipate contradictory tendencies, acknowledge contrasting interests, [and] appreciate genuine concerns.

It is true that leaders sometimes struggle with 'the delicate balance in giving employees control over their own work processes without at the same time losing control over what employees do' (Ford and Fottler, 1995: 22). Hence, the ability to retain the balance between power and control is a real challenge for organisations in implementing employee empowerment practices. It is important to remember that the distribution of power and the exercise of control is not the same in every company: 'the ability of managers to exercise this control varies within different organisational and cultural contexts' (Davies and Mills, 1999: 175).

At Small Organisation, the majority of employees had not even heard the word 'empowerment', and were unaware that this was practised in the organisation. In this sense, this study supports the views of Denham Lincoln et al. (2002: 288) that, 'In terms of management policy, our view is that organisations should either stop using the term (employee empowerment) and spare their employees the disillusionment, or explain clearly and honestly what they do and do not mean by it.' This argument gains support when one considers employees' responses at Large and Small Organisations. In the former case, many employees had been quite enthusiastic about the EP programme and the events in which they had participated. However, they were disillusioned by the fact that when they returned to the workplace 'nothing changed'. In contrast, at Small Organisation, where the term 'employee empowerment' was not used, there was little indication of employee disillusionment.

At Large Organisation, employees were disillusioned by the inconsistency of practice at different sites and the lack of collaboration and support from managers. These findings would appear to be in keeping with the contingency view of new forms of work organisation articulated by Geary (2003: 399) as illustrated:

> New forms of work organisation, it is argued, do not have uniform effects but are likely to be contingent on a series of factors, such as the manner in which change is introduced, whether employees and their representatives are involved, employees' prior experiences and expectations, whether any provision is made for employment security, and the extent to which human resource policies are adapted to support their introduction.

An interesting finding of my study is that even in organisations adept in the use of TQM and the EFQM Excellence Model, employee empowerment may have little to do with power or its redistribution. Furthermore, a number of employees in the case organisations of my study, did not appear to seek more power in the political sense, but more discretion and responsibility for decision-making and control over their own work situations, which has resonance with the social work literature. Participants wanted greater scope for utilising their capabilities which is perceived to have an increase in internal locus of control, self-efficacy and self-esteem of employees (Huq, 2010). In this sense, Gutierrez (2001: 210) defines empowerment not only as the process of increasing 'political power' but also as increasing 'personal and interpersonal power', leading to psychological empowerment. Hence, in my view, 'Managers and leaders need to create an environment that makes employees feel "powerful" within themselves, so that they are able to make decisions and carry them out responsibly' (Huq, 2010: 88).

There is also a noticeable change in employees' attitudes and expectations for a more meaningful way of life at work. To illustrate, Davies and Quinn (1999: 1) observe the changing and demanding expectations of employees regarding the role of business and their attitudes towards working life: 'the public's overall ethical expectations of the role of business in wider global society has coincided with the individual's changing expectations for a more meaningful, more empowered, and less controlled, working life.' A vast amount of knowledge exists in organisations that remain unused and untapped, and alluding to this, Clutterbuck and Kernaghan (1995: 12) point out: 'Most companies still squander it (knowledge) in a way they would never dream of if they were wasting tangible raw materials.' Worse still, according to Gandz (1990: 79), a high level of educated human capital is being wasted, as people are not allowed to contribute their intelligence:

We have relatively highly educated human assets, many of whom are working and contributing at a fraction of their potential; the creative, innovative energy in this asset base is enormous. If it is to be liberated, we must start to think much more seriously than we have traditionally done of investing in human resource development rather than expensing people. Only through making such investments will we be able to improve our business processes continuously, utilising both our human and other assets to maximum benefit for the business organisations, employees within those organisations and our society as a whole.

Employee empowerment should not be viewed as a commodity to be acquired or tick marked for the benefit of receiving quality awards. It must be viewed as a process of transforming of people's lives that is developed through action and continuous learning. On a personal level, for people, whether in management or non-management position, it requires a process of transformation constructed through positive actions. Individuals need to learn how to overcome feelings of helplessness through increased self-esteem and self-efficacy. This helps to generate self-confidence leading to psychological empowerment, as individuals and groups are not empowered unless they believe themselves to be so. It is wise to accept that empowerment does not happen overnight and it is not a quick fix, hence Kieffer (1984: 27) states: 'Empowerment is inescapably labor-intensive.' In the management world, the aspects of training, learning skills for empowerment and realisation of the time and resources have not been given adequate attention. Hence, empowerment is not just about learning new skills, it is also about '[individuals] reconstructing and reorienting deeply engrained personal systems of social relations' (Kieffer, 1984: 27).

As noted in the social work literature, feeling more powerful is important for service users, because people need to gain control over factors whether they are social, political or psychological, which are critical to overcoming feelings of oppression, powerlessness and disempowerment. It has been enlightening to know that the reason why disempowered people find themselves powerless is because they lack control over the decisions and the resources that affect their lives. In this sense, empowerment is viewed as an anti-oppressive practice in social work; this means that efforts are made to remove or reduce as far as possible, the oppressive circumstances that service users may face. Therefore, through the sharing of power, service users can make decisions, particularly those that affect their life situations (Denney, 1998; Means et al., 2003).

In its widest sense, employee empowerment may be viewed as including marginalised people and groups: employees who are farthest down the ladder have access to knowledge, information and a 'say' in decision-making which effect their lives at work. When individual employees do not have the power to take decisions they lack confidence in carrying out tasks, which in turn leads to low self-efficacy and self-esteem. The danger is that feelings of powerlessness and disempowerment can cause damage not only to individuals, but in the end the organisation suffers as well. These negative outcomes of lack of power, feelings of powerlessness and being disempowered, need to be highlighted. Appelbaum et al. (1999: 250) argue that 'employee empowerment will be achieved if employees feel valued, supported, have high self-esteem.' This resonates with Kieffer's (1984) argument that 'feeling more powerful' is more important than 'having more power' in the political sense.

It is interesting to note the psychological implications of employee empowerment and how internal locus of control, self-efficacy, self-esteem and self-confidence play an important part. Rosenthal et al. (1998: 170) highlight that in contemporary enterprising culture: 'the values of self-actualisation, freedom and "respect for the individual"' need to be given significant importance, which has implications for the higher motivational needs of individuals (Maslow, 1943). As Wilson (2004: 146) notes, the strength of Maslow's (1943) theory 'lies in the fact that it supports management practices that encourage employee autonomy and personal growth as these will enable employees to satisfy self-esteem and self-actualisation needs.' Conger and Kanungo (1988) conclude from their studies that employee empowerment gives employees more personal control.

Clearly, the need for employees to feel as if they have some control over their work is important and this is agreed by several authors across management, social work and psychology literature. When people feel they have some control over their work and are empowered to take decisions, they are more likely to accept the consequences of them. In other words, employees are more committed to actions based on decisions that they have taken themselves than they are to actions that are based on decisions taken by others (Greenberg and Baron, 2000).

Thus, empowerment is about change on several levels, such as people having to learn new behaviours and new skills, and new ways of interacting with other people, the environment, social conditions and systems that may be oppressive. As Freire (1972) argues, it is about the development of critical consciousness, and the ability to think against the status quo that enables people to act together, to change oppressive social conditions. Hence, in Sheppard's (1995: 26) view the social work role is 'the raising of consciousness, or conscientisation, a concept drawn from Freire (1972).'

Within social work and community health, it is noticeable that the practice of empowerment is clearly focused on people, either as a group, or as individuals. Any intervention therefore focuses on assisting individuals or groups of people to improve the quality of their lives on both the micro and macro level. Drawing knowledge from the social work literature has been valuable in deepening our understanding of employee empowerment and the importance of psychological empowerment. We have also learnt that interventions that provide genuine opportunities for individuals to participate may help them develop a sense of psychological empowerment. Hence training, coaching, supporting employees are all important parts of the people empowerment strategy.

In a growing global market, where new ideas grow quickly and innovation is rife, those organisations whose employees are psychologically empowered will be the ones who are able to look after customers' needs and respond quickly. Customers distinguish the organisation's services from those of other companies who sell the same services or products by experiencing the empowered employees' *distinctive* levels of service, and if necessary customers are prepared to pay a premium price.

As mentioned in Part I, SHRM is not just about hiring people; organisations need to have a planned approach with regards to recruitment, in order to achieve a competitive edge. Competitors may buy and recruit the smartest and skilled people to gain competitive advantage, but these *smartest and skilled* people may not necessarily be psychologically empowered, in order to work within an empowered culture. As previously argued, those are the organisations who will survive who have employees who are empowered; high achievers; resilient and able to cope with unstable markets.

Another important conclusion is that a complex journey such as employee empowerment cannot be considered without appropriate leadership. In order to empower employees, it is imperative that leaders have the necessary skills, such as coaching, counselling, negotiating and enabling.

In many instances, people in management and non-management positions at Large Organisation felt that the organisation was paying 'lip service' and they feared that it was going back to the old 'command and control' culture. Furthermore, there was hardly any evidence of the management behaviour as described by the CEO, namely, directing, coaching and supporting. One explanation of why the CEO's enthusiasm may not have been shared by all managers could be, as Fenton-O'Creevy (2001) suggests, that when change has the effect of overloading managers, they may fall back on the command and control approach rather than supporting new initiatives. A large number of employees reported they have not noted any significant change in the dominant management style. These perceptions are, of course, very different to those expressed by the CEO and, to a lesser extent, by senior management. While some senior managers, in particular, understood the philosophy and principles underlying the EP programme at a cognitive level, nevertheless at the affective level, they feared that too much empowerment could adversely affect day-to-day operations; one senior manager referred to a 'descent into anarchy', revealing an interesting difference between espoused theory and theory in use.

As previously stated in the Prologue, although political focus is important, nevertheless, organisations must consider the wider issues of the psychological implications of employee empowerment and how it may affect individuals, including people in non-management, management and leadership positions.

If employees are unhappy because organisations are not treating them like human beings who can use their brains, then it is obvious that questions can arise in employees' minds – 'why should I work for an organisation that does not believe in me?' These have psychological implications regarding employees' self-efficacy and self-esteem. In such cases, employees may feel that the organisation is not treating them fairly and it is letting their people down. There are several general leadership models and none of them are right or wrong. But, for the 'people-oriented' leadership style in an empowered organisation, the right and wrong way is quite apparent. The right way is to value and understand what people need and listen to how they want to be supported at work and the wrong way is not to value people's needs and not to allow them to have a say in processes or have an input into strategic decisions of the organisation, which is contrary to employee empowerment and SHRM principles.

But, not everybody who is a leader can understand this. During my research some employees commented, 'just because a person gets a leadership position, it is not necessary that he/she understands how to lead'. Leadership is very much about trying to understand people first. It is about actively listening to people, what the people want, what their needs are from basic to self-actualisation needs; giving them direction, coaching and support. This is the essence of leadership in an empowered organisation, it is about enabling people to achieve goals.

Another important point is that organisations need to support leaders as well. Just having the skills of directing, coaching and supporting employees is not enough – leaders also need freedom and to be empowered to use these skills. Giving autonomy alone will not result in leaders feeling empowered. Leaders need to feel that they are capable and competent and psychologically empowered to work within an empowered culture.

It is in the interest of organisations to be aware that, without the psychological empowerment of all employees, including leaders, it will be difficult to have any continuity in their employee empowerment programmes. Hence, my argument, *psychological empowerment is the glue that has a chance to hold the employee programme together, strategies alone will not do.*

This book raises awareness how important it is to listen to people and find out why they are unhappy in order to make the necessary changes that are needed to make the organisation a happy and fair place to work within an employee empowerment culture. This in turn makes a win-win situation for the people and the organisation. Clearly, leadership is critical; it can be the difference between success and failure in the practice of employee empowerment in organisations, as Bennis (1984: 16) cautions:

> *If I have learned anything from my research, it is this: the factor that empowers the work force and ultimately determines which organisations succeed or fail is the leadership of those organisations.*

The complexities of employee empowerment and the role of leaders have been largely under-estimated and it is obvious that organisations struggle with employee empowerment in practice. Effective utilisation of human resources is a strategic issue for organisations, as hierarchical organisations struggle to survive. The growing trend for downsizing and merging of organisations means that they can no longer maintain the 'command and control' approach as employees are given more responsibility and expected to take decisions. However, simply burdening employees with extra responsibility without empowering them does not deliver results, as is evident from my case study, particularly when neither the employer nor the employee understands or knows what 'being empowered' means.

It is true that the competitive nature of the global marketplace and business environment have made effective utilisation of human resources in organisations a strategic issue. Hammuda and Dulaimi (1997: 289) state: 'Any company that cannot deliver to its customers the product and service with better quality, and at a faster pace and a lower price than that of its global competitors may soon be out of business.'

Organisations are struggling to meet the increasing demands for flexibility and quality, hence the argument that employee empowerment is necessary for the survival and success of organisations. But, as I have argued throughout my discussions, this raises several questions: how will organisations practice employee empowerment from a post-modern perspective? Do organisations have a 'framework' for guidance to implement employee empowerment? Have organisations given their employees tools, resources and opportunities to work and behave in empowered ways? Are leaders in organisations aware of the particular 'people-oriented' skills that employees prefer in an empowered organisation (Huq, 2010)?

There is agreement in the management literature that the main problem is lack of evidence-based case studies and the availability of any first-hand information regarding the difficulties and issues that organisations actually face when implementing employee empowerment. Hence, from this point of view, findings from my case studies reveal important facts that give us insight into knowledge about the practical aspects of implementation. Participants of my study have spoken honestly and I have tried to bring attention to the high and low points, for the benefit of organisations, who genuinely want to practice employee empowerment. In the post-modern age, as Fook (2012: 45), remarks: 'It is in fact about applying knowledge in a reasoned way, based on values and in relation to context.'

This book is my humble effort to look for possibilities rather than focus on problems. It is a first attempt to examine the empowerment model from two disciplines – management and social work. It is clear that such an exercise was necessary to bridge some of the gaps with regards to the understanding of empowerment at the conceptual and practice levels. The essence of the 'Framework for Implementing Employee Empowerment Model D' is about 'humanising' the workplace, in line with SHRM and neo-modernist theories.

This book makes a number of important contributions to the knowledge of employee empowerment, which has frequently been criticised for its lack of research. These contributions are significant because it is apparent that lack of knowledge is damaging, it is disabling organisations, as they do not achieve what they set out to achieve via employee empowerment.

The 'Framework for Implementing Employee Empowerment Model D' provides an opportunity for leaders in both management and social work to create empowering environments for their organisations. Model D as a tool and a framework reaches out to both the aforementioned disciplines, enabling leaders to play a positive role in 'humanising' their workplaces.

In this book, I have discussed the concerns in the management literature with regards to the ambiguity and confusion surrounding the meaning of employee empowerment. The management literature reports that employee empowerment is shrouded with ambiguity and it is difficult to understand what it comprises of. After *'unravelling the mystery'* of the themes of employee empowerment in the management literature, namely, power-sharing, participative decision-making, devolution of responsibility and people-oriented leadership style (Huq's Model A), it was important to draw the empowerment themes from the social work literature to enhance our understanding of empowerment in this discipline, namely, access to information, collaboration and enablement (Huq's Model B). These key themes from both the disciplines, that is, merging management and social work, led to the birth of a new set of multi-disciplinary themes, which I have termed a *'kaleidoscope of themes'*, Huq's Model C.

It is apparent that these themes, in Huq's Model C, have an impact with regards to employees' locus of control, self-efficacy and self-esteem. This led to the scoping for a new model of employee empowerment, which I have named Huq's Model of Employee Empowerment, Huq's Model D, leading to a platform for psychological empowerment. In this respect, Morrell and Wilkinson's (2002: 128) suggestion was extremely useful: '[a] ... framework ... can offer a method for categorising and thereby assessing any "empowering" initiative.'

There is a great onus on leaders in empowered organisations to lead with understanding and knowledge about employee empowerment and a style of leadership that is 'people-oriented'. To reiterate Belasco's (1989: 12) point: 'If we are to deal with the serious competitive problems facing our nation, we must change the way we do business. The only way to accomplish this needed change is to empower people to execute change ... The future of our country depends on our ability to become masters of empowerment.'

It is hoped that my framework, Huq's Model of Employee Empowerment, Huq's Model D, will be useful not only for mastering the knowledge with regards to employee empowerment, but also mastering the tool for practical implementation, enabling leaders to be true 'leaders of empowerment'.

Bibliography

Adams, R. (1990). *Self-Help, Social Work and Empowerment*. London: Macmillan.

Adams, R. (1996). *Social Work and Empowerment*. London: Macmillan.

Adams, R. (2003). *Social Work and Empowerment*, 3rd edn. New York: Palgrave Macmillan.

Allport, G.W. (1937). *Personality: A Psychological Interpretation*. London: Constable.

Alpander, J.C. (1991). Developing Managers' Ability to Empower Employees. *Journal of Management Development*, 10(3), 13–24.

Appelbaum, S.H., Hebert, D. and Leroux, S. (1999). Empowerment: Power, Culture and Leadership – A Strategy or Fad for the Millennium? *Journal of Workplace Learning: Employee Counselling Today*, 11(7), 233–54.

Argyris, C. (1998). Empowerment: The Emperor's New Clothes. *Harvard Business Review*, May, 98–105.

Arnold, H.J. and Feldman, D.C. (1986). *Organisational Behavior*. USA: McGraw-Hill.

Ashness, D. and Lashley, C. (1995). Empowering Service Workers at Harvester Restaurants. *Personnel Review*, 24(8), 17–32.

Austen-Smith, J. (1994). People Empowerment. *Logistics Information Management*, 7(6), 28–31.

Bandura, A. (1977). Self-Efficacy: Toward a Unifying Theory of Behavioral Change. *Psychological Review*, 84, 191–215.

Bandura, A. (1986). *Social Foundations of Thought and Action: A Social Cognitive View*. New Jersey: Prentice Hall.

Bandura, A. (1995). *Self-Efficacy in Changing Societies*. Cambridge: Cambridge University Press.

Banister, P., Burman, E., Parker, I., Taylor, M. and Tindall, C. (1994). *Qualitative Methods in Psychology*. Buckingham: Open University Press.

Barling, J. and Beatlie, R. (1983). Self-Efficacy Beliefs and Sales Performance. *Journal of Organisational Behavior Management*, 5, 41–51.

Barney, J. (1991). Firm Resources and Sustained Competitive Advantage. *Journal of Management*, 17(1), 99–120.

Baron, R.A. and Byrne, D. (2000). *Social Psychology*. Massachusetts: Allyn & Bacon.

Baron, R.A. and Greenberg, J. (1990). *Behavior in Organisations, Understanding and Managing the Human Side of Work*. Massachusetts: Allyn & Bacon.

Barrett, K., Crimando, W. and Riggar, T.F. (1993). Becoming an Empowering Organisation: Strategies for Implementation. *Journal of Rehabilitation Administration*, November, 159–67.

Beirne, M. (2006). *Empowerment and Innovation: Managers, Principles and Reflective Practice*. UK: Edward Elgar.

Belasco, J.A. (1989). Masters of Empowerment. *Executive Excellence*, 6(3), 11–12.

Bennis, W. (1984). The 4 Competencies of Leadership. *Training and Development*, August, 14–19.

Beresford, P. and Croft, S. (1993). *Citizen Involvement: A Practical Guide for Change*. Basingstoke: Macmillan.

Bernstein, W.M. (2003). 'Empowerment': A Task for the Self, Not the Organisation. *Organisation Development Journal*, 21(1), 75–80.

Besterfield, D.H., Besterfield-Michna, C., Besterfield, G.H. and Besterfield-Sacre, M. (1995). *Total Quality Management*. New Jersey: Prentice Hall.

Bird, F.B. (1999). Empowerment and Justice. In Quinn, J.J. and Davies, P.W.F. (eds), *Ethics and Empowerment*. Basingstoke: Macmillan, 41–89.

Block, P. (1987). *The Empowered Manager: Positive Political Skills at Work*. San Francisco: Jossey-Bass.

Bolin, F.S. (1989). Empowering Leadership. *Teachers College Record*, 91(1), 81–96.

Boudrias, J.S., Morin, A.J.S. and Brodeur, M.M. (2012). Role of Psychological Empowerment in the Reduction of Burnout in Canadian Healthcare Workers. *Nursing and Health Sciences*, 14(1), 8–17.

Bowen, D.E. and Lawler III, E.E. (1992). The Empowerment of Service Workers: What, Why, How, and When. *Sloan Management Review*, Spring, 31–9.

Braye, S. and Preston-Shoot, M. (1995). *Empowering Practice in Social Care*. Buckingham: Open University Press.

Breton, M. (1994). On the Meaning of Empowerment and Empowerment-Oriented Social Work Practice. *Social Work with Groups*, 17(3), 23–37.

Brewer, J.D. (2000). *Ethnography*. Buckingham: Open University Press.

Bricker-Jenkins, M., Barbera, R., Young, C. and Beemer, M. (2013). Poverty Through the Lens of Economic Rights. In Saleebey, D. (ed.), *The Strengths Perspective in Social Work Practice*, 6th edn. USA: Pearson, 255–77.

Burdett, J.O. (1991). What is Empowerment Anyway? *Journal of European Training*, 15(6), 23–30.

Burke, R.J., Mustafa, K., Wolpin, J., Yirik, S. and Koyuncu, K. (2014). Organizational Empowerment Practices, Psychological Empowerment and Work Outcomes among Male and Female Front-Line Service Employees in Five-Star Turkish Hotels – Signs of Progress. *An International Journal of Management Studies*, 4(2), 39–45.

Bystydzienski, J.M. (1992). *Women Transforming Politics, World Wide Strategies for Empowerment*. USA: Indiana University Press.

Cameron, K. and Caza, A. (2005). Developing Strategies and Skills for Responsible Leadership. In Doh, J.P. and Stumpf, S.A. (eds), *Handbook on Responsible Leadership and Governance in Global Business*. Cheltenham: Edward Elgar, 87–111.

Carter, J.D.T. (2009). Managers Empowering Employees. *American Journal of Economics and Business Administration*, 1, 41–6.

Chiang, C. and Jang, S. (2008). The Antecedents and Consequences of Psychological Empowerment: The Case of Taiwan's Hotel Companies. *Journal of Hospitality & Tourism Research*, 32(1), 40–61.

Chiles, A.M. and Zorn, T.E. (1995). Empowerment in Organisations: Employees' Perceptions of the Influences on Empowerment. *Journal of Applied Communication Research*, 23(1), 1–25.

Christensen Hughes, J.M. (1999). Organisational Empowerment: A Historical Perspective and Conceptual Framework. In Quinn, J.J. and Davies, P.W.F. (eds), *Ethics and Empowerment*. Basingstoke: Macmillan, 197–234.

Claydon, T. and Doyle, M. (1996). Trusting Me, Trusting You? The Ethics of Employee Empowerment. *Personnel Review*, 25(6), 13–25.

Clement, A. (1994). Computing at Work: Empowering Action by 'Low-level Users'. *Communication of The ACM*, 37(1), 53–63.

Clutterbuck, D. and Kernaghan, S. (1995). *The Power of Empowerment, Release the Hidden Talents of Your Employees*. London: Kogan Page.

Collins, D. (1996a). Whither Democracy? Lost Debates in Management Empowerment. *Empowerment in Organisations*, 4(1), 12–24.

Collins, D. (1996b). Control and Isolation in the Management of Empowerment. *Empowerment in Organisations*, 4(2), 29–39.

Conger, J.A. (1989). Leadership: The Art of Empowering Others. *The Academy of Management Executive*, 3(1), 17–24.

Conger, J.A. and Kanungo, R.N. (1988). The Empowerment Process: Integrating Theory and Practice. *Academy of Management Review*, 13(3), 471–82.

Corsun, D.L. and Enz, C.A. (1999). Predicting Psychological Empowerment among Service Workers: The Effect of Support-Based Relationships. *Human Relations*, 52(2), 205–24.

Cotton, J.L. (1993). *Employee Involvement*. London: Sage.

Crosby, P.B. (1979). *Quality is Free: The Art of Making Quality Certain*. New York: McGraw-Hill.

Cunningham, I. and Hyman, J. (1999). The Poverty of Empowerment? A Critical Case Study. *Personnel Review*, 28(3), 192–207.

Cunningham, I., Hyman, J. and Baldry, C. (1996). Empowerment: The Power to Do What? *Industrial Relations Journal*, 27(2), 143–54.

Daft, R.L. (1999). *Leadership, Theory and Practice*. USA: The Dryden Press.

Dahl, R.A. (1957). The Concept of Power. *Behavioural Science*, 2, 201–15.

Dalrymple, J. and Burke, B. (1995). *Anti-Oppressive Practice, Social Care and the Law*. Buckingham: Open University Press.

D'Annunzio-Green, N. and Macandrew, J. (1999). Re-Empowering the Empowered: The Ultimate Challenge? *Personnel Review*, 28(3), 258–78.

Davies, M. (ed.) (2000). *The Blackwell Encyclopaedia of Social Work*. Oxford: Blackwell.

Davies, P.W.F. and Mills, A. (1999). Ethics, Empowerment and Ownership. In Quinn, J.J. and Davies, P.W.F. (eds), *Ethics and Empowerment*. Basingstoke: Macmillan, 170–94.

Davies, P.W.F. and Quinn, J.J. (eds) (1999). *Ethics and Empowerment*. Basingstoke: Macmillan.

Deming, W.E. (1986). *Out of the Crisis: Quality, Productivity and Competitive Position*. Cambridge: Cambridge University Press.

Denham, N., Ackers, P. and Travers, C. (1997). Doing Yourself Out of a Job? How Middle Managers Cope with Empowerment. *Employee Relations*, 19(2), 147–59.

Denham Lincoln, N., Travers, C., Ackers, P. and Wilkinson, A. (2002). The Meaning of Empowerment: The Interdisciplinary Etymology of a New Management Concept. *International Journal of Management Reviews*, 4(3), 271–90.

Denney, D. (1998). *Social Policy and Social Work*. New York: Oxford University Press.

Denscombe, M. (2002). *Ground Rules for Good Research: A 10 Point Guide for Social Researchers*. Buckingham: Open University Press.

Denzin, N.K. (1989). *Interpretive Interactionism.* California: Sage.

Denzin, N.K. and Lincoln, Y.S. (1998a). *The Landscape of Qualitative Research, Theories and Issues*. Thousand Oaks: Sage.

Denzin, N.K. and Lincoln, Y.S. (1998b). *Strategies of Qualitative Inquiry*. Thousand Oaks: Sage.

Denzin, N.K. and Lincoln, Y.S. (1998c). *Collecting and Interpreting Qualitative Materials*. Thousand Oaks: Sage.

Dessler, G. (2001). *Leading People and Organisations in the 21st Century*. New Jersey: Prentice Hall.

DuBois, B. and Miley, K.K. (2005). *Social Work: An Empowering Profession*, 5th edn. USA: Pearson Education.

Dubrin, A.J. (1994). *Applying Psychology: Individual and Organisational Effectiveness*. New Jersey: Prentice Hall.

Du Gay, P. and Salaman, G. (1998). The Cult[ure] of the Customer. In Mabey, C., Salaman, G. and Storey, J. (eds), *Strategic Human Resource Management*. London: Sage, 58–67.

Dupuy, F. (2004). *Sharing Knowledge: The Why and How of Organisational Change*. Hampshire: Palgrave Macmillan.

Edmonstone, J. and Havergal, M. (1993). Empowerment: Holy Grail or a Blinding Case of the Obvious? *Health Manpower Management*, 19(2), 22–8.

Ellis, R.A. and Taylor, M.S. (1983). Role of Self-Esteem within the Job Search Process. *Journal of Applied Psychology*, 68, 632–40.

Fahlberg, L.L., Poulin, A.L., Girdano, D.A. and Dusek, D.D. (1991). Empowerment as an Emerging Approach in Health Education. *Journal of the Institute of Health Eduction*, 22(3), 185–93.

Farnham, D., Hondeghem, A. and Horton, S. (2005). *Staff Participation and Public Management Reform: Some International Comparisons*. Basingstoke: Palgrave Macmillan.

Farzaneh, J., Farashah, A. and Kazemi, M. (2014). The Impact of Person-Job Fit and Person-Organisation Fit on OCB: The Mediating and Moderating Effects of Organisational Commitment and Psychological Empowerment. *Personnel Review*, 43(5), 672–91.

Fenton-O'Creevy, M. (2001). Employee Involvement and the Middle Manager: Saboteur or Scapegoat? *Human Resource Management Journal*, 11(1), 24–40.

Fincham, R. and Rhodes, P. (2005). *Principles of Organisational Behaviour*, 4th edn. Oxford: Oxford University Press.

Fink, A. (2005). *Conducting Research Literature Reviews, From the Internet to the Paper*, 2nd edn. Thousand Oaks: Sage.

Flick, U. (2002). *An Introduction to Qualitative Research*, 2nd edn. London: Sage.

Fook, J. (2012). *Social Work: A Critical Approach to Practice*. London: Sage.

Ford, R.C. and Fottler, M.D. (1995). Empowerment: A Matter of Degree. *Academy of Management Executive*, 9(3), 21–31.

Forrest, D. (2000). Theorising Empowerment Thought: Illuminating the Relationship between Ideology and Politics in the Contemporary Era. *Sociological Research Online*, 4(4), 1–21.

Foy, N. (1994). *Empowering People at Work*. Aldershot: Gower Publishing Limited.

Frans, D.J. (1993). A Scale for Measuring Social Worker Empowerment. *Research on Social Work Practice*, 3(3), 312–28.

Freire, P. (1972). *Pedagogy of the Oppressed*. Harmondsworth: Penguin.

Freire, P. (1996). *Pedagogy of the Oppressed*. Translation by Myra Bergman Ramos. Harmondsworth: Penguin.

Friedmann, J. (1992). *Empowerment: The Politics of Alternative Development*. Massachusetts: Blackwell.

Gable, G. (1994). Integrating Case Study and Survey Research Methods: An Example in Information Systems. *European Journal of Information Systems*, 3(2), 112–26.

Gandz, J. (1990). The Employee Empowerment Era. *Business Quarterly*, 74–9.

Geary, J. (2003). New Forms of Work Organisation: Still Limited, Still Controlled, but Still Welcome? In Edwards, P. (ed.), *Industrial Relations: Theory and Practice*, 2nd edn. Oxford: Blackwell, 338–67.

Ghoshal, S. and Bartlett, C.A. (1997). *The Individualized Corporation*. London: Harper.

Gibson, R. (1997). *Rethinking the Future*. London: Nicholas Brealey.

Gilbert, T. (1995). Nursing: Empowerment and the Problem of Power. *Journal of Advanced Nursing*, 21, 865–71.

Gist, M.E. (1987). Self-Efficacy: Implications of Organisational Behavior and Human Resource Management. *Academy of Management Review*, 12(3), 472–85.

Goski, K.L. and Belfry, M. (1991). Achieving Competitive Advantage through Employee Empowerment. *Employment Relations Today*, Summer, 213–20.

Graen, B.G. and Uhl-Bien, M. (1995). Relationship-Based Approach to Leadership: Development of Leader-Member Exchange (LMX) Theory of Leadership Over 25 Years: Applying a Multi-Level Multi-Domain Perspective. *Leadership Quarterly*, 6(2), 219–47.

Greasley, K., Bryman, A., Dainty, A., Price, A., Soetanto, R. and King, N. (2005). Employee Perceptions of Empowerment. *Employee Relations*, 27(4), 354–68.

Greenberg, J. and Baron, R.A. (2000). *Behavior in Organisations: Understanding and Managing the Human Side of Work*, 7th edn. New Jersey: Prentice Hall.

Guterman, N.B. and Bargal, D. (1996). Social Worker's Perceptions of their Power and Service Outcomes. *Administration in Social Worker*, 20(30), 1–20.

Gutierrez, L.M. (2001); Working with Women of Colour: An Empowerment Perspective. In Rothman, J., Erlich, J.L. and Tropman, J.E. (eds), *Strategies of Community Intervention*, 6th edn. Itaska, IL: Peacock.

Hales, C. (2000). Management and Empowerment Programmes. *Work, Employment and Society*, 14(3), 501–19.

Hammer, M. (1997). Beyond the End of Management. In Gibson, R. (ed.), *Rethinking the Future*. London: Nicholas Brealey, 95–105.

Hammer, M. and Champy, J. (1993). *Reengineering the Corporation: A Manifesto for Business Revolution*. London: Nicholas Brealey.

Hammuda, I. and Dulaimi, M.F. (1997). The Theory and Application of Empowerment in Construction: A Comparative Study of the Different Approaches to Empowerment in Construction, Service and Manufacturing Industries. *International Journal of Project Management*, 15(5), 289–96.

Hardy, C. (1985). The Nature of Unobtrusive Power. *Journal of Management Studies*, 22(4), 384–99.

Hardy, C. and Leiba-O'Sullivan, S. (1998). The Power Behind Empowerment: Implications for Research and Practice. *Human Relations*, 51(4), 451–83.

Hartline, M.D. and Ferrell, O.C. (1996). The Management of Customer-Contact Service Employees: An Empirical Investigation. *Journal of Marketing*, 60(4), 52–70.

Hasan, S.T.S. (2010). A Review on an Employee Empowerment in TQM Practice. *Journal of Achievements in Materials and Manufacturing Engineering*, 39(2), 204–10.

Hashemi, S.M.K., Nadi, H.K., Hosseini, S.M. and Rezvanfar, A. (2012). Agricultural Personnel's Proactive Behavior: Effects of Self Efficacy Perceptions and Perceived Organizational Support. *International Business and Management*, 4(1), 83–91.

Hellriegel, D., Slocum Jr., J.W. and Woodman, R.W. (1989). *Organisational Behavior*. USA: West Publishing Company.

Herschel, R.T. and Andrews, P.H. (1993). Empowering Employees in Group Work. *Information Strategy: The Executive's Journal*, Spring, 36–42.

Heslin, P. (1999). Boosting Empowerment by Developing Self-Efficacy. *Asia Pacific Journal of Human Resources*, 37(1), 52–64.

Hill, F. and Huq, R. (2001). Employee Empowerment – In Theory and in Practice: What Does it Mean? Integrated Management, Proceedings of the *6th International Conference on ISO 9000 & TQM*, 292–8.

Hill, F. and Huq, R. (2004). Employee Empowerment: Conceptualisations, Aims and Outcomes. *Total Quality Management*, 15(8), 1025–41.

Hitt, M.A., Miller, C.C. and Colella, A. (2006). *Organisational Behaviour: A Strategic Approach*. USA: John Wiley & Sons.

Hoepfl, H. (1994). Empowerment and the Managerial Prerogative. *Empowerment in Organisations*, 2(3), 39–44.

Holt, G.D., Love, P.E.D. and Nesan, J.L. (2000). Employee Empowerment in Construction: An Implementation Model for Process Improvement. *Team Performance Management: An International Journal*, 6(3/4), 47–51.

Honold, L. (1997). A Review of the Literature on Employee Empowerment. *Empowerment in Organisations*, 5(4), 202–12.

Hosking, D.M. and Morley, I.E. (1991). *A Social Psychology of Organizing People, Processes and Contexts*. Hertfordshire: Harvester Wheatsheaf.

Houtzagers, G. (1999). Empowerment, Using Skills and Competence Management. *Participation and Empowerment: An International Journal*, 7(2), 27–32.

Huczynski, A. and Buchanan, D. (2001). *Organisational Behaviour: An Introductory Text*. UK: Prentice Hall.

Humphries, B. (1996). *Critical Perspectives on Empowerment*. Birmingham: Venture.

Huq, R. (2008). *An Investigation of What Employee Empowerment Means in Theory and in Practice*. PhD Doctoral Research. Queen's University Belfast. UK.

Huq, R. (2010). *Employee Empowerment the Rhetoric & Reality*. Devon: Triarchy Press.

Huq, R. and Hill, F. (1999). An Exploration of Empowerment at the Theoretical and Practical Levels. *March, 17th International Labour Process Conference*, School of Management, Royal Holloway, University of London, UK.

Huq, R. and Hill, F. (2005). An Attempt to Clarify Employee Empowerment by Drawing Knowledge from the Social Work Literature, Track: Organisational Behaviour. *September, 8th Annual Irish Academy of Management Conference,* Galway Mayo Institute of Technology, Ireland.

Huselid, M.A. (1998). The Impact of Human Resource Management Practices on Turnover, Productivity, and Corporate Financial Performance. In Mabey, C., Salaman, G. and Storey J. (eds), *Strategic Human Resource Management.* London: Sage, 104–27.

Islam, T., Khan, S.R., Ahmad, U.N.U., Ali, G. and Ahmed, I. (2014). Organizational Learning Culture and Psychological Empowerment as Antecedents of Employees' Job Related Attitudes: A Mediation Model. *Journal of Asia Business Studies,* 8(3), 249–63.

Ivancevich, J.M. and Matteson, M.T. (1993). *Organisational Behaviour and Management.* USA: Irwin.

Johnson, P.R. (1994). Brains, Heart and Courage, Keys to Empowerment and Self-Directed Leadership. *Journal of Managerial Psychology,* 9(2), 17–21.

Johnson, P. and Duberley, J. (2000). *Understanding Management Research: An Introduction to Epistemology.* London: Sage.

Jones, P. and Davies, A. (1991). Empowerment: A Study of General Managers of Four Star Hotel Properties in the U.K. *International Journal of Hospitality Management,* 10(3), 211–17.

Joo, B. and Shim, J.H. (2010). Psychological Empowerment and Organisational Commitment: The Moderating Effect of Organisational Learning Culture. *Human Resource Development International,* 13(4), 425–41.

Juran, J.M. (1988). *Juran on Planning for Quality.* New York: The Free Press.

Kaler, J. (1999). Does Empowerment Empower? In Quinn, J.J. and Davies, P.W.F. (eds), *Ethics and Empowerment.* Basingstoke: Macmillan, 90–114.

Kanter, R.M. (1984). *The Change Masters: Corporate Entrepreneurs at Work.* London: Allen & Unwin.

Kappelman, L.A. and Richards, T.C. (1996). Training, Empowerment, and Creating a Culture for Change. *Empowerment in Organisations*, 4(3), 26–9.

Kark, R., Shamir, B. and Chen, G. (2003). The Two Faces of Transformational Leadership: Empowerment and Dependency. *Journal of Applied Psychology*, 88(2), 246–55.

Keller, T. and Dansereau, F. (1995). Leadership and Empowerment: A Social Exchange Perspective. *Human Relations*, 48(2), 127–46.

Kieffer, C.H. (1984). Citizen Empowerment: A Development Perspective. *Prevention in Human Services*, 3, 9–36.

Kirst-Ashman, K.K. (2003). *Introduction to Social Work and Social Welfare: Critical Thinking Perspectives*. USA: Thomson Learning.

Kizilos, P. (1990). Crazy about Empowerment. *Training*, 27(12), 47–56.

Knol, J. and Linge, R.V. (2009). Innovative Behaviour: The Effect of Structural and Psychological Empowerment on Nurses. *Journal of Advanced Nursing*, 65(2), 359–70.

Koberg, C.S., Boss, R.W., Senjem J.C. and Goodman, E.A. (1999). Antecedents and Outcomes of Empowerment. *Group and Organisation Management*, 24(1), 71–91.

Kondo, Y. (1997). Quality as a Source of Empowerment. *Proceedings of the Second International Conference on ISO 9000 and TQM: Business Excellence*, 251–60.

Kouzes, J.M. and Posner, B.Z. (1987). *The Leadership Challenge: How to Get Extraordinary Things Done in Organisations*. USA: Jossey-Bass.

Laschinger, H.K.S., Leiter, M., Day, A. and Gilin, D. (2009). Workplace Empowerment, Incivility, and Burnout: Impact on Staff Nurse Recruitment and Retention Outcomes. *Journal of Nursing Management*, 17, 302–11.

Lashley, C. (1994). Is There Any Power in Empowerment? *Conference Paper, Council for Hospitality*, April, 2–21.

Lashley, C. (1996). Research Issues for Employee Empowerment in Hospitality Organisations. *International Journal of Hospitality Management*, 15(4), 333–46.

Lashley, C. (2001). *Empowerment, HR Strategies for Service Excellence*. Oxford: Butterworth-Heinemann.

Lashley, C. and McGoldrick, J. (1994). The Limits of Empowerment: A Critical Assessment of Human Resource Strategy for Hospitality Operations. *Empowerment in Organisations*, 2(3), 25–38.

Lawler, E.E., Mohrman, S.A. and Ledford, G.E. (1995). *Creating High Performance Organisations: Practices and Results of Employee Involvement and Total Quality Management in Fortune 1000 Companies*. San Francisco: Jossey-Bass.

Leach, D.J., Wall, T.D. and Jackson, P.R. (2003). The Effect of Empowerment on Job Knowledge: An Empirical Test Involving Operators of Complex Technology. *Journal of Occupational and Organisational Psychology*, 76, 27–52.

Leavy, B. (1994). The Craft of Case-Based Qualitative Research. *Irish Business and Administration Research*, 15, 105–29.

Lee, M. and Koh, J. (2001). Is Empowerment Really a New Concept? *International Journal of Human Resource Management*, 12(4), 684–95.

Legge, K. (1995). *Human Resource Management: Rhetorics and Realities*. London: Macmillan.

Leiba, T. and Weinstein, J. (2003). Who are the Participants in the Collaborative Process and What Makes Collaboration Succeed or Fail? In Weinstein, J., Whittington, C. and Leiba, T. (eds), *Collaboration in Social Work Practice*. London: Jessica Kingsley, 63–82.

Logan, M.S. and Ganster, D.C. (2007). The Effects of Empowerment on Attitudes and Performance: The Role of Social Support and Empowerment Beliefs. *Journal of Management Studies*, 44(8), 5–15.

Long, R.F. (1996). Empowerment – A Management Style for the Millennium? *Empowerment in Organisations*, 4(3), 5–15.

Lord, J. and Hutchinson, P. (1993). The Process of Empowerment: Implications for Theory and Practice. *Canadian Journal of Community Mental Health*, 12(1), 5–22.

Lorsch, J.W. (1995). Empowering the Board. *Harvard Business Review*, January–February, 107–17.

Mabey, C., Salaman, G. and Storey J. (1998). Strategic Human Resource Management: The Theory of Practice and the Practice of Theory. In Mabey, C., Salaman, G. and Storey J. (eds), *Strategic Human Resource Management*, London: Sage Publications Ltd.

McAuley, J., Duberley, J. and Johnson, P. (2007). *Organisation Theory: Challenges and Perspectives*. Edinburgh: Pearson Education.

McLeod, J. (2001). *Qualitative Research in Counselling and Psychotherapy*. London: Sage.

Mangundjaya, W.L. (2014). Psychological Empowerment and Organizational Task Environment in Commitment to Change. *International Journal of Business and Management*, 2, 119–26.

Marchington, M. (1995). Fairy Tales and Magic Wands: New Employment Practices in Perspective. *Employee Relations*, 17(1), 51–66.

Marchington, M. and Wilkinson, A. (2000). Direct Participation. In Bach, S. and Sisson, K. (eds), *Personnel Management*, 3rd edn. Oxford: Blackwell, 340–64.

Martin, J. (2005). *Organisational Behaviour and Management*, 3rd edn. London: Thomson Learning.

Martin, L. and Vogt, J.F. (1992). No Sense of Trespass: Empowerment through Informational and Interpersonal Licence. *Organisational Development Journal*, 10(1), 1–8.

Maslow, A.H. (1943). A Theory of Human Motivation. *Psychological Review*, 50, 370–96.

Maslow, A.H. (1954). *Motivation and Personality*. New York: Harper.

Mattaini, M.A., Lowery, C.T. and Meyers, C.H. (1998). *The Foundations of Social Work Practice: A Graduate Text*, 2nd edn. Washington, DC: National Association of Social Workers (NASW) Press.

Means, R., Richards, S. and Smith, R. (2003). *Community Care, Policy and Practice*, 3rd edn. Basingstoke: Palgrave Macmillan.

Menon, S.T. (1999). Psychological Empowerment: Definition, Measurement, and Validation. *Canadian Journal of Behavioural Science*, 31(3), 161–4.

Moon, C. and Stanworth, C. (1999). Ethics and Empowerment: Managerial Discourse and the Case of Teleworking. In Quinn, J.J. and Davies, P.W.F. (eds), *Ethics and Empowerment*. Hampshire: Macmillan, 326–43.

Morgaine, C.A. (1993). A Language of Empowerment. *Home Economics*, Spring, 15–21.

Morgan, G. (1986). *Images of Organisation*. California: Sage.

Morrell, K. and Wilkinson, A. (2002). *Perspectives on Practice: Empowerment: Through the Smoke and Past the Mirrors?* London: Routledge.

Murrell, K.L. (1985). The Development of a Theory of Empowerment: Rethinking Power for Organisation Development. *Organisation Development Journal*, Summer, 34–8.

Nesan, L.J. and Holt, G.D. (2002). Assessment of Organisational Involvement in Implementing Empowerment. *Integrated Manufacturing Systems*, 13(4), 201–11.

Neumann, J. (1992/3). 'Empowerment' and the Authoritarian: Psychodynamics in the Service of Organisational Change. *The Tavistock Institute Review*, 25–30.

Oakland, J.S. (1989). *Total Quality Management*. London: Heinemann.

Ogden, S., Glaister, K.W. and Marginson, D. (2006). Empowerment and Accountability: Evidence from the UK Privatised Water Industry. *Journal of Management Studies*, 43(3), 521–55.

Ojeifo, E. and Winstanley, D. (1999). Negotiated Reality: The Meaning of Empowerment. In Quinn, J.J. and Davies, P.W.F. (eds), *Ethics and Empowerment*. Basingstoke: Macmillan, 271–99.

Parker, E.L. and Price, R.H. (1994). Empowered Managers and Empowered Workers: The Effects of Managerial Support and Managerial Perceived Control and Worker's Sense of Control over Decision Making. *Human Relations*, 47(8), 911–28.

Parrott, L. (2002). *Social Work and Social Care*, 2nd edn. London: Routledge.

Parrott, L. (2007). *Values and Ethics in Social Work Practice*. Exeter: Learning Matters.

Parsloe, P. (1996). *Pathways to Empowerment*. Birmingham: Venture.

Parsons, R.J. (1991). Empowerment: Purpose and Practice Principle in Social Work. *Social Work with Groups*, 14(2), 7–21.

Pastor, J. (1996). Empowerment: What It Is and What It Is Not. *Empowerment in Organisations*, 4(2), 5–7.

Patton, M.Q. (1987). *How to Use Qualitative Methods in Evaluation*. California: Sage.

Patton, M.Q. (2002). *Qualitative Research and Evaluation Methods*, 3rd edn. Thousand Oaks: Sage.

Payne, M. (2000). *Anti-Bureaucratic Social Work*. Birmingham: Venture Press.

Pearlstein, R.B. (1991). Who Empowers Leaders? *Performance Improvement Quarterly*, 4(4), 12–20.

Pearson, C.A.L. and Chatterjee, S.R. (1996). Implementing Empowerment through Sub-Unit Clusters: A Western Australian Case Study. *Empowerment in Organisations*, 4(3), 16–25.

Peters, T. (1987). *Thriving on Chaos, Handbook For a Management Revolution*. London: Guild Publishing.

Peters, T. (1994). *The Pursuit of Wow!* London: Macmillan.

Peters, T. and Waterman, R.H. (1982). *In Search of Excellence*. New York: Harper & Row.

Pfeffer, J. (1994). *Competitive Advantage through People: Unleashing the Power of the Work Force*. Boston: Harvard Business School Press.

Pierson, J. and Thomas, M. (2002). *Collins Dictionary: Social Work*. London: Collins.

Potterfield, T.A. (1999). *The Business of Employee Empowerment: Democracy and Ideology in the Workplace*. USA: Greenwood Publishing Group.

Prestby, J.E., Wandersman, A., Florin, P., Rich, R. and Chavis, D. (1990). Benefits, Costs, Incentive Management and Participation in Voluntary Organisations: A Means to Understanding and Promoting Empowerment. *American Journal of Community Psychology*, 18(1), 117–49.

Pring, R. (2000). *Philosophy of Educational Research*. London: Continuum.

Psoinos, A. and Smithson, S. (2002). Employee Empowerment in Manufacturing: A Study of Organisations in the UK. *New Technology, Work and Employment*, 17(2), 132–48.

Quinn, J.J. and Davies, P.W.F. (eds) (1999). *Ethics and Empowerment*. Basingstoke: Macmillan.

Rappaport, J. (1984). Studies in Empowerment: Introduction to the Issue. *Prevention in Human Services*, 3, 1–7.

Rappaport, J. (1987). Terms of Empowerment/Exemplars of Prevention: Toward a Theory of Community Psychology. *American Journal of Community Psychology*, 15(2), 121–48.

Ripley, R.E. and Ripley, M.J. (1992). Empowerment, the Cornerstone of Quality: Empowering Management in Innovative Organisations in the 1990s. *Management Decision*, 30(4), 20–43.

Ripley, R.E. and Ripley, M.J. (1993). Empowering Management in Innovative Organisations in the 1990s. *Empowerment in Organisations*, 1(1), 29–40.

Ritchie, J. (2003). The Applications of Qualitative Methods to Social Research. In Ritchie, J. and Lewis, J. (eds), *Qualitative Research Practice: A Guide for Social Science Students and Researchers*. London: Sage, 24–46.

Robson, C. (1993). *Real World Research: A Resource for Social Scientists and Practitioner Researchers*. Oxford: Blackwell.

Rosenthal, P., Hill, S. and Peccei, R. (1998). Checking out Service Evaluating Excellence, HRM and TQM in Retailing in The Theory of Practice and the Practice of Theory. In Mabey, C., Salaman, G. and Storey, J. (eds), *Strategic Human Resource Management*. London: Sage, 170–81.

Rubin, H.J. and Rubin, I.S. (1995). *Qualitative Interviewing: The Art of Hearing Data*. Thousand Oaks: Sage.

Sahoo, C.K. and Das, S. (2011). Employee Empowerment: A Strategy towards Workplace Commitment. *European Journal of Business and Management*, 3(11), 46–55.

Saleebey, D. (2013). *The Strengths Perspective in Social Work Practice*. London: Pearson.

Schein, E.H. (1993). How Can Organisations Learn Faster? The Challenge of Entering the Green Room. *Sloan Management Review*, Winter, 85–92.

Schuler, S.R. and Jackson, S.E. (1999). *Strategic Human Resource Management*. Oxford: Blackwell.

Seibert, S.E., Silver, S.R. and Randolph, W.A. (2004). Taking Empowerment to the Next Level: A Multiple Level Model of Empowerment, Performance, and Satisfaction. *Academy of Management Journal*, 47(3), 332–49.

Sheppard, M. (1995). *Care Management and the New Social Work: A Critical Analysis*. USA: Whiting and Birch Ltd.

Shera, W. and Page, J. (1995). Creating More Effective Human Service Organizations through Strategies of Empowerment. *Administration in Social Work*, 19(4), 1–15.

Shipper, F. and Manz, C.C. (1992). Employee Self-Management without Formally Designated Teams: An Alternative Road to Empowerment. *Organisational Dymanics*, 48–61.

Siegall, G. and Gardner, S. (2000). Contextual Factors of Psychological Empowerment. *Personnel Review*, 29(5/6), 703–22.

Sigler, T.H. and Pearson, C.M. (2000). Creating an Empowering Culture: Examining the Relationship between Organisational Culture and Perceptions of Empowerment. *Journal of Quality Management*, 5, 27–52.

Silzer, R. and Dowell, B.E. (2010). Strategic Talent Management Matters. In Silzer, R. and Dowell, B.E. (eds), *Strategy-Driven Talent Management: A Leadership Imperative*. San Francisco: John Wiley & Sons, 3–72.

Simons, R. (1995). Control in an Age of Empowerment. *Harvard Business Review*, March–April, 80–88.

Smith, J.A. (1996). Evolving Issues for Qualitative Psychology. In Richardson, J.T.E. (ed.), *Handbook of Qualitative Research Methods for Psychology and the Social Sciences*. Leicester: British Psychological Society, 189–201.

Snape, D. and Spencer, L. (2003). The Foundations of Qualitative Research. In Ritchie, J. and Lewis, J. (eds), *Qualitative Research Practice: A Guide for Social Science Students and Researchers*. London: Sage, 1–23.

Sommer, R. and Sommer, B. (2002). *A Practical Guide to Behavioural Research, Tools and Techniques*, 5th edn. New York: Oxford University Press.

Spreitzer, G.M. (1995). Psychological Empowerment in the Workplace: Dimensions, Measurement, and Validation. *Academy of Management Journal*, 38(5), 1442–65.

Spreitzer, G.M. (1996). Social Structural Characteristics of Psychological Empowerment. *Academy of Management Journal*, 39(2), 483–504.

Spreitzer, G.M., Kizilos, M.A. and Nason, S.W. (1997). A Dimensional Analysis of the Relationship between Psychological Empowerment and Effectiveness, Satisfaction and Strain. *Journal of Management*, 23(5), 679–704.

Stanton, A. (1990). Empowerment of Staff: A Prerequisite for the Empowerment of Users? In Carter, P., Jeffs, T. and Smith, M. (eds), *Social Work and Social Welfare Yearbook 2*. Buckingham: Open University Press, 122–33.

Staub-Bernasconi, S. (1991). Social Action, Empowerment and Social Work – An Integrative Theoretical Framework for Social Work and Social Work with Groups. *Social Work with Groups*, 14(3–4), 35–51.

Staw, B.M., Sutton, R.I. and Pelled, L.H. (1994). Employee Positive Emotion and Favorable Outcomes at the Workplace. *Organisation Science*, 5(1), 51–71.

Stewart, J.G., McNulty, R., Griffin, M.T.Q. and Fitzpatrick, J.J. (2010). Psychological Empowerment and Structural Empowerment among Nurse Practitioners. *Journal of the American Academy of Nurse Practitioners*, 22(1), 27–34.

Strauss, A. and Corbin, J. (1998). Grounded Theory Methodology: An Overview. In Denzin, N.K. and Lincoln, Y.S. (eds), *Strategies of Qualitative Inquiry*. Thousand Oaks: Sage Publications.

Sykes, J.B. (ed.) (1976). *The Concise Oxford Dictionary of Current English*, 6th edn. London: Oxford University Press.

Thomas, K.W. and Velthouse, B.A. (1990). Cognitive Elements of Empowerment: An 'Interpretive' Model of Intrinsic Task Motivation. *Academy of Management Review*, 15(4), 666–81.

Thomas, M. and Pierson, J. (1995). *Dictionary of Social Work*. London: Collins Educational.

Tjosvold, D., Hui, C. and Law, K.S. (1998). Empowerment in the Manager-Employee Relationship in Hong Kong: Interdependence and Controversy. *The Journal of Social Psychology*, 138(5), 624–36.

Toffler, A. (1991). *Power Shift*. New York: Bantam Books.

Tuuli, M.M. and Rowlinson, S. (2009). Performance Consequences of Psychological Empowerment. *Journal of Construction Engineering and Management*, 135(12), 1334–47.

Velthouse, B.A. (1990). Creativity and Empowerment: A Complementary Relationship. *Review of Business*, 12(2), 13–18.

Wagner, J.I.J., Cummings, G., Smith, D.L., Olson, J., Anderson, L. and Warren, S. (2010). The Relationship between Structural Empowerment and Psychological Empowerment for Nurses; A Systematic Review. *Journal of Nursing Management*, 18(4), 448–62.

Walton, J. (1999). *Strategic Human Resource Development*. England: Pearson Education.

Walton, R.E. (1985). From Control to Commitment in the Work Place. *Harvard Business Review*, March–April, 77–84.

Weber, A.L. (1991). *Introduction to Psychology*. USA: HarperCollins.

Weinstein, J., Whittington, C. and Leiba, T. (eds) (2003). *Collaboration in Social Work Practice*. London: Jessica Kingsley.

Whetten, D.A. and Cameron, K.S. (1991). *Developing Management Skills*. New York: HarperCollins.

Whittington, C. (2003). Collaboration and Partnership in Context. In Weinstein, J., Whittington, C. and Leiba, T. (eds), *Collaboration in Social Work Practice*. London: Jessica Kingsley, 13–18.

Wilkinson, A. (1998). Empowerment: Theory and Practice. *Personnel Review*, 27(1), 40–56.

Wilkinson, A. and Brown, A. (2003). Managing Human Resources for Quality Management. In Dale, B.G. (ed.), *Managing Quality*, 4th edn. Oxford: Blackwell.

Williams, J. (1995). Education for Empowerment: Implications for Professional Development and Training in Health Promotion. *Health Education Journal*, 54, 37–47.

Willmott, H. (1994). Business Process Re-Engineering and Human Resource Management. *New Technology, Work and Employment*, 23, 34–46.

Wilson, F. (1995). Managerial Control Strategies Within the Networked Organisation. *Information Technology & People*, 8(3), 57–72.

Wilson, F.M. (2004). *Organisational Behaviour and Work: A Critical Introduction*, 2nd edn. Oxford: Oxford University Press.

World Economic Forum (2015). Crisis in Leadership Underscores Global Challenges. Available at: http://www.weforum.org/news/crisis-leadership-underscores-global-challenges (accessed 17 February 2015).

Yang, S.B. and Choi, S.O. (2009). Employee Empowerment and Team Performance: Autonomy, Responsibility, Information and Creativity. *Team Performance Management*, 15(5/6), 289–301.

Yoon, J., Han, N.C. and Seo, Y.J. (1996). Sense of Control among Hospital Employees: An Assessment of Choice Process, Empowerment, and Buffering Hypotheses. *Journal of Applied Social Psychology*, 26(8), 686–716.

Zastrow, C.H. (2003). *The Practice of Social Work: Applications of Generalist and Advanced Content*, 7th edn. USA: Thomson Learning.

Zhang, X. and Bartol, K.M. (2010). Linking Empowering Leadership and Employee Creativity: The Influence of Psychological Empowerment, Intrinsic Motivation, and Creative Process Engagement. *Academy of Management Journal*, 53(1), 107–28.

Zimmermann, M.A. (1990). Taking Aim on Empowerment Research: On the Distinction Between Individual and Psychological Conception. *American Journal of Community Psychology*, 18(1), 169–77.

Zimmermann, M.A. (1995). Psychological Empowerment: Issues and Illustrations. *American Journal of Community Psychology*, 23(5), 581–99.

Zimmerman, M.A., Israel, B.A., Schulz, A. and Checkoway, B. (1992). Further Explorations in Empowerment Theory: An Empirical Analysis of Psychological Empowerment. *American Journal of Community Psychology*, 20(6), 707–27.

Index

Note: **bold** page numbers indicate figures.

If you have found this book useful you may be interested in other titles from Gower

The Self as Enterprise
Foucault and the Spirit of 21st Century Capitalism
Peter Kelly
9780754649632 (hardback)
9781409450702 (e-book – PDF)
9781409473572 (e-book – ePUB)

The Fulfilling Workplace
The Organization's Role in Achieving Individual and Organizational Health
Ronald J. Burke and Cary L. Cooper
9781409427766 (hardback)
9781409427773 (e-book – PDF)
9781409460459 (e-book – ePUB)

Equality, Diversity and Opportunity Management
Costs, Strategies and Leadership
Tony Morden
9781409432784 (hardback)
9781409432791 (e-book – PDF)
9781409474562 (e-book – ePUB)

GOWER

The Culture Builders
Leadership Strategies for Employee Performance
Jane Sparrow
9781409437246 (paperback)
9781409437253 (e-book – PDF)
9781409483922 (e-book – ePUB)

The Velvet Revolution at Work
The Rise of Employee Engagement,
the Fall of Command and Control
John Smythe
9781409443247 (paperback)
9781409443254 (e-book – PDF)
9781472400574 (e-book – ePUB)

Human Nature
A Guide to Managing Workplace Relations
Greg Clydesdale
9781472416797 (hardback)
9781472416803 (e-book – PDF)
9781472416810 (e-book – ePUB)

Visit **www.gowerpublishing.com** and

- search the entire catalogue of Gower books in print
- order titles online at 10% discount
- take advantage of special offers
- sign up for our monthly e-mail update service
- download free sample chapters from all recent titles
- download or order our catalogue